THE UNDERWORLD IN TWENTIETH-CENTURY POETRY

PR
605
O,85T49
2009
web

BL

THE UNDERWORLD IN TWENTIETH-CENTURY POETRY

FROM POUND AND ELIOT TO HEANEY AND WALCOTT

Michael Thurston

palgrave
macmillan

THE UNDERWORLD IN TWENTIETH-CENTURY POETRY
Copyright © Michael Thurston, 2009.

All rights reserved.

First published in 2009 by
PALGRAVE MACMILLAN®
in the United States—a division of St. Martin's Press LLC,
175 Fifth Avenue, New York, NY 10010.

Where this book is distributed in the UK, Europe and the rest of the world,
this is by Palgrave Macmillan, a division of Macmillan Publishers Limited,
registered in England, company number 785998, of Houndmills,
Basingstoke, Hampshire RG21 6XS.

Palgrave Macmillan is the global academic imprint of the above companies
and has companies and representatives throughout the world.

Palgrave® and Macmillan® are registered trademarks in the United States,
the United Kingdom, Europe and other countries.

ISBN: 978–0–230–62046–9

Library of Congress Cataloging-in-Publication Data

Thurston, Michael, 1965–
    The underworld descent in twentieth-century poetry: from Pound and
    Eliot to Heaney and Walcott / Michael Thurston.
        p. cm.
    ISBN 978–0–230–62046-9 (alk. paper)
    1. English poetry—20th century—History and criticism. 2. American
poetry—20th century—History and criticism. 3. Voyages to the otherworld
in literature. 4. Hell in literature. I. Title.

PR605.O85T49 2010
821'.9109—dc22   2009013916

A catalogue record of the book is available from the British Library.

Design by Newgen Imaging Systems (P) Ltd., Chennai, India.

First edition: December 2009

10 9 8 7 6 5 4 3 2 1

Printed in the United States of America.

For Abby, Katie, and Megan
and for E.S.W.

CONTENTS

ACKNOWLEDGMENTS

Parts of chapter 2 appeared in somewhat different form in "Contexts, Choruses, and Katabases (Canonical and Non-): Some Methodological Implications of Cary Nelson's Recovery Work," which was published in *Cary Nelson and the Struggle for the University: Poetry, Politics, and the Profession*, ed. Michael Rothberg and Peter K. Garrett (Albany: State University of New York Press, 2009). Books take time, and time to write requires money. For time to work on this book, and the money that made that time possible, I am grateful to the Mellon Foundation and the Provost / Dean of Faculty at Smith College. For additional research funding, I would like to thank the office of the Associate Provost / Dean for Academic Development and the Committee for Faculty Compensation and Development at Smith. Thanks to the staffs of the Mortimer Rare Book Room at Smith and the Humanities Reading Room of the British Library for guidance and assistance, and to my research assistants: Sarah Bolts, Aria Cabot, and Emily Powers. Thanks, also, to the Haymarket, where much of this book was written (and all of it was rewritten) beneath portraits of Walter Benjamin and Antonio Gramsci.

Books take the author's time; they also take the time of those colleagues generous enough to offer theirs. For their helpful questions and suggestions, I am grateful to members of the American and Canadian Studies Seminar at the University of Birmingham (and to Helen Laville for inviting me to present my work to the group), to the audiences at conferences (at Cambridge University, Queen's University, and the University of Illinois) at which material for this book was explored, and, especially, to members of the 2007–2008 Undergrounds and Underworlds Colloquium at Smith College's Kahn Liberal Arts Institute. This book benefits, too, from interactions with students in classes where I have tried some of the readings out, especially from the sharp matriculants of the English program at the University of Sarajevo, where I presented parts of the book in lectures. I have enjoyed the support, the critical engagement, and the patience of friends and colleagues at Smith, who read drafts of chapters, asked provocative and productive questions, suggested poems or works of scholarship, and otherwise lived out the collaborative ideal of academic life: Nancy Bradbury, Dawn Fulton, Michael Gorra, Betsey Harries, Rick Millington, Kevin Rozario, and Emily Wojcik. I wish Ron Macdonald, who encouraged this project before it had even become a project, were here to see what came of it, and I'm grateful for the Vergilian guidance of his *Burial-Places of Memory*.

Books take time away from the family, and I want to thank mine—Abby, Katie, and Megan—for putting up with the time I needed to write this book, and for making home such a paradise to emerge into after my sojourns in the Underworld.

PERMISSIONS

The author gratefully acknowledges the permission to quote from the following:

Edna St. Vincent Millay, "Sonnets from an Ungrafted Tree" (copyright 1923, 1951 by Edna St. Vincent Millay and Norma Millay Ellis). Reprinted with permission of Elizabeth Barnett, Literary Executor, The Millay Society.

Jon Stallworthy, "War Poet," parts of which were published in the *Times Literary Supplement* (7 November 2008), and parts of which remain unpublished. Reprinted with permission of Jon Stallworthy.

INTRODUCTION

On a summer evening, a man enters a cave, carrying not only some minimal provisions (beer, potato crisps) but also candles, a typewriter, and paper. He types questions and awaits the answers, transmitted through his own typing (leaving in the resulting typescript "touch-typing mistakes of apparent oracular provenance").[1] His central question, one at which he has arrived only after crawling "through the tunnel of daylight" and having "reached the chorus of noise in this black cavity," one that is refined and repeated over the course of his sojourn in the cave, is "How should I reform my life?"[2] The man is driven to the question by his failings, most immediately a failure to act and help a victim of assault, but, it is suggested, also a series of failures in relationships. The cave's oracle answers in typically cryptic fashion: "A ccp, nomayomopm pf / A combination of drips outside in the now dark tunnel sounded exactly li m like someone moving belongings out of a car," and, later, "engage in hunting other things where settle son who speaks only once and that a moment of dan-ger...your fate to have no son but he is the first person you meet after leaving your sperm in the cave..."[3] The questioning man stays all night in the cave, moving deeper when beckoned by the oracle, losing along the way much of what he brought in with him—torch, crisps, candles, even the typewriter—and finding additional voices (espe-cially that of a woman he has loved) and ever more elaborate answers to questions he cannot quite articulate. Six hours and sixteen pages after entering, the inquirer leaves the cave to embark on the new life he sought to find through his consultation with the oracle. From the stormy early morning, he looks back to find the cave "nut-calm" and "as black as the inside of your nutty skull."[4]

Douglas Oliver's experimental text, *In the Cave of Suicession*—which was published in Cambridge, England, by the avant-garde poetry press Street Editions in 1974 (and which I have just summarized)—nicely condenses the key elements of a topos at once ancient and actively present: the descent into the Underworld in search of pro-phetic wisdom. The Underworld descent tradition actually conflates two narrative topoi—the *nekuia*, in which the shades of the dead are

invoked and confronted, and the *katabasis*, in which the protagonist
actually enters (literally "goes down" into) the Underworld; I will
return to this distinction below. My point for now is that the story
Oliver tells (both *katabasis* and *nekuia*) is one of the oldest in Western
literature: the protagonist, usually at the nadir of his journey, at a dark
moment of exhaustion, confusion, or despair, is driven to seek counsel
and guidance from the past preserved and the prophetic vision vouch-
safed to a tutelary figure in the Underworld. Oliver's entryway into
the Underworld is more explicitly related to female genitalia than we
find in his epic models (though even in those, the Underworld carries
strong associations with the female: Odysseus, Aeneas, and Dante are
all assisted by women in their Underworld experiences, and a good
deal of Odysseus's sojourn with the shades involves women, from his
mother through what classicists have called the "parade of women").
Moreover, Oliver's explicit relation of the cave to the mind, his strong
suggestion that the descent into the cave is a descent into the self,
is a modern wrinkle probably not imaginable to Homer or Vergil
(though Dante might be read in such terms). Nevertheless, Oliver's
is an Underworld descent that largely conforms to the conventions
of the long tradition in which such descents appear either as a crucial
episode or as a large part of the entire narrative in many of the classic texts of Western literature: Odysseus's encounter with the shade
of Tiresias becomes Aeneas's meeting with his father, Anchises, in
Vergil's *Aeneid*. Aeneas's trip into the classical Underworld becomes
Dante's descent into a medieval Christian's Hell in *Inferno*. Dante's
Inferno is echoed by Milton's Satan in *Paradise Lost*. Milton in turn
provides a backdrop for William Blake in *The Marriage of Heaven and
Hell*. Setting out on his own descent into the Suicide Cave and, more
than that, setting out his self-referential narrative of self-scrutiny along
the narrative lines of this ancient topos, Oliver at once imbues his own
story with the deep cultural resonance of the Underworld descent and
provides himself an opportunity to revise the terms of this cultural
legacy (by introducing the chance errors of touch-typing, for example,
to foreground language and poetic production themselves).

In casting his questioner's journey in the structure of an
Underworld descent, though, Oliver participates not only in a long
tradition comprising classic texts but also in a fashion current among
his own contemporaries and recent predecessors. Twentieth-century
poets made a habit of going to Hell, from Ezra Pound in his rewriting of the Odyssean *nekuia* to Derek Walcott's katabatic journey
into the volcano Soufriere on St. Lucia. At the very moment Oliver
has his questioner consult the oracle in Derbyshire's Suicide Cave,

James Merrill was decades into a long-running dialogue with other-worldly spirits, conducted through a Ouija board in his Stonington, Connecticut dining room. Even Oliver's widow, Alice Notley, would go on to publish her own Underworld poem, *The Descent of Alette*, in 1996.[5] What were these poets, thousands of years after the example of Odysseus, doing with the Underworld descent? Or, to shift the emphasis from intention to effect, what was the Underworld descent doing *for* Pound and T.S. Eliot, Sterling Brown and Hart Crane, Edna St. Vincent Millay and H.D., Seamus Heaney and Tony Harrison, and many other poets? These are the questions that animate this book.

* * *

Before turning to modern poems that deploy the descent narrative, it will be useful to sketch (very briefly) the tradition upon which those poets draw, and since the Underworld descent is part of Western literature from its beginnings, it behooves us to begin at its beginnings. Odysseus's invocation of Tiresias's shade in the eleventh book of the *Odyssey* is perhaps the tradition's inaugural moment, though it draws upon even older materials—not only other accounts of Odysseus's adventures but also the legends of Heracles's descent into Hades as he completed his labors, the myths surrounding Persephone and Demeter, and the history of ritual visits to (often subterranean) oracles, including a well-known pilgrimage to Tiresias's shrine in Boeotia.[6] The Underworld episode falls just short of midway through the epic, after Odysseus's long sojourn on Circe's island. Directed by Circe to "consult the soul of Theban Tiresias," Odysseus leads his (barely willing) men to the shores of the Cimmerian lands, upon which the sun, even at its apogee, never shines. Following Circe's instructions, Odysseus digs a pit, pours into it libations to the dead, and finally cuts the throats of sacrificial sheep so that their blood fills the pit. The ritual summons the shades of all kinds of the dead from Erebus: brides and bachelors, old men and young women, and, especially, warriors. Among this crowd, Odysseus first recognizes Elpenor, who had died in a drunken fall as the crew prepared to leave Circe's island. Elpenor begs Odysseus to conduct the obsequies necessary for his soul's rest, and almost as soon as Odysseus agrees, the hero's mother, Anticleia, of whose death Odysseus was unaware, appears. Odysseus is grief-stricken, but he cannot let his mother's shade near the blood until Tiresias has drunk from the pit. The prophet promptly appears and, once he has drunk the sacrificial blood, he relates the important information that Poseidon is enraged at Odysseus, that Odysseus and his crew must not touch the cattle of the sun god, and that even if he does everything right Odysseus will return only after more time passes and only after having lost his ship and his companions. He will then have to kill the suitors who have spent the last dozen or more years wooing his wife, consuming his livelihood, and perpetrating violence upon his people. This is the information for which Odysseus has come, but when it is his turn to speak, the hero asks not about the sun god or the suitors or the sacrifice he must make to Poseidon, but about Anticleia; how, Odysseus wonders, can he make his mother recognize him? What follows is a series of colloquies between Odysseus and shades other than the prophet whose wisdom he came to seek. He first speaks with Anticleia, who catches him up on the state of things in Ithaca (and whom he cannot embrace, though he tries three times), then hears the tales of several other women. Odysseus then meets the shades of his fellow combatants in the Trojan War. Agamemnon tells of his own murder, Achilles says that he would rather serve as another man's slave than rule over the dead in the Underworld, and Ajax, who still bears a grudge over losing Achilles's armor to Odysseus, says a profound nothing at all. Finally, after glimpsing the punishments meted out by Minos, the judge of the dead—Tantalus tempted by the fruit out of reach, Sisyphus pushing his stone up the hill, all part of what classicists now argue is a later interpolation—Odysseus leaves the pit and rejoins his companions and they sail on (to disregard some of Tiresias's advice).

The eleventh book of the *Odyssey* narrates a *nekuia*; while he interacts with the shades of the dead, Odysseus does not actually descend into the Underworld. Instead he remains in a liminal space created by ritual, a space he is able to leave at will. The word *nekuia* derives from the Greek word for death in order to name the invocation of the shades. It distinguishes an episode of invocation from an actual physical descent, which is called a *katabasis*, from the Greek "*katabanein*" (which combines the preposition "*kat*," meaning "to go down," and the verb "*banein*" or "to go"). Though *katabanein* literally means "to go down" it has a variety of technical meanings, including "to disembark (a ship)." Homer does not use this specific verb in relation to Odysseus' journey to Hades, which is appropriate since his hero does not actually descend into the Underworld. Other accounts of Odysseus' "*katabasis*" (and the accounts of other heroes' Underworld journeys) are more literal and do involve a true descent. Some of these accounts were probably common enough in Homer's day, so that it appears he *chose* not to have Odysseus actually descend into

Hades. Or does he? Homer does use the opposite of *"katabanein"*—*"anabanein"*—when Elpenor anticipates Odysseus's departure from Hades. More than this, characters who meet Odysseus in Hades tend to refer to his journey as an actual "descent." What really distinguishes *nekuia* from *katabasis*, then, is perhaps a matter more of emphasis than of actual generic difference; while Odysseus may or may not descend into the Underworld, the emphasis of the episode is on his interaction with spirits. In similar stories that involve their heroes' actual descent into Hades—the tradition of the *katabasis*—more attention is given to description of the physical space of the Underworld and of its inhabitants. They literalize, for whatever reason, what is symbolic in the Homeric text. The canonical antecedent for this katabatic tradition is the sixth book of Vergil's *Aeneid*.

Like Odysseus in Book XI, Aeneas in Book VI is at a crucial low point of his journey. He has recently left Carthage after a disastrous affair with the Carthaginian queen, Dido, and, in a moment of great symbolism, has lost his helmsman, Palinurus, so that his ship loses its way. Aeneas is able, though, to reach Cumae, where he asks the Sibyl, a prophetess of Apollo, to help him cross the Acheron into Hades so that he can consult the shade of his father, Anchises. Where Odysseus is directed by Circe to consult Tiresias, Aeneas is obeying his father's direction; this is just the first of many times when Vergil takes advantage of the chance to compare Roman virtue favorably to Greek culture by revising his poetic antecedent, thereby writing revision in as a key component of the *katabasis* itself. As if to show his awareness of the Greek past against which he sets his (pre)-Roman hero, Vergil has Aeneas appeal to precedent as he pleads his case with the Sibyl, arguing that if such Greeks as Orpheus, Pollux, Theseus, and Hercules have entered the Underworld, he should be able to as well. It is at this point that the Sibyl famously replies that it is easy to descend (*Facilis descensus Averno*), but the way back up, well, "There is the trouble, there is the toil."[7]

That allegedly easy way down into the Underworld takes a good deal longer to recount than Odysseus's ritual, and it offers Vergil more opportunities to revisit and revise his model, engaging in a process that reinforces both specific content that will become conventional in the Underworld descent and the dynamic of revision that critics like David Pike and Ronald Macdonald argue characterizes the topos. For example, Aeneas encounters the unburied Palinurus, just as Odysseus had met Elpenor. Vergil's encounter is reminiscent of Homer's and the repetition here highlights the anxiety over how one is remembered as a key component of the descent's emotional and cultural repertoire. But when Palinurus begs for Aeneas either to bury him so that his shade can cross over to Hades or to help him across the Styx, echoing Elpenor's plea for Odysseus to build a tomb to him, Vergil alters what he finds in Homer and refuses to grant his hero this power over his mate's immortal fate. Where Odysseus promises to memorialize Elpenor, the Sibyl calms Palinurus with the promise of future fame in the form of a coastal point named for him. Much is going on here. First, the episode is one of many examples of what Macdonald describes as Vergil's deployment of "a specific Homeric intertext to foreground the unique character of his own poem and hero."[8] David Pike makes a similar argument, writing that "the Homeric *nekuia* and the tradition it represents are present in the *Aeneid* as objects of its satirical descent. Vergil makes his voice manifest in large part through traces of his rereading and rewriting of Homer."[9] Just as important as this revisionist impulse is the way that Vergil makes an implicit gesture of cultural evaluation here, lodging the power to commemorate in supernatural hands (thereby demonstrating Roman piety), and making the mode of commemoration geographic rather than architectural (thereby suggesting Roman permanence). In a similar way, as Macdonald shows, Vergil uses Aeneas's encounter with Charon, the boatman who ferries souls over the Styx, to contrast and rank an outmoded Greek heroism characterized by chaotic and selfish violence with the new Roman model, saturated with virtue and pietas, the latter embodied by the hero who bears a golden bough and sheathes his sword, and who wants to take away nothing but the advice he seeks from his father.[10]

We could pile up more examples, but the point is made. The tradition of the descent into the Underworld is a tradition of revision, of innovation against the horizon of the past. Much, though, remains the same from Underworld to Underworld during the centuries after Vergil, centuries during which the narrative is ubiquitous in European writing, and one key consistency is the emphasis on the fates of those who dwell in the Underworld as a way to criticize the writer's culture. The *katabasis* recurs in a wide range of apocalyptic and vision literature from the first century through the middle ages, gaining through these retellings many of the details that have come to seem compulsory, many of which relate to the project of cultural critique. Dating from around the middle of the third century CE, for example, are the *Apocalypse of St. Peter* and the *Apocalypse of St. Paul*, in which appear descriptions of Hell and the torments of sinners that not only seem to follow the punishments described in the *Aeneid* but also already resemble scenes that show up in Dante's *Inferno* a

thousand years later. Here, for illustration, is an exemplary passage
from the *Apocalypse of St. Peter*:

> And behold, again a place! And there a pit, large and full. In it those
> who have denied righteousness. And angels of punishment go around
> there in it and ignite the fire of their punishment.[11]

Peter's Apocalypse goes on to describe the tortures endured by murderers, especially of children, frauds, blasphemers, and usurers (the
last of whom are condemned to a pit full of excrement, an image we
will meet again in Pound's Canto XIV). The *Apocalypse of St. Paul*
is similarly at once shocking and familiar in its handling of sinners:
blasphemers gnaw their own tongues, adulterers hang by their hair
and eyebrows in a river of fire. Central to both of these visions is
the great truth that the descending visionary discovers in Hell: the
absolute necessity of belief in the Incarnation and Resurrection of
Christ. Just as Odysseus and Aeneas found the guidance they needed
in commitments to home and ancestors, these early Christian *katabases* locate their analogous prophetic wisdom in orthodoxy. Even
more important, though, is the way the lovingly described torments,
each for a specific failure to believe and act that orthodoxy, at least
implicitly condemn the dominant culture that surrounds the writers
in the second and fourth centuries.

The orthodoxy of the late antique apocalypses is embodied
in a guardian angel (a Christianized Vergil) in the most popular
descent into Hell before Dante's *Inferno*, the twelfth-century *Visions
of Tondal*. In this descent narrative we see even more clearly the
katabatic intention to achieve effects in the world. Composed in
Regensburg around 1150, the *Visions of Tondal* was enormously
popular; 243 manuscripts survive. Of these, over 100 are vernacular
translations from the text's original Latin.[12] As Roger Wieck writes,
the readers of (and hearers about) these manuscripts used the text
for a specific purpose: "The *Visions of Tondal* provided an instructive
and practical treatise on subjects that dominated the genuinely pessimistic spirituality of the late Middle Ages...The *Visions* was one of
several devotional texts...that were frequently bound up together as
a single book...Read by the pious, these stories encouraged the performance of penance in this world so as to avoid greater tribulations
in the next."[13] Just as in the antique apocalypses, this cultural work
would have been performed largely by the graphic description of
what awaits sinners in Hell, scenes witnessed by the worldly knight,
Tondal, when he falls into a fit at dinner and his soul leaves his body

and visits Hell. Among the most famous of the knight's otherworldly adventures was an episode in which, after being shown a narrow, nail-studded bridge over a boiling lake full of ravenous beasts—the bridge that thieves must cross as their punishment—Tondal is forced to cross the bridge himself, pulling along a cow that he had stolen in his youth.[14] The image of Tondal and his cow appears in a number of artists' renditions of Hell, including Hieronymous Bosch's in his "Hay-Wain" *Hell*.[15]

Popular as *Tondal* was among late medieval and early modern readers, though, he has been all but completely eclipsed by the pilgrim-poet figure who moves through Hell, Purgatory, and Paradise in Dante's *Divine Comedy* (c. 1307–1320). Dante's descent into Hell marks a crucial moment in the descent tradition for where the Apocalypses of St. Peter and St. Paul, the *Visions of Tondal*, and the various narratives of Underworld descent recounted by Gregory of Tours (in his *History of the Franks*), Gregory the Great (in his *Dialogues*), the Venerable Bede (in his *Ecclesiastical History of England*), and others offered the Underworld as a real place,[16] their chronicle style enhancing the verisimilitude of their narrated adventures, Dante's terza rima stanzas and allegorical language emphasized the literary character of his enterprise:

> When I had journeyed half of our life's way,
> I found myself within a shadowed forest,
> for I had lost the path that does not stray.[17]

Like Odysseus and Aeneas, Dante is at a low point in his journey when he makes his way to the Underworld. Like his predecessors, he finds in that Underworld both guidance (in the form of Vergil) and a series of interlocutors anxious over how they are remembered in the world. Also like his predecessors, Dante revises what he finds in previous accounts of Underworld descents. Where Tondal sees a Lucifer bound but fiercely powerful, squeezing the souls from the damned and exhaling them into the torments of Hell, Dante discovers a creature that consumes the damned without volition or apparent awareness, a mass frightening in its lack of power and will. More importantly, though, Dante also places his predecessors in the Underworld. Vergil, who mapped the territory in its canonical form, now guides a poet whose Christian vision will supersede his own, and Ulysses, hero of the Homeric epic Vergil himself had revised, is encountered suffering the torment reserved for those who gave false counsel, as if to suggest that the pagan poem is one the new poet must correct if the truth is to be told. Dante thus illustrates what Pike calls the "characteristic strategy" of the Underworld descent:

> The descent into the underworld functions simultaneously as a repository for the past and as a crucible in which that repository is melted down to be recast as something other than what it had been. The most characteristic strategy of the descent is to stress its own complexity and novelty in contrast with a simple and outmoded past, a past newly reconstituted as such by the new act of descent.[18]

I would argue, though, that the relationship between new descent and "outmoded" is one of interdependence; Dante gets nowhere, after all, without Vergil as a guide.

Though Dante's revision of the tradition of the Underworld descent is a deeply traditional way of deploying the topos, the *Inferno* still stands out as an important moment in the tradition's development. I have suggested that the difference between the *nekuia* and the *katabasis* is one of emphasis, with the invocation of the shades emphasizing the key encounter with the prophet and the descent emphasizing the geography of the Underworld and the fates of those who dwell there. More than any of his predecessors, Dante synthesizes these impulses, combining the necromantic importance of the shades' speech and the katabatic critique arising from the shades' locations. We see this throughout the poem in the figure of Vergil, who passes on a good deal of philosophical wisdom to Dante (along with the more immediately important practical knowledge needed for moving through Hell, escaping some sticky situations there, and dealing with the shades who call out to the poet). We might also recall Dante's famous encounter with his mentor, Brunetto Latini, in Canto XV; the shade's encouraging speech to Dante—revealing to him his future fame, as long as he purifies himself of Florentine corruption, in a way reminiscent of Anchises's revelation of Rome's future to Aeneas—takes place even as Brunetto continues his march across fiery sands, his punishment for sodomy. More than this, though, Dante strongly emphasizes an element of the Underworld encounter that is often much more subtle and understated in the antique models: the chastisement of the visitor by the shades. In moments like Canto X, when Farinata tells Dante he will never return to Florence, or Canto XXIV, when Vanni Fucci tells Dante that his party, the Whites, will be defeated at Pistoia, or Canto XXXII, when the Guelph traitor, Bocca degli Abati, rants at Dante, we see the poet exposing himself, his party, and his poetic project to critique. This combination of self-examination (through the challenges posed by revenant spirits) and self-encouragement (through the revelations of mentor shades) is a central component of the contemporary Underworld descent poem. After this survey, the utility of the Underworld descent for modern poets ought to be obvious. These deeply traditional narrative moments—the descent and the invocation—have at their hearts the contemplation of tradition itself; the descending hero seeks guidance precisely from those who have come before him. Odysseus meets with Tiresias and also with his mother and other members of his family, with Achilles and other members of his Achaian army. Aeneas takes his course directly from his father, Anchises. Dante follows his predecessor poet, Vergil, into the depths of the Inferno. Discussing the *Odyssey* but suggesting the applicability of his insight to the epic tradition generally, George DeForest Lord suggests that the hero's alienation, his recognition that the resources of his world and himself are exhausted, leads him to conclude that only the past can disclose his future:[19]

> Only by traveling to the perimeter of the world can he escape [Circe's] charmed circle and reorient himself by visiting the shades of his great forbears, from whom he learns about both his past and his future. The *nekuia*, then, is at once the initiatory ritual and turning point of this hero's journey, just as Vergil makes the descent into the underworld the central experience of Aeneas' voyage.[20]

Having become "Nobody," as he identifies himself to the Cyclops, having lingered with the witch Circe, lost his men to their dehumanizing, bestial desires, and lost his own sense of mission and direction, Odysseus must undergo a rehearsal of the past in order to know his future course. Aeneas, after the disastrous dalliance with Dido, and Dante, coming to himself in the darkness of the middle of his life's road, follow suit and seek their way forward through an engagement with the past as well. In her study of contemporary fictions modeled on the descent into the Underworld, Rachel Falconer argues that writers working after the Second World War do something similar in their *katabases*: "Katabatic narrative offers contemporary writers a positive structure for representing the process by which a self is created out of adversity."[21]

The past of most pressing concern to poets working through their own moments of exhaustion, confusion, and despair is often the past of their own medium, and so perhaps the most important thing about the descent and invocation topoi is the fact that, as scholars have long argued, they are interwoven with poets' concerns about poetry. Indeed, they have, from early on, structured poets' thinking about their vocation and their relationship at once to the poetic past and to the demands of their own circumstances. Pike remarks that "the ancient motif of the descent to the underworld...has over the millenia gathered around itself an ever-increasing constellation of meanings," and goes on to argue that "the topographical movement of descent and return within the motif...makes the descent a fundamentally allegorical form: the core fact of death is imbued with the hero's individual past, the past of his society, and the past of the motif itself."²² Similarly, Macdonald finds in the "Janus episode" a figure for specifically literary course-setting.²³ Because the language a poet receives is a "burial-place," Macdonald argues, the Underworld descent is an entry into the poetic past that enacts a relinquishing rehearsal of that past and a turn toward the future, a transformation of history into the discourse of fate. The descent is able to serve this function because "in the underworld all pasts are made equally present." The Underworld therefore offers "a chance to discover a new order in the past, in which the voice of the present has an authentic claim to be heard."²⁴ That which is in the Underworld is dead, but it retains a powerful influence on the living poet. The journey to the Underworld, Macdonald writes, "has something like the effect of liberating the poet from repressed material that he would otherwise have to repeat."²⁵ The literary past can be mastered only when the living poet undergoes the chastening but ultimately enabling journey down into it and demonstrates his or her ability at once to survive the ordeal and to one-up the dead.

Each deployment of the Underworld descent also addresses the specific exigencies of its own historical moment. I have mentioned the critique of Greek civilization in Book VI of the *Aeneid*, but we should also note that the parade of a glorious future that Anchises reveals to Aeneas is the glorious Roman past that Vergil narrates so as to justify the new empire of Augustus. In his *Inferno*, Dante meets figures involved in the contemporary Florentine conflicts (between Guelfs and Ghibellines) that resulted in his own exile from the city in 1302. Indeed, some of the contemporaries Dante consigns to Hell were still alive at the time of the poem's composition, so that the machinery of the Underworld's evaluative space, its cartography of crime and punishment, is applied for purposes of cultural critique. While Hell itself is timeless, the specific revenants Dante encounters there are, in some cases, written in for reasons quite timely during the struggle between forces of Florentine autonomy and Papal authority and those of Hohenstaufen imperial ambition that raged around the poet as he wrote. In a similar way, William Blake—who engraved an illuminated version of the *Inferno*—mobilized the familiar components of the Underworld descent with politically and culturally subversive aims in his *Marriage of Heaven and Hell*. Visiting a printing house in Hell (playing on the "printer's devils" who operated presses and referring obliquely to the politically radical press that produced revolutionary tracts and pamphlets in the early 1790s), Blake discovers a prophetic wisdom useful in his own worldly struggles, a series of proverbs that challenge the dictates of monarchical and religious authority in England. Moreover, Blake witnesses a "diabolical" method of writing, which he resolves to bring with him as a literary and artistic praxis in the world above. On one level, he thereby grounds and justifies the acid-engraving technique with which he produced his illuminated books. On another level, though, Blake makes an implicit argument for the role of literature in society: to "cleanse the doors of perception" and enable revolutionary change. This imperative is one to which I pay particular attention in this book's second part, for it informs the specific anxiety by which a number of contemporary poets have been beset and which they have attempted to work out through the conventions of the descent into the Underworld or the invocation of the shades of the dead. The Dantean combination of self-critique and self-justification and the Blakean explicitness about poetry's world-altering power inform a series of poetic explorations of poetry's power to influence the world (or its lack of such power) and of the ethical problems that arise from either that power or its absence.

* * *

My aims in this book are not primarily etiological. It is, however, useful to hazard some guesses about why the Underworld descent, especially in forms other than allusions to the myth of Persephone (which were popular throughout the nineteenth century), rose to poetic prominence in the 1910s. One historical fact not to be ignored is the frequency with which Europeans and Americans of the late nineteenth and early twentieth centuries experienced actual subterranean space. David Pike begins his 2005 book, *Subterranean Cities*, by locating the roots of contemporary obsessions with "all things underground" to the "complex drainage systems, underground railways, utility tunnels, and storage vaults" of the nineteenth-century city.[26] He goes on to demonstrate in rich detail the transformations wrought on the urban imagination by the increasing habitation of underground spaces, especially the underground railways that began to operate in London and Paris in the 1860s and 1870s.[27] In her *Notes on the Underground*, Rosalind Williams points to the Industrial Revolution's expansion of mining as well as the building of canals and railroad tunnels in addition to the urban underground on which Pike focuses. With the Industrial Revolution, she writes, "underground enterprises became proximate, central, and large-scale, rather than remote, peripheral, and small-scale."[28] Decades before ground was broken for London's Metropolitan Line, Marc Isambard Brunel and his son, Isambard Kingdom Brunel, were engineering their famous Thames Tunnel (though it took almost twenty years to complete the three-mile link between Rotherhithe and Wapping; the tunnel was begun in 1826 and did not open until 1843). And even before Brunel developed the shield that would enable digging beneath the bed of the Thames, miners in Yorkshire and Wales were excavating tunnels and galleries to exploit the coal seams of their mountainous regions. Both Williams and Pike persuasively argue that the widespread experience of underground spaces had profound effects on modern culture in Europe and England. When, during the International Exposition of 1867, Parisians and tourists, including visiting royalty, entered the new sewers (the system had expanded tenfold since 1800), they engaged, Williams writes, in the construction of a new social infrastructure and a new consciousness shaped by the new technological infrastructure of the Underground.[29] Pike argues that the late nineteenth century, with the development of underground urban transportation, was "the first occasion that the majority of the population, and especially the middle class, spent any significant amount of time below the earth," and that, as a result, those underground spaces were imaginatively transformed.[30]

Both Pike and Williams spend a good deal of time analyzing the literary and artistic, as well as architectural, evidence of the transformative effects of the Underground on consciousness as well as the transformations wrought on the Underground by human creative will and ingenuity, and the archive of nineteenth-century literature and art that worked to interpret and influence the Underground is rich indeed. Not only does Victor Hugo include a lengthy digression on and a climactic episode in the sewers, in which he locates history and truth, in *Les Miserables* (1862), and not only does H.G. Wells imagine a race of people utterly transformed by subterranean existence in *The Time Machine* (1895), but a wide range of writers, from Eugene Sue in *Les Mysterés de Paris* to Marcel Allain and

Pierre Souvestre in their serial, *Fantomas*, from Pierce Egan in *Life in London* (1823) to Alice Meynell in "The London Sunday," go underground to dramatize and make sense of this new level of contemporary urban life. From time to time, the mythological Underworld is brought to bear in these interpretive efforts. Pike quotes French architect Louis Heuzé, for example, writing of the excavation of tunnels for the Métro, worrying over the toxic effects that might follow when the "fetid heritage of past generations" (as opposed to the historic truth Hugo locates in the sewers) is revealed and decrying the "mephitic exhalations" that might be released in the process of digging.[31] He writes that Hector Guimard's famous Métro entryways were "translated into angry visions of hell," and describes a 1905 Guillaume drawing in which Dante and Vergil stand beside a crowded Métro car whose glowing top "reinforces the Dantesque recollection of infernal flames."[32]

But the cultural texts examined by both of these important authors really explore the "underground" as opposed to "underworld" of the urban and industrial nineteenth century. If the texts use the latter as they set out to understand the former, they still do not explain the motives for doing so, the attractive power of that specific vocabulary of imagery and narrative.[33] I want to conclude this section by pointing to two cultural trends that might have highlighted the *nekuia* and *katabasis* as potentially useful schema for poets in the twentieth century. The first is the renewed and energetic scholarly attention paid to these topoi by classicists in the first two decades of the twentieth century. The Oxford classicist J.A.K. Thomson's 1914 *Studies in the Odyssey* explored the origins of the figure of Odysseus in ancient Greek mythology and religion. Thomson's work painstakingly locates those origins in Boeotia, crucially by locating the *nekuia* of Book XI there and by arguing that this "Visit to the Dead" is not only "an original part of the Odysseus saga" but also that "there is no part older than that."[34] Thomson was not alone among influential classicists bringing new attention to the *nekuia* through a methodological focus on ancient Greek ritual and religion. His work is indebted to that of Jane Harrison, whose *Prolegomena to the Study of Greek Religion* (1903) and *Themis* (1912) grounded the Odyssean *nekuia* in ancient rituals of blood sacrifice, exorcism, and oracular consultation.[35] The work of Thomson and Harrison, as well as that of their colleague Gilbert Murray, was dispersed through British culture of the early twentieth century not only by their books but also by their teaching at Oxford and Cambridge, teaching in precisely the field studied by so many writers and others who would go on to influence modern writing.

Almost certainly more important to most modern poets than these classicists' renewed attention to the ancient Underworld descent was the widespread popularity of Dante among cultural elites of the early twentieth century. Whereas the Homeric *nekuia* might have achieved a higher cultural profile due to new scholarship from the 1880s through the 1910s (Harrison's earliest work on the episode was published in her 1882 *Odyssey in Art and Literature*), Dante and the *Inferno* were continually visible throughout the nineteenth century. Translated by Henry Wadsworth Longfellow, Dante Gabriel Rosetti, and others, famously illustrated by the artist Gustave Doré (and less famously, until later, by William Blake), and engaged at length in poetry and prose by writers ranging from Percy Shelley (in *Prometheus Unbound* and *A Defence of Poetry*), Robert Browning, John Ruskin, Alfred Tennyson, and Rosetti, Dante was a figure much on the mind of nineteenth-century poets.[36] It is out of that attention to Dante that Yeats, in 1896, derived the insights he published in a series of essays on Blake's illustrations for the *Divine Comedy*, insights he revisited and revised over the next thirty years in what Steve Ellis has described as Yeats's "attempt to re-define some of the central problems of Romantic poetic theory."[37] The core of Dante's importance for Yeats is an aspect of the earlier poet that might have appealed to many writers grappling with the way things seemed to fall apart during the twentieth century's second decade; as Ellis writes, "it was above all in the imposition of regularity on a world of disordered conflict that Yeats felt he was following the Dante who 'saw all things set in order.' "[38]

Yeats brought some attention to Dante through his prose (from the 1896 essays through *A Vision* in 1937), but Dante was much more effectively popularized by Ezra Pound, who lived with Yeats at Stone Cottage and worked as his secretary during the winters of 1913–1916. By that time, Pound had already published his *Spirit of Romance* (1910), a study of medieval Provencal and Tuscan poets leading up to and including Dante, and that book grew out of lectures he had been giving in London since shortly after his arrival in the city in 1908. He was almost as tireless a promoter of Dante as of his own work, and in his *Draft of XVI Cantos*, first published in 1925, Pound effectively assimilated these two projects by modeling the two penultimate cantos (XIV and XV) on Dante's vision of Hell. That book begins with the Underworld that predates and prefigures Dante's, the portal opened on the sands of the Cimmerian Lands in the eleventh book of the *Odyssey*, so that in Pound we find these two infernal strands of early twentieth-century culture—the classicists' renewed attention to the *nekuia* and the continuation of interest in Dante—intertwined. This suggests a third impetus for the poetic visits to the Underworld with which this book is concerned: the model and influence (as guide to follow or example to reject) of Pound himself.

*   *   *

The factors I have dealt with here—the modern European's frequent experience of underground spaces, the cultural prominence of Dante, and the revival of scholarly interest in the *nekuia* in the first decades of the twentieth century—coalesce in the work of poets who served in the First World War. Many of these poets not only endured subterranean lives in trenches and dugouts on the Front, but they also brought to those experiences their knowledge of mines, sewers, and underground railways, their reading of classical and medieval texts, including the *Odyssey* and the *Inferno*, and, in some cases, their knowledge of contemporary debates among classicists like Harrison and Thomson. Robert Graves's 1917 poem, "The Escape," is perhaps the most explicit in its deployment of the *katabasis*. Graves writes in the poem's introductory note that he had been mistakenly reported dead and he goes on in the poem to narrate his experience of this brief "death" in terms of the classical Underworld of Hades. He finds himself "half-way down the road / To Lethe" and is only saved from the "vapours of forgetfulness" by Proserpine herself.[39] Pursued by the angry shades of those who must remain dead, Graves flees, only to be confronted by Cerberus, whom he finally pacifies with "army biscuit smeared with jam" and "morphia...bought on leave."[40]

While Graves's is the most explicit Underworld poem of the Great War, Wilfred Owen's "Strange Meeting" is the most powerful, not least because it synthesizes the classical topos and the contemporary spaces of trench and mine, subordinating the specifics of the classical Underworld to the importance of the encounter with the dead at the poem's heart. Both poems are in rhyming couplets (though Owen's rhymes are more often slant), but where Graves casts his Underworld descent in a tartly ironic tone and in the indicative mood, Owen casts his in the shadow of figuration: "It seemed that out of battle I escaped / Down some profound dull tunnel."[41] His speaker finds no analogue for Cerberus or Proserpine. Instead, when he probes the "encumbered sleepers" in the tunnel and is confronted by one who stands and stares at him in recognition, the speaker simply knows by the man's "dead smile" that he is "in Hell." Rather than the topography familiar from the Hells of Dante or Vergil, Owen's tunnel, both in its description and in the poet's diction, is based on the familiar mines of his youth. The tunnel is, for example, "groined," a product of human engineering rather than supernatural design (though the agent of the groining is "titanic wars," the adjective preserving an attenuated connection to the ancient Greek mythological Underworld). Jon Stallworthy has noted the poem's resonance with a pit explosion at a nearby colliery (12 January 1918) and quotes Owen himself writing of how he mixes up "the War" with "a poem on the Colliery Disaster" ("Miners," with its "poor lads / Left in the ground").[42] Stallworthy goes so far as to trace Owen's "vision of a subterranean Hell" through not only "Miners" but also "Cramped in that funneled hole," "The Kind Ghosts," "Deep under turfy grass and heavy clay," and all the way back "to the Calvinist Hell of which Owen must have heard at his mother's knee."[43]

The most important contrast between the two poems is to be found in their climactic encounters. Where Graves grapples with Cerberus and ultimately succeeds in escaping by drugging the dog, Owen more quietly, less comically, and more finally engages in a colloquy with a dead enemy soldier. Owen's narrative not only draws on different elements of the Underworld descent, on episodes like Odysseus's encounter with the shade of Achilles and Aeneas's provocative appearance to the shades of the dead Achaians, but it also (as a result) focuses on a truth different from the one Graves delivers. Where Graves escapes (and this conclusion is emphasized by the poem's title), demonstrating thereby the insufficiency of received myths against the experience of trench warfare with the irony Paul Fussell has famously argued the Great War bequeaths to modern memory,[44] Owen's speaker is condemned not only to remain in Hell and not only to accept his mortality but also to confront his own complicity in the mass murder of the Front. He makes good on the Underworld descent tradition's promise of profound wisdom, but the truths he hears from the poem's revenant will allow him neither to find his way home like Odysseus nor to found a city like Aeneas. Most readers see the poem's conclusion as its climax; it is in the last few lines that the speaker learns his interlocutor's identity ("I am the enemy you killed, my friend") and, through that, must face his own guilt. But in a moment whose importance Owen marks by crafting with slant rhymes a quatrain among the couplets, the shade delivers an even more devastating wisdom: "I mean the truth untold," the dead soldier says, "Now men will go content with what we spoiled, / Or, discontent, boil bloody, and be spilled."[45] The dead soldier offers a truth that can only be found in this Underworld, a truth available only to the dead: the pity of war is the lost value of men's "glee," which might have made many laugh, of their courage, mystery, wisdom, and mastery (key terms a few lines after those I have quoted). Achilles, the greatest and most famous warrior, immortal through his martial deeds, tells Odysseus in Book XI that he would rather live an unknown slave than suffer the afterlife as a renowned hero. The dead soldier in Owen's poem makes a similar point—the loss entailed by any individual death, whether the enemy soldier's, the speaker's, or some other happening elsewhere on the Front, the loss entailed by any among the myriad deaths of a war is inexpressible. He goes on to make a pessimistic prophecy: the disaster of these deaths will not leave a lesson that will improve the world and the generations that follow will either complacently continue in their misguided ways or take up arms in doomed attempts to right their course.

While underground spaces along the front lines might have suggested the Underworld to some classically trained English poets in the 1910s, the Underworld descent has offered itself to the poets of later, and less obviously subterranean, wars as well. In chapters 2 and 3, I will have something to say about the *nekuia* and *katabasis* in the 1930s and 1940s and its use for engaging first anxieties about and then the reality of aerial bombardment, but I want here to offer, as two termini of the war-as-Hell line whose first stations are Graves's and Owen's poems, a poem of the Vietnam War and a contemporary poem (2007) that imaginatively returns to the Great War. In Doug Anderson's "Erebus" (1994), the second-person protagonist ("you") dreams he is back in Vietnam, "naked, / stumbling along a paddy dike across an open field."[46] Hearing Aretha Franklin's "Respect," a song familiar to him from the mortar pits of his combat experience, the protagonist enters a village and finds himself surrounded by the dead.

Unlike Owen's speaker, Anderson's protagonist is brought face to face not with those for whose deaths he is responsible but with those whose lives he tried, as a medic, to save. His encounter performs a type of work often present in the Underworld descent narratives but just as often overshadowed by eye-catching scenes of eternal punishment and crucial scenes of prophetic wisdom: the healing of the hero's heart when he is reassured by one among the dead that he has done right. A key antecedent for Anderson is the passage in *Aeneid* VI when Aeneas meets the shade of Priam's son Deiphobus. Upset by the prince's appearance (his face is cruelly mutilated), Aeneas apologizes for failing to find and bury his body and describes the obsequies he performed in its absence. Deiphobus grants Aeneas the peace Dido denies him when he implores her shade just fifty lines earlier. In its final half-line—"Let us sleep now"—Owen's poem suggests a note of communion that might lead to a similar moment of reassurance, but we are denied any positive conclusion. Anderson's poem, by a survivor of the war who recollects his experience in the relative tranquility of life two decades later, imagines its protagonist being comforted by the shades. They thank him for his attempts to save them, for his practices of care under fire. They offer to clothe him, to make him comfortable beside their fire. And, most important, they extend to him assurances he had offered them in their agonies: "You're going to be fine, my man, you're going home."[47] The Underworld, in which both warriors and civilian victims gather, offers the descending hero not only guidance for his journey but also comfort and community (an offer, as I will show in chapter 3, that Yeats explores, heartbreakingly, in his late poem "Cuchulainn Comforted").

In his recent poem, "War Poet," Jon Stallworthy uses the Underworld descent of a poem like "Strange Meeting" to frame an Orphic backward glance at the experience of soldiers in the Great War. If that sentence seems to mesh diverse strands of the motif, it is accurate to Stallworthy's poem, for just as Stallworthy shows the roots of Owen's poem in Shelley's *Revolt of Islam* and in contemporary colliery explosions as well as the classical katabasis, his "War Poet" derives from a variety of Underworlds: the "Doom" (a scene of the dead rising from their graves to be judged at the Apocalypse, with the sinners heading down to Hell), the sixth book of the *Aeneid* (which provides the poem's epigraph), Dante's *Inferno* (whose terza rima Stallworthy uses in the second and fifth of his poem's seven parts), and the myth of Orpheus. The poem opens with a meditation on the "Doom" painted over the chancel arch in the Church of St. James the Great in South Leigh:

> Back to South Leigh for evensong
> and, in the sermon, watched the long
> arm of the sun restore the Doom.[48]

The scene provokes a memory of the speaker's fellow soldiers, during the First World War. Like Anderson's poem, Stallworthy's offers a sort of comradeship in the Underworld ("my own lot"), but Stallworthy's speaker, unlike Anderson's, is "reprieved" while his fellows are "detailed for Hell." Condemned to live, he is also condemned to remember, and much of the poem reconstructs his painful losses during the war—of consciousness when he is wounded by shelling, of his beloved, memories of whom drew him back from the infernal darkness of that unconsciousness, and of his own sense of himself and his capacity for self-control. Stallworthy imposes something like the chiasmic structure of the *katabasis*, bringing his speaker to a broken-hearted nadir in part five (cast in a single stanza that melds haiku with the terza rima of part two):

> Heart, full as the moon
> was full, a broken ring now,
> an empty sky soon.[49]

From this low point, the speaker emerges (though fitfully—as the Vergilian epigraph has it, the descent into Avernus is easy, but it is hard work to climb back out) through imagery of bells and light in part six (both carrying liturgical as well as romantic significance), and, finally, through the act of artistic production itself, which orders and contains even the experiences of loss the poem surveys.

*   *   *

As these poems show, the classical topoi of the Underworld descent appears in war poems from both ends of the twentieth century, but if I have been surprised by anything in the research for and writing of this book it has been by the relative infrequency with which later war poets (or even other poets of the First World War) have recurred to the Underworld descent motif. Similarly, while Rachel Falconer dates the irruption of the infernal into history at the Holocaust's bureaucratizing of genocide and while some of the descent *narratives* she analyzes address that catastrophe, it is difficult to find poetic Underworld descents that represent the Holocaust. War is, infamously, Hell, but the hells into which most twentieth-century poets have ventured tend to stage other kinds of conflicts. Chief among these are three, which make up the focal points for the chapters that follow: the poet's conflict with the literary past, the poet's conflict with elements of his or her own society, and the poet's conflict with herself or himself over the degree to which poetry can or should affect contemporary historical and political events. My focus in this book, then, is not why poets avail themselves of the *nekuia* and *katabasis* but instead what poets do with the *nekuia* and *katabasis*.

PART 1

1

DECLARATIONS OF INTERDEPENDENCE: THE NECROMANTIC CONFRONTATION WITH TRADITION

In this chapter I read deployments of the *nekuia* by two central modernist poets, Ezra Pound and T.S. Eliot. Both Pound and Eliot saw the poetic landscape that surrounded them as something of a wasteland—used up and played out. Each sought to reinvigorate poetry through a mode of experimentation and invention deeply dependent upon the resources inherent in the literary tradition. In the deliberately monumental and cannily marketed projects that consolidated a sense of modernism—Pound's 1925 *A Draft of XVI Cantos* and Eliot's 1922 *The Waste Land*—each poet had recourse to the ancient tradition of the descent into the Underworld to consult the prophet Tiresias. In the 1917 *Three Cantos* that made up his first attempt at the long poem that would come to dominate his career, and in the final version of that long poem's first Canto (1925), Pound staged a *nekuia* through which he at once enacted and justified the poetic practices by which he would "make it new." At the center of *The Waste Land*, Eliot also stages an encounter with Tiresias, who, I will argue, represents the tradition against and through which Eliot works. As Pound does in Canto I, Eliot in "The Fire Sermon" makes a forceful declaration of interdependence. I conclude this chapter with a brief look at a countertradition that coexists with Pound and Eliot and continues to the present: the feminist revision of the necromantic encounter, which emphasizes the dynamic of interdependence by modeling collaboration rather than competition.

* * *

Throughout the late 1910s, Ezra Pound cast about for the right opening and form for the ambitious long poem he had begun composing in 1915 and had considered at least since 1908.[1] The *Three Cantos* first published in *Poetry* in 1917 shows one ultimately rejected version:

> Hang it all, there can be but one *Sordello!*
> But say I want to, say I take your whole bag of tricks,
> Let in your quirks and tweeks, and say the thing's an art-form,
> Your *Sordello*, and that the modern world
> Needs such a rag-bag to stuff all its thought in;
> Say that I dump my catch, shiny and silvery
> As fresh sardines flapping and slipping on the marginal cobbles?[2]

In this opening gesture, Pound thematizes belatedness, explicitly addresses a poetic predecessor, expresses his anxiety over that predecessor's influence, and thinks out loud about the poetic form his age demands. From the beginning, Pound makes his ambitions clear. He wants to write a capacious and comprehensive poem, a "forty-year epic,"[3] a "poem including history."[4] The "catch" of poetic wisdom Pound's project might yield, a "fresh" haul that offers nourishment, could go to waste simply slipping on the "marginal cobbles" (a phrase that suggests peripheral improvisation as much as the stones of the street).

At the same time, Pound addresses the agonistic relationship between a poet and his precursors. Robert Browning's long narrative poem *Sordello* (1840) offers a model "bag of tricks," a set of formal and structural devices that might enable Pound to stuff into his "poem of some length" the disparate materials he needs it to contain. Browning crafted what Ronald Bush has called "a new kind of narrative poetry—a poetry that portrays not just an action but an authentically modern dramatization of the way an action acquires significance within an individual intelligence."[5] *Sordello* is a narrative flexible enough to include the results of Browning's medievalist research and the emotional content of his own experience, to include, as Pound puts it, "the half or third of [his] intensest life."[6]

There is a problem, though, and Pound announces it in his first line. "Hang it all, there can be but one *Sordello*." Pound cannot simply repeat the older poet's innovations. Instead, in these "*Three Cantos*" that are to begin a "forty-year epic," he must work through Browning's poem and through the tradition Browning had himself synthesized and addressed to find his own "art-form." That process leads him through an extended critique of Browning (in *Three Cantos* 1) and an elaboration of the paratactic method that will dominate the early Cantos in their final version, especially the juxtaposition of a flat and fallen present with moments of illumination (spiritual and artistic) in the past. Pound's critique of Browning is intertwined with a stab at the new form his long poem will take, a form built on Pound's experiments in the 1910s with the luminous detail, the image, and the vortex, a form comprising fragments (of historical information, literary text, commentary, episodes from personal experience) juxtaposed to dramatize artistic wandering in the darkness.[7]

All this gets especially interesting at the end of *Three Cantos*, when Pound forces the moment to its crisis by going to Hell. In some readings, Pound and his poem have *been* in a hell of sorts, encountering the shades of bygone artists since the opening invocation of Browning and *Sordello*.[8] At the end of *Three Cantos* 3, however, Pound explicitly invokes the *nekuia* of Odysseus in *Odyssey* XI. A revised version of this passage, which is the penultimate moment of *Three Cantos* 3, opens Canto I in the 1925 *A Draft of XVI Cantos* and has been readers' introduction to *The Cantos* ever since. In its position as the conclusion of *Three Cantos*, the encounter with the Underworld shades restates and refocuses the poem's thematic engagement with the problem of belatedness. In what follows, I read the episode first to show what work it does for Pound at the conclusion of *Three Cantos* and then to show how the *nekuia* performs a different task when revised, reframed, and removed to the beginning of the 1925 *A Draft of XVI Cantos*.

Ronald Bush writes that Odysseus "is one of a series of heroes lost in individual dark nights,"[9] but Pound's framing of the episode suggests not simply Odysseus's wandering but also the poet's own struggle to wrest that wandering into language of his own:

> Uncatalogued Andreas Divus,
> Gave him in Latin, 1538 in my edition, the rest uncertain,
> Caught up his cadence, word and syllable
> . . . .
> I've strained my ear for—*ensa*,—*ombra*, and—*ensa*
> And cracked my wit on delicate canzoni——
> Here's but rough meaning:
> "And then went down to the ship, . . .[10]

Pound focuses here not on the narrative dark night Bush describes but on matters of translation and poetic form, the problems of "cadence, word and syllable." He emphasizes the difficulties of carrying these over from one language into another, writing that he has expended enormous efforts ("strained my ear," "cracked my wit") on the linguistic and cultural specificities of form.

The passage thus framed exemplifies Pound's solution. Where the speaker offers "rough meaning," a cursory reading of the first few lines of his rendering shows that this "roughness" might mean something other than hastily literal:

> And then went down to the ship, set keel to breakers,
> Forth on the godly sea;
> We set up mast and sail on the swarthy ship,
> Sheep bore we aboard her, and our bodies also
> Heavy with weeping. And winds from sternward
> Bore us out onward with bellying canvas—
> Circe's this craft, the trim-coifed goddess.[11]

As numerous readers have noted, the patterns of assonance, consonance, and alliteration, as well as the syntactic archaism (the inversion in "Sheep bore we aboard her") and odd diction ("swarthy ship") resemble the voice Pound had crafted for his translation of the Anglo-Saxon "Seafarer":

> May I for my own self song's truth reckon,
> Journey's jargon, how I in harsh days
> Hardship endured oft.[12]

The combination of frame and form focuses on two related literary problematics: the construction of a textual throat that can give voice to the literary tradition, and the specific networks of transmission through which that tradition comes into this constructed throat in the first place. The "cadence, word and syllable" Pound crafts for the *nekuia* embody his sense of the episode's age (Pound wrote in a 1935 letter that "the *Nekuia* shouts aloud that it is older than the rest...").[13] As Hugh Kenner writes, Pound's version of English poetry's oldest form offers a suitable set of vocal cords for the sounding of the Western tradition's oldest narrative, ritual, and topos; the form bears an analogous relationship to its content.[14] At the same time, the frame here foregrounds the roads texts travel to their translators. Pound has not been looking into Chapman's Homer, nor has he been reading the epic in Greek. The mediation of Divus, as much as the age of the episode, accounts for the form Pound's passage takes; he has worked at "—*ensa*, —*ombra*, and —*ensa*" not because they are in Homer but because they are in the mediating versions through which Odysseus has wandered on his way to Pound. Kenner again: "The Canto is not simply...a passing through the [Odyssean] knot of newer rope. It is also *about the*

fact that self-interfering patterns persist while new ways of shaping breath flow through them."[15]
        At the end of *Three Cantos* 3, then, Pound arrives at something like the beginning (of Western literature, of English poetry). What, though, is the significance of Odysseus' descent for Pound's project? Leon Surette argues that the *nekuia* condenses the ritual climax of the Eleusinian mysteries, in which initiates acted out a descent into Hades and an encounter with Persephone.[16] Hugh Witemeyer argues that Odysseus offers the "protean archetype of a mythical hero" out of which the historical figures who become the poem's "minor heroes" must be shown to emerge.[17] Perhaps. Part of the episode's attraction for Pound, though, is simply the episode's ancient character. As Bush writes, Pound's belief that the *nekuia* predates the rest of the *Odyssey* would have been influenced by such scholars as Jane Harrison and James Alexander Ker Thomson. Thomson's 1914 *Studies in the Odyssey*, for example, makes its case emphatically: "But is the Visit to the Dead an original part of the Odyssean saga? The answer is, yes; THERE IS NO PART OLDER THAN THAT."[18] Moreover, it is specifically the visit to Tiresias that is most ancient; Thomson writes that "the core of the Odyssean *nekyia* [*sic*] is an actual, very ancient Boeotian tradition of a visit to consult Tiresias."[19]
        Why is the episode's vast age so important for Pound? Bush suggests that Odysseus' blood offering to Tiresias was "at once an affirmative communion with the Olympian gods and a fearful purificatory exorcism of the chthonic powers."[20] Pound's translation would, therefore, participate in these ritual resonances, a participation made more important, Bush points out, by Pound's choice to start his translation at the line where Dante begins Ulysses' speech in the *Inferno* and also perhaps by his decision to end it with a reference to Hermes ("Argicida"), who conducted souls to the Underworld.[21] What this adds up to for Bush is that Odysseus is another in the series of individuals wandering in the darkness; he must, with the rest of those figures, be quieted and purged. Kenner reads Odysseus' significance more positively. The *nekuia* is an "autochthonous knot," a "pattern persisting undeformable while many languages have flowed through it."[22] As such, it offers a model for translation (in which the conveyance of this "energized pattern" from one language to another is the goal), which is to say, since Pound found in translation a "model for the poetic act," that the *nekuia* stands as the first instance of something like *poetry*.[23] Pound's arrival at *Odyssey* XI, in this reading, is something like an arrival at the primal source of the poetic, a source that will energize Pound's project (which is, as the Divus

frame suggests, to focus poetry on its own processes, including the processes by which it is transmitted and reshaped). I want to suggest another possibility, one not unrelated to these but different from them at least in emphasis. Pound opens *Three Cantos* concerned about belatedness, about his need for a new form like but not like Browning's *Sordello*. He arrives ultimately at Hades and Odysseus's invocation of Tiresias, at an ancient narrative of a more ancient rite in which the dead spirit is consulted for guidance. The arrival at the *nekuia* comes through a frame focused on poetic practice; the guidance sought here is not for the way back to Ithaca but for a way out of *Sordello*. *Three Cantos* finds their end in the beginning and in their beginning; Pound's translation of the *nekuia* dramatizes the search for a method undertaken in the very first line. The stakes of that search are also suggested by the translated passage; the first shade Odysseus encounters is that of Elpenor, the shipmate who died at Circe's island and was left unburied; he begs Odysseus for a memorial. Elpenor's plight echoes the worry of the speaker in "The Seafarer": He will be unremembered, his mortality final and complete.[24] If Frank Lentricchia is correct when he writes that Pound "was haunted for his entire career by the suspicion that he was not original," then Elpenor's is the fate Pound fears and is one keen goad to found a new (immortally memorable) poetics.[25]

We might therefore expect, at this climactic moment, a profound statement of poetics from Tiresias, but Pound cuts off his translation after the prophet speaks just one sentence. *Odyssey* XI gives Tiresias about forty lines after he drinks the blood; during his speech, he warns Odysseus about the obstacles he will encounter, describes the situation he will find at home, and offers instructions for dealing with both (and the book goes on for another five hundred lines detailing Odysseus' colloquies with other shades).[26]

Pound cuts the passage where he does because the content of Tiresias' advice is less important for his purposes than the fact of it. The passage's allegorical correspondences clarify its function. Pound is the poet on a quest for a new form. Odysseus is a figure for him. Odysseus seeks guidance from Tiresias, a prophet long sought out for his wisdom, even after his death. Pound seeks guidance from the tradition that begins with Odysseus' *nekuia*. Odysseus fights off other shades until Tiresias arrives and drinks and speaks. In a similar way, Pound has fought his way through other forms, fashions, and progenitor poets, shades who cannot offer the wisdom he needs. Indeed, he has fought his way all the way back to the beginning of the tradition, the summoning of the dead prophet from Hades. Odysseus gets

his guidance by offering blood to Tiresias. Pound gets his by offering something like it, the textual body he has fashioned through his
attention to "cadence, word and syllable" (and, perhaps, the bodily
straining and cracking entailed by the effort). Odysseus must hear the
prophet traditionally consulted. Pound must hear the tradition itself
as prophet.

Pound's *nekuia* suggests a conclusion quite different from David
Pike's analysis of the descensus ad inferos trope. Throughout his
analysis, Pike notes the relationship between the trope of the descent
and the anxiety of poetic influence. The scene bears a frisson of one-
upmanship as it plays out the justification of new poetics against the
backdrop of exhausted conventions. As Pike writes, "to be found in the
underworld, a person must be dead."[27] Pound, though, is not motivated by what Pike calls "the mortification of [his] predecessors."[28]
The prophet is indeed dead, and since he is a synecdoche for a literary
tradition, the tradition the prophet represents is dead too, powerless
and captive. At the same time, though, the hero requires the prophet's
wisdom, so much so that he engages in a perilous descent and performs the rites of summoning and sacrifice. In a similar way, the tradition's resources are enlivened by the poet who conjures them. The
function of the *nekuia* at the end of *Three Cantos* 3, then, is to declare
not the poet's independence from but instead the poet's interdependence with the tradition, to establish him as the one who grants new
life to the dead tradition by feeding it with the blood of his innovation
while acknowledging his fundamental need for the tradition's buried
wisdom. As Lentricchia puts it, "Ezra Pound, Odyssean poet, makes
his descent into the West's literary underworld in order to conjure the
ghosts of writers past in a poetry of reading. Homer's hero summons
the dead with the ritual of blood sacrifice; Pound, with the blood of
scholarly poetic labor, would summon Homer..."[29] He would, moreover, summon Homer to sanction his own innovative poetic project,
a project that crucially involves foregrounding the processes of composition and transmission themselves. Homer's blessing would, not
incidentally, guarantee Pound's own immortality in literary memory
and figuratively bury poor Elpenor.

So far so good, but between 1917 and 1925, when he published
A Draft of XVI Cantos with Three Mountains Press in Paris, Pound
relocated the *nekuia* to the beginning of Canto I. His translation of
Odyssey XI is now one of the most famous opening gestures in modern poetry: "And then went down to the ships." The *Three Cantos* of
1917 is thus made obsolete, scrubbed from *The Cantos*, relegated to
an appendix in the most readily available selection of Pound's shorter

poems. Why the shift? What different work does the *nekuia* do in its new, and now canonical, position?

The bibliographic features of *A Draft of XVI Cantos*—the volume's large size and decorative cover, its fine printing on special paper, its red-printed capitals, its Henry Strater illuminations—all enhance the archaism of what is now the opening Canto's narrative and style. As numerous critics have said, these features constitute an artifactual allusion to medieval illuminated manuscripts; they position the book as part of a tradition of monumental codices and in so doing they materially enact the poetics of transmission that is the poem's chief innovation and achievement.[30] Even in the subsequent, undecorated versions, though, the *nekuia* works differently as Canto I than as the end of *Three Cantos* 3. I want to point out three key changes and to suggest the new work these changes make the *nekuia* do for Pound's "forty-year epic."

We should first note the revisions Pound makes in the translation itself between its 1917 and 1925 versions. Many of these, especially for the first sixty-five lines or so, are fairly insignificant: alterations of capitalization, punctuation, lineation, and, in some cases, syntax. A couple of diction changes—"dreory" for "dreary"—thicken the atmosphere of archaism ("dreory," from the Anglo-Saxon *dreorig* at once adds some literal blood to the passage and points up the stylistic connection to the roots of English poetry in Anglo-Saxon verse). The end of the translation, though, is more heavily revised. The 1917 version follows Tiresias' speech ("Odysseus, shalt / Return through spiteful Neptune, over dark seas, / Lose all companions") with reference to Odysseus's further encounters with the shades:

> Foretold me the ways and the signs.
> Came then Anticlea, to whom I answered:
> "Fate drives me on through these deeps; I sought Tiresias."
> I told her news of Troy, and thrice her shadow
> Faded in my embrace.
> Then had I news of many faded women—
> Tyro, Alemena, Chloris—
> Heard out their tales by that dark fosse, and sailed
> By sirens and thence outward and away
> And unto Circe buried Elpenor's corpse.[31]

Two lines of white space intervene before Divus is commanded to "Lie quiet." In the 1925 version, the passage is condensed and reordered:

> "Lose all companions." And then Anticlea came.
> Lie quiet Divus. I mean that is Andreas Divus,

In officina Wecheli, 1538, out of Homer.
And he sailed, by Sirens and thence outward and away
And unto Circe.[32]

What gets cut? Elpenor's burial, for one thing, which leaves the anxiety of innovation an open and pressing question. More importantly, perhaps, most of Odysseus's human, as opposed to poetic, concerns are deleted; the 1925 version includes none of Odysseus's attempts to embrace his mother, Anticlea, and no sympathetic hearing of the "faded" women's tales. Pound's cuts keep the focus tight on issues directly pertaining to his poetic project.

Second, the reshuffling of lines that makes "Lie quiet Divus" precede rather than follow "sailed . . . outward and away" is worth a moment's attention, for it suggests a shift in that poetic project itself. Where the *Odyssey* translation's frame in *Three Cantos* 3 positioned the passage so it could exemplify a theory of translation and, through translation, of poetry, with the route the narrative took to Pound (via Divus) duly (but only duly) noted, the incomplete frame in Canto I (no introduction for the translation and then the abrupt interruption of the ego scriptor cantilenae addressing Divus) diminishes the importance of translation ("cadence, word and syllable") while emphasizing that of transmission ("In officina Wecheli, 1538, out of Homer," a line that illustrates one element of what Jerome McGann means when he calls *The Cantos* a "poem including bibliography").[33] In 1917, Pound's attempt at immortalizing innovation comprised explicit attention to translation and, through that, the specific forms thought might take in particular languages. By 1925, Pound has resolved instead on the specific bibliographic routes a narrative takes through various languages and historic moments. He therefore foregrounds Divus as his source and deemphasizes his own work of translation.

In addition, the brief return to the *Odyssey* after the "footnote" to Divus (Pound names the Sirens and Circe, two female presences that distract and obstruct and threaten Odysseus on his quest), leads differently into the Canto's concluding lines, subordinating questions of style to the newly central narrative of transmission. *Three Cantos* 3 provides a smooth transition from the *nekuia* to a Latin translation of the Second Homeric Hymn to Aphrodite: Pound's description of the colophon in Divus' translation leads to a description of the volume's contents, which include G.D. Cretensis's Latin translations of Homeric hymns as well as Divus' *Odyssey*. This transition suggests an opposition between Divus' translation of Odysseus' journey and Georgius' translations of the apostrophes to Aphrodite.

Writing that Divus's "thin clear Tuscan stuff / Gives way before the florid mellow phrase," Pound suggests that the shift here outlines an aesthetic conflict (consonant with the 1917 frame's emphasis on style in translation). *A Draft of XVI Cantos'* Canto I makes a more abrupt transition to a much shorter quotation from the Homeric Hymn. Pound deletes the stylistic comparison and simply juxtaposes Cretensis's Latin "Venerandam" to the end of the *Odyssey* translation. As John L. Foster writes, this highlights the importance of Aphrodite as a "patron of the protagonist" and opening avatar of the female principle that will recur throughout the poem.[34]

While Odysseus sails away, however, the poem does not. Instead, it shifts (through the Homeric hymn) from the mythological narrative of the *Odyssey* to the literary narrative of the *Aeneid*. The Aphrodite praised as "Venerandam" is Aeneas' mother. Argicida ("slayer of Argos") refers to Hermes, who conducts dead souls to Hades with his golden staff. Aeneas obtains this "golden bough" and offers it to Persephone as he undertakes his own journey into the Underworld. *Three Cantos* 3 ends at this point, with Hermes' golden bough, one descent leading directly to another by way of the books out of which Pound reads them. Canto I deletes the transition so that Odysseus' continued journey is juxtaposed with the more fragmentary focuses on Aphrodite and Hermes that conclude the Canto. The revision at once eliminates an evocation of divine beauty (the longer quotation from the Homeric Hymn) and suggests that even Odysseus does not sail out of the Underworld. Canto I's concluding phrase ("So that:") makes his descent and its literary descendent (the *Aeneid*) the opening gambits in the dramatic narrative of the Western literary tradition and in the dramatic narrative that subsequent Cantos will explore.

Finally, and most important, what difference does it make that the *nekuia* that was the closing moment of *Three Cantos* 3 now, with the revisions I have described, appears as Canto I? How does this shift alter the work the invocation does? Witemeyer writes that Pound moved the episode to the front of his poem because "Pound could not 'hang his shimmering garment on' any of the historical figures who were his minor heroes."[35] Leon Surette suggests that the *nekuia* as an opening gesture foregrounds the Cantos' relationship to the Eleusinian mysteries.[36] I find more persuasive the notion that Pound's shifting of the *nekuia* follows from the way the poem changed and developed as he worked on the Cantos between 1917 and 1925. Different critics point to different moments as key in the revision and elaboration of this poetics. Christine Froula's analysis of Canto IV from its earliest drafts (in 1915) through its final form suggests that Pound's work on this Canto led to the structuring principle of the "subject rhyme," the recognition and indication of thematic parallels in historical episodes.[37] Thomas Grieve locates the important moment in Pound's work on the long poems whose composition falls between *Three Cantos* and *A Draft of XVI Cantos*: "Hugh Selwyn Mauberley" and "Homage to Sextus Propertius."[38] Alternatively, Lawrence Rainey's painstaking reconstruction of Pound's work on the Malatesta sequence (Cantos VIII–VI) leads him to argue that that work (in 1922 and 1923) "marked a catalytic moment" and "precipitated a radical revision of all the earlier cantos, crystallizing the design for the larger poem, which until then had remained obscure to Pound himself."[39] Similarly, critics differ (understandably) on the purposes that undergird Pound's poem as a whole. While Lentricchia argues that Pound seeks to purify language by scraping away the abstract and isolating the particular, Bush writes that Pound sought to unify poetry and action, the gulf between which had defeated Browning (or at least his protagonist, Sordello), while Froula argues that Pound attempts to "find a poetic form to embody a changing experience of history."[40] Whatever the crucial moment and whatever the broad purpose, most readers agree on the constituents of Pound's modernist poetics: discontinuity, fragmentation, juxtaposition, the image, the incorporation of historical documents, the palimpsestic overlay of materials from different eras to demonstrate their spiritual congruence. Pound moved the *nekuia* to the beginning, in part, in order to justify that poetics in the way the descent topos made available: through a confrontation with the tradition he sought at once to declare dead on arrival and to enliven with his own innovating breath.

Ultimately, the removal of the *nekuia* to Canto I is a product of Pound's solution of the problem introduced in the first line of *Three Cantos* 1: the recognition of belatedness. The descent in search of prophetic wisdom is an admission of that belatedness. Rather than succumbing to it, though, Pound thematizes it and bases his poetic innovations upon it. He will undertake the work left for a poet in the wake of "the one *Sordello*," the self-referential sifting and recombining of the best that has already been thought and written. Opening his poem with the ritual invocation to Tiresias (and with Elpenor's plea), Pound foregrounds the interdependence of poet and tradition (and the stakes of innovation); these are the conclusion at which he arrives in August 1917's issue of *Poetry*, and they become the starting point and subject matter in the deluxe volume printed in Paris in 1925. Moreover, the jump directly into Homer (deleting the quotation marks that would indicate the passage's mediated status) evinces a confidence lacking in the long lead-up to the *nekuia* in *Three Cantos*.

Now the poem's first gesture is not an anxious encounter with an ancestor poet but a powerful and empowering mastery of the tradition at its ancient, chthonic, and ritual roots. Beginning at the beginning, with the dawn of Western literature in Odysseus' descent, with poetry's descent into prehistory, legend, and necromancy, and in the voice of something like the beginnings of English poetry in Anglo-Saxon alliterative verse, Pound promises that the poetics he here enacts and the project he here inaugurates will synthesize the vast literary tradition of the West (an ambition made even more vast as the poem proceeds and the East comes into play as well). The opening passage, a translation of a translation whose footnote makes explicit the dynamics of transmission, promises that through his poetic innovations Pound will make his poem one that truly includes (all of) history.

* * *

Pound's revision of *Three Cantos* emphasizes the poet's relationship to tradition by placing it—thematically, formally, and even theoretically— right at the beginning of his poem. Writing at the same time, often with Pound's editorial input, T.S. Eliot locates a necromantic encounter with Tiresias (and the tradition he represents) not at the beginning but right at the very heart of *The Waste Land*. By that I mean first of all that the Tiresias episode is simply at the geographic center of the poem: the vision occurs in the middle of "The Fire Sermon," the third of the poem's five parts. The necromantic episode is located not only in the poem's middle section but right in the middle of that middle section, framed by the other episodes into which "The Fire Sermon" is divided.[41] Tiresias therefore appears in the central position within the section as well as within the poem as a whole.

Eliot explains Tiresias's centrality in his notes to the poem. There, he famously writes:

> Tiresias, although a mere spectator and not indeed a "character," is yet the most important personage in the poem, uniting all the rest. Just as the one-eyed merchant, seller of currants, melts into the Phoenician Sailor, and the latter is not wholly distinct from Ferdinand, Prince of Naples, so all the women are one woman, and the two sexes meet in Tiresias. What Tiresias sees, in fact, is the substance of the poem.[42]

Eliot's character-focused account here is instructive both for its thematic emphasis on the meeting of the sexes and its indications about the poem's procedure of juxtaposing thematically resonant fragments. Eliot's note offers Tiresias as a synthesis of the poem's narrative and formal concerns. I will begin my discussion of the *nekuia* in *The Waste Land* by arguing that among those concerns is the same sense of belatedness and the concomitant anxiety that motivated Pound. Both this anxiety and the Underworld descent as a means for managing it are present in Eliot's work long before *The Waste Land*, as early as "The Love Song of J. Alfred Prufrock," in which Eliot arrived at a provisional solution. That solution did not hold, though, and Eliot in the early 1920s must once more negotiate the potentially disabling weight the Tradition imposes on the individual poet. Just as Pound's resolution in *Three Cantos* 3 is revised in Canto I, Eliot's resolution in "Prufrock" is replaced by the one at which he arrives through the transformation of "He Do the Police in Different Voices" into *The Waste Land* in 1921–1922. I will argue that Tiresias and his vision in the "violet hour" passage of "The Fire Sermon" constitute an allusion to the Odyssean *nekuia* through which Eliot, like Pound, establishes and justifies a new poetic project built upon an avowed interdependence with the literary tradition.

The anxiety of the young poet in the face of the powerful voices in the literary tradition he inherits is palpably present in Eliot's first major poem, "The Love Song of J. Alfred Prufrock" (published in *Poetry* in 1915 but written in 1910 and 1911). There, a part of what threatens speech (and the speaker) is an overwhelming sense of belatedness, a sense that what he wants to say has already been said. In the Underworld of that poem, we find Eliot first encountering what he will come to call "Tradition" as an enervating and disabling force. Tiresias' vision in "The Fire Sermon"'s *nekuia* is a revision of Eliot's problematics of poetry, power, and predecessors in "Prufrock."

That "Prufrock" plays out in a figurative Underworld is not obvious but neither is it obscure. The poem's epigraph quotes Guido da Montefeltro in Dante's *Inferno*; to Dante, Guido says "If I thought that my reply would be to someone who would ever return to earth, this flame would remain without further movement; but as no one has ever returned alive from this gulf, if what I hear is true, I can answer you with no fear of infamy."[43] The epigraph strongly suggests that the words that follow are spoken in an Underworld and that their speakers assume that their speech will not be heard in the world of the living. Under the shadow of this allusion, the opening lines' evocation of various demimondes (of French Symbolisme, of the urban waterfront or red-light district) read also as descriptions of a "submonde." Where but in Hell would the evening be "spread out against the sky / Like a patient etherised upon a table"? The images of sawdust and oyster shells, the bits left over after the life in trees and oysters has been consumed, takes on a hellish cast, as does the yellow fog that creeps and curls up a few lines later.

From the beginning, the poem emphasizes the inefficacy, and even the danger, of speech. The opening strophe names a number of speech acts, but each is somehow negative: "muttering," "tedious argument," an "overwhelming question" whose asking is forestalled. As the poem continues, it forges an increasingly intense connection between speech and violence (specifically, violence the speaker fears will be directed at him). The speech of the unspecified "They" will emphasize his physical deterioration (itself reminiscent of those exhausted fragments in the opening description). Voices are "dying with a dying fall"; one is fixed "in a formulated phrase"; a casually devastating "That is not what I meant at all" threatens the worth even of an utterance that might squeeze "the universe into a ball"; and, finally, "human voices wake us and we drown."

When we accept the speaker's invitation—"Let us go then you and I"—we follow him into a space of "muttering retreats" characterized by detritus (sawdust, oyster shells). These images of exhaustion are fit metonyms for the "retreats" and fit emblems for the linguistic bits and pieces—the allusions and partial quotations—that "mutter" in them. Those allusions emphasize the deadly danger of overly ambitious speech (precisely the sort of thing that might be met with the dismissive "That is not it, at all").

Eliot would not, I think, accept an equation of poetry with prophecy ("That is not what I meant at all"). Nevertheless, as Eliot would agree, the two genres share aspects of invocation and authority, as well as similar rhetorical repertoires. Poetry might be prophecy's replacement in a fallen age; it is, after all, the locus of speech trained on verities rather than velleities (those light inclinations that resemble "talking of Michelangelo" and are implicitly damned in "Portrait of a Lady"). Whether prophet, poet, or Polonius-like courtier, though, Prufrock is thwarted, preemptively "cut off" by the speech acts that surround him and that saturate his own so that he finally, frustrated, shouts (in the poem's only line punctuated with an exclamation mark): "It is impossible to say just what I mean!"[44] Formulated phrases, whether those of the society women Prufrock fears or of the poets Prufrock quotes, are, at least potentially, silencing.

The solution Eliot develops in 1910–1911 hinges on the difference between speech and song. Even as Prufrock's inarticulate performance suggests anxiety over those poets' influence, Eliot finds in their formulated phrases the means for saying just what he means. Or, perhaps, for singing just what he means, for while speech is beset with danger and difficulty, the speaker hears "the mermaids singing each to each" with apparent ease. On one hand, theirs is a siren song; the mermaids can be seen as figures for the women who populate the poem and emasculate Prufrock. On the other hand, though, it is around their song that the poem itself becomes most lyrical. Eliot composes tercets here, the series interrupted by the single line "I do not think that they will sing to me." He regulates the meter; where earlier passages seem intentionally to keep off kilter, these lines are emphatically iambic (with some initial anapestic substitutions). He rhymes: "peach," "beach," "each"; "back," "black"; "brown," "drown." By the final stanza, the speaker seems to have followed their song to "the chambers of the sea," spaces that metaphorically bear rhythm and poetic form within them (not only in the sea's tidal ebb and flow, but also in "chambers," rendered in Italian as "stanzas"). The danger, finally, comes less from the mermaids and their song than from "human voices" like those of Prufrock's society. It is upon their interruption that the poetic dreamworld collapses and "we drown."

In this way, Eliot's title—"Love Song"—claims for poetry the power to articulate, to seduce, to decorate, and, most of all, to create spaces apart from prosaic "human voices." In such a poetic space, other voices, other singing voices at least, are not to be feared. In that space, Eliot can sing just what he means not in spite of but by virtue of the stanzaic chambers other poets have built. He can do so by becoming a medium for the expression of those other poets' songs, making meaning of those snatches of old tunes.

I choose the word "medium" in that last sentence with some premeditation, for "The Love Song of J. Alfred Prufrock" is the first provisional attempt at a relationship between a poet and the poetic tradition that Eliot develops in a more nuanced way in "Tradition and the Individual Talent," an essay whose argument hinges on the notion of the poet as a medium. The first paragraph of the essay's middle section ends with Eliot's insistence that what makes the mature poet mature is not his/her "being necessarily more interesting, or having 'more to say,'" but the fact that he/she is "a more finely perfected medium in which special, or very varied, feelings are at liberty to enter into new combinations."[45] What Eliot means by "medium" here is "catalyst," as he makes clear in a famous analogy that compares the poet to "the shred of platinum" that, when "introduced into a chamber containing oxygen and sulphur dioxide" produces "sulphurous acid."[46]

The Oxford English Dictionary also defines "medium" as "an inter-mediate agency, means, instrument or channel," and, in a more specific sense of this denotation, "a person who is supposed to be the organ of communications from departed spirits." These necromantic meanings of "medium" seem also to be in play as Eliot writes about the poet's relationship to tradition. We might first simply note the essay's preoccu-pation with "dead poets" and, more simply, "the dead": "the most indi-vidual parts of his work may be those in which the dead poets...assert their immortality most vigorously"; "you must set him...among the dead."[47] More importantly, we must understand how Eliot sees the poet's task in providing a voice for the dead. Tradition is, in part, what Eliot calls "the historical sense," which "compels a man to write...with a feeling that the whole of the literature of Europe from Homer...has a simultaneous existence and composes a simultaneous order."[48] The work of the poet is to act as a medium for "the mind of Europe," a voice for that "whole of the literature of Europe from Homer," and this work famously entails "a continual surrender of himself as he is at the moment to something which is more valuable," a "continual self-sacrifice, a continual extinction of personality."[49] Setting aside those last phrases' echoes of necromantic ritual, we can hear in the pun of "medium" sufficient evidence for thinking of Eliot's "tradition" as an Underworld into which the poet/hero must descend and out of which he will bring that wisdom—the tradition's, not his own—that will let his new work thrive.

As "Tradition and the Individual Talent" suggests, Eliot's 1910–1911 negotiation of poetic anxiety does not satisfactorily hold through the decade. By the early 1920s, Eliot needs to rethink and reenact an enabling relationship with his poetic forebears. The *nekuia* at the vio-let hour is the key to that renegotiation. I am claiming that Tiresias' appearance in the poem makes a structural allusion to the *nekuia*. My claim first requires me to show that Eliot locates Tiresias in the Underworld.[50] The first bit of evidence for this location is Tiresias' presence itself. Long dead, he can only inhabit the Underworld (a door to which Odysseus opens in the *nekuia*). Moreover, as critics have noted, much of the poem's diction, imagery, and allusion suggest that its space of speaking is an (if not the) Underworld.[51] The Cumaean sybil's speech in Eliot's epigraph (from Petronius' *Satyricon*[52]) and the title of the first section ("The Burial of the Dead") foreground a living death that is elaborated in the poem's famous opening lines:

> April is the cruellest month, breeding
> Lilacs out of the dead land, mixing

Memory and desire, stirring
Dull roots with spring rain.[53]

The buried can see roots stirring, can be warmed by snow, can be fed and kept (somehow) alive with "dried tubers," and so the scene here seems to be at least an "under-earth." Its more specifically Underworld character is indicated in the first "Unreal City" passage: "A crowd flowed over London Bridge, so many, / I had not thought death had undone so many" (14). Here, according to his own notes, Eliot alludes to the third and fourth cantos of Dante's *Inferno*, in which Dante enters the Gates of Hell and encounters first the lukewarm (aware during life of neither good nor evil) and then the unbaptized in Limbo.[54] The crowd described is (or seems) a crowd of the dead, shades in an "Unreal City." The fact that they appear in an allusion highlights another hellish aspect of the poem. It is to a large extent a tissue of allusion and quotation, a text emphatically composed of others. Those texts—Ezekiel, Ecclesiastes, *Tristan und Isolde, The Tempest*, "Le sept vieillards," the *Inferno*, The White Devil, "Au Lecteur," to name the first few—are by dead authors. Their quoted (or misquoted or partially quoted) lines, then, are the speech of dead shades (as must be the speech of, say, the one who concludes "The Burial of the Dead" by calling out to Stetson, whom he recognizes from the second century BCE battle of Mylae).

Eliot's notes direct us to the legends of the Holy Grail and the fertility cults whose rituals Fraser describes in *The Golden Bough*, both of which have to do with the quest to renew a land laid waste. While the notes do not adduce the epic tradition so explicitly, the quest motifs analogously echo it. Like Parsifal, Odysseus and Aeneas are on quests whose successful completion will guarantee the proper course of natural and historical cycles. The poem's epigraph amplifies these echoes; its Sybil is the one who helps Aeneas into the Underworld with the golden bough. Tiresias at the center of the poem at once cinches the epic connection and performs his familiar necromantic function. If the wasteland (or *The Waste Land*) that readers enter is an Underworld, then what propels us, at least in part, is the search for prophetic wisdom. When we meet Tiresias midway through "The Fire Sermon," he provides it.

Now that we have established where and why Tiresias speaks, we can consider what he sees and narrates, for it is in the style and substance of Tiresias's vision that Eliot establishes the necessary relationship with his poetic predecessors:

I Tiresias, though blind, throbbing between two lives,
Old man with wrinkled female breasts, can see

> At the violet hour, the evening hour that strives
> Homeward, and brings the sailor home from the sea,
> The typist home at teatime . . . (31)

The prophet goes on to describe the typist's flat (littered with under-
wear), to show her heating canned food for a meal, and, finally, to
narrate her evening with a "young man carbuncular," a "small house
agent's clerk." That evening culminates in a decidedly seamy sexual
episode. At the center of the center of the poem, then, "at the violet
hour" of a necromantic confrontation with the prophet who holds the
wisdom necessary for the successful completion of a quest, Tiresias
the seer offers the vision of bad sex in a London bed-sit.

Exemplifying the inextricability of desire and power, the episode
condenses the concerns that shape numerous other fragmentary narratives in the poem. Sometimes those narratives are dramatized. "A
Game of Chess," for example, stages two affairs or marriages in trouble, while "The Fire Sermon" depicts the precariously aquatic sexual
adventures of Elizabeth and Leicester. More often, they are allusively
present; Tristan and Isolde, Antony and Cleopatra, Aeneas and Dido
all appear only in fragments. These show up, respectively, as a few
quoted lines from Wagner's opera, a pastiche of Enobarbus' lines
describing Cleopatra's barge in Shakespeare's *Antony and Cleopatra*,
and a one-word reference ("laquearia") to Dido's banquet in the
Aeneid. In each of these cases, sexual desire is interwoven with power,
whether the power struggle between lovers (or between rivals in love)
or the political power at stake because of the lovers' identities as heads
of state. While the narratives do not all end in the same way, they do
all at least suggest unpleasant endings. While neither the upper-class
woman nor Lil (from "A Game of Chess") seems destined for the
dramatic suicides of Dido and Cleopatra, neither has good prospects
for fulfilling relationships either.

Perhaps more important than the narrative and allusive elements
of the poem invoked and subsumed by Tiresias' vision is the conventional association of traditional poetic forms with the same knot of
sex and power the episode ties. It is precisely through his handling
of form at this point in the poem that Eliot conducts his complex
negotiation with the tradition that threatens to silence him. More
specifically, it is in his handling of the sonnet, that paradigmatic lyric
condensation of desire, power, and poetic prowess, that Eliot makes
his declaration of interdependence.

While Eliot cast the whole "At the violet hour" passage in "He
Do the Police in Different Voices" in rhyming quatrains, the final

version, arrived at partly through the editorial offices of Pound, rhymes irregularly. Through the first twenty lines, only one whole quatrain remains. The climax of the scene, though, falls into a very regular rhyme scheme: the fourteen-line passage beginning "The time is now propitious" and ending "finding the stairs unlit" (32–33), permitting the assonance of "kiss" and "unlit" to substitute for a couplet rhyme, reads as a pretty good Shakespearean sonnet. Not only do the quatrains and couplet rhyme as the form demands (almost), but the stanzas also compose discrete tropic units. The first plays on the meanings of "engage," so that invitation, betrothal, and combat all are connotatively at work. The second emphasizes the last of these with its military diction. The third shifts attention to Tiresias and his typicality (or, better, the typicality of the episode itself, since even the famed prophet has "foresuffered" it). The couplet at once returns us to the "lovers" and implies a comment on the scene; "gropes" links the clerk's assault on the typist with his assault on the stairs so that the darkness of the stairs seems also to embrace the action we have just witnessed.

Like Pound, Eliot stages a confrontation with Tradition at its inaugural moment, in its most ancient and ritual guise. Simply by doing so, according to David Pike's reading of the descensus trope, Eliot demonstrates his advancement of and over the tradition; it is dead and he is at once alive and able to bring it to some kind of renewed life. The clerk leaves a place of light (the typist's second act upon returning home is to light the stove, and the sun's rays are shown to fall upon her "drying combinations") and enters the darkness. In that darkness are stairs, which separate the flat from the world around it (a world that is, as the clerk leaves, dark). They provide the back end of a chiasmus whose front end they imply. As Ronald Macdonald has written, the descent into the Underworld is characterized by a similarly chiasmic structure. The hero takes a path (or a series of ritual steps) down, encounters whomever he encounters, and retreats.[55] The path down and back is dark, the moment of encounter one of both literal and figurative illumination. We might read the clerk, then, as making a visit that structurally echoes the *nekuia*. If so, the carbuncular clerk is a pimply Odysseus and the typist is linked with Tiresias, the latter connection suggested not only by aural similarity but also, and more forcefully, by Tiresias's self-descriptions, each of which emphasizes his female attributes ("Old man with wrinkled female breasts," "old man with wrinkled dugs") and by a staged intensification of his identification with the typist. Tiresias calls attention to himself as narrator three times, each time raising the stakes of his vision. At the

beginning of the passage, he can simply "see . . . The typist." After
his description of her flat, Tiresias indicates not only his vision but
also his visionary capacity: "Perceived the scene, and *foretold* the rest"
(emphasis mine). Finally, between the scene's climactic "assault" and
the young man's departure, Tiresias shifts from foretelling to foresuf-
fering, from vision to empathy: "And I Tiresias have foresuffered all /
Enacted on this same divan or bed."

We might go one step further: the clerk/hero is the poet who visits
at the violet hour to take from the transcriber/tradition what might
be of use to him. To take it, we might add, by force, in an "assault."
That word suggests a connection between the clerk and the silencing
Tereus, which makes the typist a figure for Philomela, whose story
is one of the key narrative referents of Eliot's numerous fragmentary
quotations and allusions. In Ovid's telling, Philomela of Athens, sister of Procne, is raped by her brother-in-law Tereus, king of Thrace,
who is overcome by desire when he sees her beauty. When she threatens to tell the world, Tereus cuts out her tongue and imprisons her,
convincing Procne that her sister is dead. For a year, Philomela weaves
a tapestry that tells her story; when it is finished, she sends it to her
sister, who understands the story, rescues Philomela, murders Itys,
her son with Tereus, and serves the boy to his father as a banquet.
When the women show Tereus what he has eaten, he chases them,
whereupon they become birds (Procne a swallow and Philomela a
nightingale) and he becomes the warrior-like hoopoe. When, a few
lines later, the typist "smooths her hair with automatic hand," that
connection is strengthened; in Ovid's account, Philomela, after the
rape, "dragged at her loosened hair."

This is, of course, just how Eliot's treatment of the tradition has
sometimes been read. In her powerful discussion of *The Waste Land*,
Maud Ellmann writes that the poem "desecrates tradition," and that it
"uses its nostalgia to conceal its vandalism, its pastiche of the tradition
that it mourns."[56] Ellmann ultimately argues that Eliot's "blasphemy"
is generative, but the one-sided aggression she posits resembles that
of the young man in Tiresias's vision. I want to argue, however, that
the mode modeled by the young man is held up for implicit critique.
At the violet hour, Eliot writes, "the human engine waits / Like a
taxi." The human dehumanized, and, more particularly, mechanized
is one of the poem's many imagistic patterns. In the context of the
human engine, the typist is no more than a copying machine. After
the assault, she is, if anything, more directly, explicitly, and irredeem-
ably mechanized: "She smoothes her hair with *automatic* hand / And
puts a record on the gramophone" (34, emphasis mine).

The woman becomes an automaton (or is left as the one she might already have been), and the music available to her is similarly mechanized.[57] If the typist is Tiresias is Tradition and the young man is the hero is the poet, then this encounter renders Tradition mechanical, its hand "automatic" and its "mind of Europe" filled with the pure products of mass culture. Moreover, the encounter leaves the poet simply groping in the dark and the object of his aggressive attentions allusively suicidal ("when lovely woman stoops to folly" quotes Olivia's song in Goldsmith's *The Vicar of Wakefield*; the song concludes "The only art her guilt to cover, / To hide her shame from every eye, / To give repentance to her lover / And wring his bosom—is to die").[58]

In his vision, then, Tiresias offers an example of how not to treat one's tradition; he offers a warning something like those the prophet proffers when Odysseus summons him. The passage dramatizes an assault by a young, brash "clerk" sartorially marked as nouveau riche. His attitude afterward is "patronising." Instead of such an assault on Tradition, the poem acts out a more complex and productive engagement with it. Speechless himself, the poet gathers fragments and shores up his ruin with them so that they signify. That the content of their signification is often negative—"fear in a handful of dust"—is beside the point. The achievement is that transformative poetic power that finally makes nonsense syllables resonate with emotional and ethical force. This much the poem would demonstrate without the gestural *nekuia* at its heart. That scene, though, serves as a strong declaration of interdependence, propounding Eliot's self-evident literary truths.

The effects are not merely local, for this "sonnet" in the middle of the poem makes more legible the significance of sonnets partially present elsewhere in the poem. At three key moments, for example, Eliot quotes lines from French sonnets. He concludes "The Burial of the Dead" with a famous line from Baudelaire's "Au Lecteur." He follows the lines about Sweeney and Mrs. Porter and begins the transition to Mr. Eugenides' proposal in "The Fire Sermon" with a quotation from Verlaine's "Parsifal." And among the fragments gathered at the poem's end is a line from Nerval's "El Desdichado." None of these sonnets is about love and power. Each, however, bears the form's conventional association with that nexus within their lines, stanzas, and rhyme schemes. Tiresias' vision is "the substance of the poem," therefore, because it comprehends and resonates through the entire poem at once narratively, thematically, allusively, and formally.

Nothing I have said so far about this central episode in *The Waste Land* demonstrates that the reader's Underworld encounter with

Tiresias has anything to do with the poet's encounter with the literary tradition or with his justification of his own poetic project against the backdrop of that tradition. Where such themes were explicit in Pound's *nekuia*, they are obscured by (or perhaps interwoven with) the thematics of desire in Eliot's. It remains, then, for me to show how the necromantic appearance of Tiresias and his vision do, in fact, dramatize and justify an engagement with tradition and poetics.

Eliot's embedded sonnet epitomizes the rhetorical deployment of form; no form in the English lyric tradition more emphatically consociates sex (or love) and power than the sonnet. More than that, the sonnet form that remains a ghostly presence in this passage is traditionally burdened by the question of poetic language's efficacy and power. At its Italian roots, the form embodies Petrarch's punned desire for Laura, for *l'auro*, the wind that empowers his speech, and for the laurel that rewards poetic prowess. (The form also frequently meditates upon the poet's self-lacerating concern over these desires and their inextricability.) In its earliest English incarnations, the sonnet is perhaps even more thoroughly attuned to the roles literary language and convention themselves play in knotting the threads of sex and power. To take just one well-known example, Thomas Wyatt's "Whoso list to hount," an adaptation of a Petrarch sonnet (*Rime Sparse*, CXC), weaves earthly desire (the hunter for the hind, the lover for the beloved) with imagery of an authority both temporal and eternal (Caesar, who might be Henry VIII, Wyatt's omnipotent rival for Anne Boleyn, and who represents rule divine and divinely mandated). More than this, in its dense texture of translation and allusion, Wyatt's sonnet reflects on its own practice, the "vayne travaill" of the poet's "werie mynde," which will never allow him either to hold the deer or to stop trying.

The sonnet-shaped prophetic vision glimpsed "at the violet hour" suggests that the literary tradition that has shaped European society over the centuries and is the bequest the young poet inherits is saturated with desire and power that, when stripped of false nobility, amount to nothing more than an automatic and automatizing grope. Later in "The Fire Sermon," Eliot shows that even in the context of nobility, the intertwining of desire and power often at the heart of the sonnet is impoverished and impoverishing. Amidst repetition of the Thames Maidens' refrain—"Weialala leia"—Eliot describes the river's course, introduces "Elizabeth and Leicester," and narrates a climactic passage that concludes with this sestet:

> On Margate Sands.
> I can connect

> Nothing with nothing.
> The broken fingernails of dirty hands.
> My people humble people who expect
> Nothing. (37)

There are several things worth underlining here. First, the passage continues the poem's pattern of thematic elaboration; love and power are intertwined along with Elizabeth and Leicester on the floor of that canoe. The speaker's attitude resembles that of the typist when she's left alone. The first line's trams pick up the taxi and automata of the "violet hour" passage, while its dusty trees echo the stone and dust scattered from "The Burial of the Dead" through "What the Thunder Said."

More pertinently for my discussion, the passage's scattering of body parts, its imagery of dirt and fragmentation, indexes the exhaustion not only of the speaker or the subject matter, but of the verbal, rhetorical, and formal bits that compose the narrative. Indeed, those images and the passage's self-referring attenuation of the Petrarchan sonnet make palpable the tradition's enervated and enervating presence. While the first eight lines of the Elizabeth and Leicester passage break (via rhyme scheme, syntax, and white space) into separate quatrains, the last six make up a perfectly rhymed Petrarchan sestet. At the same time, the partial metrical regularity of the first eight lines (mostly iambic feet, lines hovering between rough trimeter and tetrameter, the eighth line a perfect iambic pentameter) degenerates dramatically in the last six. This degeneration culminates, and the form literally disappears, in the final line's one-word trochee: "Nothing."

There is an easy negative reading here, one sanctioned and perhaps even invited by "Prufrock": a tradition whose narrative and whose rhetorical forms consociate love, desire, and power renders one who would speak all but speechless. The sestet depends on an impoverished vocabulary; "nothing" is repeated three times in six short lines, and many of the other words—"Sands," "broken," "fingernails," "dirty," "humble"—connote dissolution and diminution. The rhyme of "nothing" with "Nothing," like the sole remaining creative ability to "connect / Nothing with nothing," is a final insult; not only is the last rhyme a simple repetition, but it is a repetition of a signifier for absence, a stunning enactment of ultimate exhaustion.[59]

This negative reading must be part of the story, but it cannot be the whole story for the passage's power derives precisely from the sources that deplete its resources. The "mind of Europe" speaks quite clearly here. B.C. Southam offers allusive glosses for more than half of the passage's lines: *Purgatorio, The Tempest, Howards End, King Lear, Heart of Darkness*, and Psalm 50.[60] Eliot is not only not prevented from speaking by these voices, he is enabled by them. And the same is true of the sonnet form. If Eliot, recuperating at Margate, can "connect / Nothing with nothing," he is nevertheless able to assemble the first three parts of his poem. That achievement suggests a more positive reading of the line: I can connect nothing with nothing, or, perhaps, "Nothing" with "nothing," and by thematizing and formally enacting the exhaustion of the tradition, Eliot paradoxically enlivens and is enlivened by it. If it is impossible for Eliot to say just what he means, it is clear that, like the allusively ubiquitous Procne and Philomela with their tapestry and birdsong, he is able, by indirect means, to say it.[61]

* * *

If it is clear that the dynamic of literary innovation both Pound and Eliot cast in necromantic form is characterized by competition, that its resolution on interdependence between living and predecessor poets is arrived at only through an agonistic confrontation, it is no less clear that an alternative dynamic is explored at the same time (and since) in poems by women. I want to conclude this chapter by examining this alternative and by showing that it, too, participates in the necromantic tradition, albeit in a way quite different in tone and in allusive texture from Pound's and Eliot's work. While the male poets, anxious over influence and belatedness, strive to supersede the tradition upon which they finally admit they depend, poets like H.D., Edna St. Vincent Millay, and, later, Adrienne Rich enact and implicitly advocate a poetics of passivity, winning the struggle with a patriarchal poetic tradition by opting out of it and, at the same time, announcing this strategy through their own allusions to narratives of Underworld descent.

Perhaps the most obvious exemplar of this countertradition is H.D.'s 1917 "Eurydice," which seems to respond directly to the poetic ambition of an Orphic poet like Pound. The poem is spoken by Eurydice, wife of the mythic poet Orpheus, after Orpheus has persuaded Hades to release her (Eurydice had died after a snakebite) and then failed to meet the god's sole condition that he not look back at Eurydice until the two had left the Underworld and reached the world above. Consigned again to the Underworld, Eurydice rails against Orpheus's "arrogance" and "ruthlessness."[62] After complaining that if he had just left well enough alone, she would have "grown from listlessness / into peace," Eurydice implies that Orpheus only came to rescue her to demonstrate his own power ("what was it you saw in my face? / the light of your own face, / the fire of your own presence?"). His vanity and ambition render her simply the ground for his performance, disposable once his purpose is achieved, and H.D. spends the middle sections of the poem registering the magnitude of Eurydice's loss. Not only does this aborted rescue interrupt her natural progression to oblivion, it also renews her knowledge of the experiences death denies her: light, the colors and fragrances of flowers, the "live souls above the earth," the earth itself.

"Such loss," Eurydice says in the poem's pivotal fifth section, "is no loss" if the cost of earthly life and sensation is the presence of the arrogant and ruthless poet. In the revaluation of values that follows this pronouncement, H.D. articulates an alternative to the agonistic poetics on display in Pound's Canto I or *Three Cantos* 3.[63] Accepting the sensory deprivation and enforced passivity of death, Eurydice finds "fervour" and "splendour" greater than the light and color of the world above: "I have the fervour of myself for a presence / and my own spirit for light." When she was simply the medium for Orpheus's ambition, Eurydice had no presence, light, or color of her own. Without Orpheus, though she loses all the presence, light, and color of the world, she is at last able to find these within herself, she is at last able to become a self. Unlike her male modernist contemporaries, H.D. does not seem to need to pit this self against other poets in order to ensure its presence and power. Indeed, she shrinks from such a confrontation, aware that if she should tell Orpheus what she has discovered, he would turn again toward her and she, in consequence, "would sink into a place / even more terrible than this."

The enabling conditions of Eurydice's new poetic power are precisely the absences that characterize the Underworld. It is black, rocky, bereft of any sensory stimulus, and even the speaking consciousness inhabiting it lacks "presence." These qualities, of course, have for centuries, if not millennia, been gendered feminine in the Western binary imagination. As Helen Sword writes, H.D.'s Eurydice seems to accept those terms, "appropriating hell, the negative space of literary marginality into which the female poet has been driven";[64] in aligning herself with absence and lack, she takes on the power to defy Orpheus, his world, and his ambition. More than this, though, she takes on fantastic existential power: "Hell must break before I am lost" (40). By refusing to strive for the immortality about which both Orpheus and Pound are so anxious (this anxiety accounts for

Orpheus's backward glance and for Elpenor's centrality in Pound's rendering of the Homeric *nekuia*), Eurydice and H.D. paradoxically achieve it. In "Sonnets from an Ungrafted Tree" (1923), Edna St. Vincent Millay stages a scene of descent for a similar purpose and with similar stakes. Millay's sequence of seventeen Shakespearean sonnets narrates a woman's return to her husband's house. (She had escaped the unsatisfying marriage only to be drawn back to care for her dying spouse.) As she cooks and cleans, Millay's unnamed protagonist recalls her husband's courtship (or what passed for courtship) and meditates upon the construction of female identity through housework. Recalling Eurydice's suspicions about Orpheus's look back, Millay symbolizes both processes of identity formation in terms of reflection. The ninth sonnet flashes back to the moment when the woman's husband, remembered as neither bright nor beautiful, got her attention by flashing a mirror in her eyes. The young couple's bond consists of no more than this. The young woman is surprised, when telling others the story, to see that "this was not so wonderful a thing," but the moment is one of stunning illumination: she is an object of desire and in the flashing moment of reflection is constituted as a subject of the discourse of romance.[65] The sonnet's couplet effectively deflates that discourse; the woman recalls feeling that "It's pretty nice to know / You've got a friend to keep you company everywhere you go." [66]

It is precisely this inescapable character of wedded "friendship" that has both driven the woman away and forced her back "into his house again" to watch over the dying of this man, "Loving him not at all," and it is to escape the interpellation into the limited and limiting subject position of "wife" that the woman undertakes a descent in the fifth sonnet. After bringing the house back to life by kindling a fire in the long-neglected hearth, the woman hears the grocer's wagon arrive. Desperate not to be seen, as if to be caught in the act of housewifery would condemn her forever to that identity, she hides in the cellar. The passage reads as a figurative death:

> Sour and damp from that dark vault
> Arose to her the well-remembered chill;
> She saw the narrow wooden stairway still
> Plunging into the earth. (50)

Millay creates the strong suggestion here that the only available escape from the positions offered by patriarchal society is in the grave. Unwilling to take that avenue, the young woman emerges and immediately reenters the identity she has tried to escape, reconstitutes herself in a vigorous routine of house-cleaning, finally polishing a stove until she can see her face, the reflection working here, as in the remembered courtship scene, to hail the woman into a subject position (which, the sonnet's last line suggests, is itself constructed through the ideological work of advertising; the newly scrubbed kitchen in which the woman sees herself is "An advertisement, far too fine to cook a supper in").[67]

We might read the descent into the cellar in the fifth sonnet as a sort of failed *nekuia* in which the woman fails to find prophetic wisdom and is left to contemplate "the empty doughnut jar" until she reemerges into the housewife's labor and identity. This early descent, though, establishes the relationship between death and freedom that the sequence's conclusion emphasizes. Sonnet XV ends with the woman's realization that "things in death were neither clocks nor people, but only dead," implying the freedom from categorization that comes with death, and in the sequence's final sonnet the woman reads the corpse of her husband in a way that clearly applies to herself and her hopes of evading patriarchally determined subject positions as well:

> She was as one who enters, sly, and proud,
> To where her husband speaks before a crowd,
> And sees a man she never saw before—
> The man who eats his victuals at her side,
> Small, and absurd, and hers: for once, not hers, unclassified. (62)

The social system defines individuals relationally, each subject the object of another's possessive attention, determined by their reflection in various discourses. Death offers a release from this relational system, an escape from gendered taxonomies. The husband's escape figures the woman's—in death she too will be free—but it also enables a degree of freedom in the present. As Sandra Gilbert writes, "Millay's protagonist feels joy that this new stranger is 'not hers, unclassified' and, by implication, exultation that she is no longer his and classified."[68] If he is no longer hers, in other words, she is also no longer his, and the unnamed forces of social suasion that brought her back to "his house" at the beginning of the sequence, forces able to act on her because of her defining relationship to her husband and because of her interpellation through the discourses of marriage and housekeeping, lose their purchase. The escape from the grocer's eyes in the fifth sonnet prefigures the escape from all the social eyes that would imprison the woman by seeing her in ideologically ordained roles.

While H.D.'s poem explicitly addresses poetry and poetics (Orpheus is a logical and long-standing figure for the poet, so that Eurydice's attacks on his arrogance and ruthlessness cannot but be read as attacks on the arrogance and ruthlessness of ambitious poets in general), Millay's treatment of these (like Eliot's in the violet hour episode) must be read out of her handling of form. Most obviously, Millay embeds a critique of the literary tradition she inherits in her ironic deployment of the sonnet. The premiere amatory form in the English lyric arsenal is deployed here to limn a relationship in which the protagonist loves her husband "not at all," in which obligation rather than attraction accounts for her begrudging presence, in which the dazzling moment of courtship is deflated as "not so wonderful a thing," and in which the husband's death (and the protagonist's death that it prefigures) is a release rather than a tragedy. In this, the sequence resembles Eliot's insistence that the sonnet's typical thematic baggage is empty and that the tradition for which the sonnet is a metonym is hollow and unsustainable; in the descent scene, Millay's protagonist looks upon an empty doughnut jar, as good a figure as any for the tradition's failure to nourish. More than this, though, Millay metaphorically writes writing itself into the sequence's final sonnet in a way that announces the death of the tradition she inherits:

> Formally the sheet
> Set forth for her today those heavy curves
> And lengths familiar as the bedroom door. (62)

The sheet that covers her husband's corpse also suggests the sheet of paper Millay addresses as she writes; the familiar curves and lengths of the husband's body, linked by simile to the bedroom where his desire once burned (perhaps), also suggest the turns and metered lines of the sonnet itself (it is "Formally," after all, that the sheet offers itself to be read).

To read the sequence's self-reference and its implicit critique of amatory conventions in this way, though, is to enact the relational objectification the poem thematically resists. We must look once more at Millay's handling of the sonnet form, then, to see how she, like her protagonist, works to evade enclosure in that relational logic. I began this discussion by calling the sequence's seventeen lyrics Shakespearean sonnets, but of course that label is not quite accurate.

While the title calls the poems "sonnets," and while each poem comprises fourteen lines of mostly regular iambic pentameter, and while each poem rhymes so that its fourteen lines are divided into three quatrains and a couplet, each poem also ends with a line fully two metrical feet longer than the thirteen that precede it. The history of the sonnet is, of course, a history of prosodic and thematic variation; poems recognized as sonnets, like George Meredith's in *Modern Love*, added not only feet but also entire lines. Nevertheless, with her elongated final lines, Millay quietly fashions a new form. Other poets had brought the six-foot alexandrine from French into their sonnet's epigrammatic couplets, but Millay's seven-foot lines, scanning almost like distichs of hymn meter or halves of Dickinson quatrains, make for an unfamiliar (and almost awkward) innovation. While her "sheet" sets forth the "curves" and "lengths" of the sonnet, "familiar as the bedroom door" to a poet who had been writing and publishing finely polished sonnets for almost ten years by this point in her career, Millay veers from the straightforward sonnet and offers instead sonnets "from an ungrafted tree," sonnets with roots of their own, "unclassified."

Millay's resolution to opt out of the Oedipal or Bloomian agon of patriarchal literary history and cultivate both an ideal and a form outside the dominant values of the literary tradition is partial and implicit; fifty years later, Adrienne Rich's similar resolution, also achieved after great success on the tradition's terms, is much more complete and explicit. "Diving into the Wreck" stages a descent and a confrontation with figures for the patriarchal literary tradition and wrests a poetic victory by refusing to compete with what confronts its speaker. Where we have seen Pound and Eliot stage struggles to demonstrate their value against the tradition and only after this struggle declare their interdependence with it, Rich, like H.D. and Millay, descends not to engage in combat but rather to explore the means for communion with "the wreck."

The title poem in a pivotal volume in Rich's career, "Diving into the Wreck" has been read in numerous ways, but rarely in terms of the *nekuia* or *katabasis*. David Kalstone writes that Rich imagines the "confusions of history and sexuality" in terms of the wreck and its cargo in order to address "the sunken treasure of personality."[69] For Wendy Martin, the poem is a counterpart to the same volume's "Phenomenology of Anger." The sunken treasure lies in "'the wreck' of civilization," which Rich's diver must accept (rather than deplore) so that she can learn from it "as a necessary prelude to beginning again."[70] Nancy Milford asks whether the wreckage is "of marriage,

or of sex, or of the selfhood within each? Is it the female body,
her own?"[71] Milford argues that the poem's descent is at once into
"female fantasy" and into "the very sources of [Rich's] poetry," its
resolution, quoting the poet, a "coming-home to . . . sex, sexuality,
sexual wounds, sexual identity, sexual politics."[72] These readings are
amplified by critics who emphasize the poem's participation in the
volume's elaboration of androgyny,[73] though some of the strongest
recent readings of the poem complicate the androgynous resolution
("I am she: I am he") in productive ways. Elizabeth Hirsh, for example, finds the poem exploring "the possibility of a relation to alter-
ity, a relation between the self or same and the other," arguing that
Rich's diver descends to "the wreck of human values" or "the wreck
of ethics."[74] Barbara Eckstein also reads the poem in terms of the
confrontation with the other, arguing that "what we acquire when we
dive into the wreck is not a place in the book of myths alongside other
myths" but, because we have encountered the "thing itself" in Rich's
careful and concrete description, "a place in the ongoing process of
revisiting and understanding the thing itself."[75]

Rich's poem invites katabatic readings, though, from its opening
moment, and it does so, I will argue, in order to stage a confrontation
with the wreck of a patriarchal literary tradition as well as the wrecks
(of personality, civilization, human values, ethics, and language) posited by these critics. As Rachel Blau DuPlessis writes, "descent, detec-
tion, and exploration are metaphors for acts of criticism. The poet, as
an undersea diver, takes a journey down to an individual and collective past..."[76] Where DuPlessis identifies the wreck as the "relations
between the sexes,"[77] I see it as the poetic tradition encountered by
Pound and Eliot in their own descents. Like Cheri Colby Langdell, I
read "Diving into the Wreck" as a revisionist response to Eliot's *Waste
Land*.[78] While the first few lines employ the imagery of scuba diving
(wetsuit, flippers, mask) and refer to contemporary filmmaker Jacques
Cousteau, the poem's very first nouns are "the book of myths" the
speaker has read and the camera she has loaded, metonyms for the
literary tradition and artistic representation respectively. The speaker's descent is one for which she prepares by reading myths, with
their own frequent narratives of descent, and one on which she brings
her own means of representation.[79] This is an artist-figure's journey,
a reckoning with the power (both to damage and to create "trea-
sures") of words, and like the others I have addressed in this chapter,
it includes a mandatory scene of abjection. "I go down," Rich writes,
twice, in the third stanza, and in the depths the speaker suffers a sea
change, crippled by her flippers and crawling "like an insect." In the

fourth stanza, this isolation and debility lead to a loss of vision and, almost, consciousness: "black I am blacking out." Whatever inherent power this prepared and armed (knife-wielding) diver/writer brought is lost in the unfamiliar "deep element." Like H.D.'s Eurydice and Millay's unnamed protagonist, Rich's speaker does not fight or try to escape. The sea into which she has descended is "not a question of power," and the way to be in this sea is passive, turned in and by the sea and not oneself. In literary terms, it is "another story," a narrative whose terms the speaker must "learn alone," without the guidance of the book of myths, an element in which she must learn to turn "without force." Her transformation proceeds through this acceptance; the speaker learns to breathe in a way appropriate to her new atmosphere and comes to feel so welcomed by the (passive and sea-swayed) beauty of the reefs that she almost forgets her purpose. Even when she remembers what she has come for, though, the speaker undertakes neither to prove her superiority to nor to differentiate herself from the drowned and damaged ruin she finds. Rather, she identifies with it, becomes it, through a deeper descent not only to but into the wreck.

Eurydice discovers in the passivity and darkness of death the power and light of a self at last able to know itself as subject rather than as an object that reflects the male poet's virtuosity. Millay's protagonist realizes the freedom from limiting subject positions brought about not only by her own eventual death but also by the death of her husband, whose body reads like the text of the sonnet tradition itself. The ruin Rich's speaker discovers and describes can be read in various ways (as we have seen), but surely one layer of significance in the penultimate stanza's catalogue is a similar literary self-reference. Rich brings to bear a range of her medium's resources even as she registers those resources' decay. The shipwreck's valuable cargo, for example, "lies" at the end of a line, its dishonesty either rescued or intensified by the next line: "obscurely inside barrels." In one reading, the phrase defines "lies" as "rests," but in another it defines the verb as "speaks untruth." The precious cargo (of words denoting precious cargo) at once awaits and dissembles. In a similar way, the speaker, identifying with the wreck and becoming multiple (mermaid, merman, figurehead), sees herself in the "half-destroyed instruments / that once held to a course." Might not these instruments be the accoutrements of verse itself, the meter and rhyme that once guided the poetic line? Might, then, the "water-eaten log" that recorded the ship's voyages, the "fouled compass" that set its course, also refer to writing, to words' purposes and maps?

If we read a critique of the patriarchal literary tradition here, and I think we should, we must also read a note of self-criticism. Like Millay, but unlike H.D., Rich began her enormously successful and oft-awarded poetic career as a master of traditional lyric form. Her first book, *A Change of World*, chosen by W.H. Auden for the Yale Younger Poets series in 1951, dexterously performed rhyming quatrains and tercets. If the wreck of poetic tradition has foundered on the rocks of the tradition's misogyny, Rich suggests that she was on the ship. She has returned, though, neither to bury nor to raise the wreck. Instead, the speaker concludes on a moment of insight very much like those we find in "Eurydice" and "Sonnets from an Ungrafted Tree." Rather than claim to supersede the wreck, though, as Pound and Eliot implicitly do, Rich has descended into it and identified with it, taking on its abject passivity, finding that her name does not appear in the book of myths. As Sword writes, Rich here appropriates "the negative space of literary marginality into which the female poet has been driven."[80] Absence from the book of myths is, as H.D.'s Eurydice might say, no loss, for the speaker has found instead of the sort of singular identity that would reassure Pound's Elpenor a collective identity with those who seek the wreck. Where Eliot gathers fragments to shore up the ruin, Rich is content to descend into the wreck, moving almost like Phlebas the Phoenician, with rather than against the sea in which the wreck is sunk, to view it almost lovingly (stroking her lamp's beam "slowly along the flank"), and to take nothing away from it other than this experience of identification and the certainty that she might be at once powerful and "unclassified."

2

KATABASIS AS CULTURAL CRITIQUE

If Pound's *A Draft of XVI Cantos* takes Odysseus's invocation of Tiresias as the model for its opening, the sequence models its climax on the katabatic descents of Aeneas and, especially, Dante. Pound establishes a powerful model for poets who set out to criticize their contemporary society (or elements of it) by condemning it to (or suggesting that it already is in or simply that it itself *is*) Hell. This chapter begins with an analysis of Pound's Cantos XIV and XV, then turns to some poems by poets who have followed Pound into Hell, adapting his path for their own purposes just as he adapts Dante's for his. My argument in this chapter comprises two claims. First, I will show how modern poets have used the *katabasis* to frame moments of cultural critique, at once deploying the narrative to dramatize problems in contemporary society and borrowing and reinvesting the cultural capital of this epic topos in order to articulate specific critiques to the tradition of European literature. In addition, I will argue that modern *katabases* tend to fall into two groups. On one hand, many of these poems either offer philosophical or aesthetic or religious transformation as the way out of the Underworld through which they figure and critique their societies or they are silent on such possibilities. On the other hand, a countertradition articulates through katabatic episodes not only critique but also explicitly political possibilities for social change. Perhaps not coincidentally, the first group tends to include the best-known modern *katabases* (Pound's "Hell Cantos," for example, or Eliot's "Burnt Norton"), while the second is made up mostly of less familiar poems.

The canonical origin of the *katabasis* in European literature is Aeneas's descent to the Underworld in Book VI of the *Aeneid*; Aeneas needs to consult his father, Anchises, in order to determine his mission and fate, and, as I suggested in the Introduction, right there at the beginning of what we might call the katabatic canon is the use of the topos for cultural critique. It is Dante, though, who most forcefully cinches the connection between Hell and the other people who comprise the culture one sets out to critique, and it is Dante who provides Pound's powerful model. The Dantean character of Pound's Hell cantos and their Underworld is announced in the first line of Canto XIV: "Io venni in luogo d'ogni luce muto." Pound quotes the fifth canto of Dante's *Inferno* ("I came to a place mute of all light") to emphasize the darkness of the place (readers who cannot understand Dante's medieval Tuscan dialect are intellectually in the dark that Pound uses the line to describe), to link that darkness to language (through the synaesthetic description of it as "mute"), and to mobilize the familiar cultural machinery of Dante's system of sins and punishments. The punishments Pound describes here are, as Ronald Bush has written, satirically scatological and downright disgusting.[1] Politicians are posed with their wrists bound to their ankles, "Faces" (and, by implication, feces) "smeared on their rumps," and forced to address the multitudes assembled in the "ooze" "through their arseholes." Profiteers are set to drink "blood sweetened with shit." It is, though, the "betrayers" and "perverters of language" whose torments are described at greatest length. As Wendy Stallard Flory has pointed out, while mothers selling their daughters off to old men are simply equated to "sows eating their litters," Pound spends nine lines detailing the filth ("foetor," "dung," "last cesspool of the universe") the falsifiers are forced to publish on their bestially "clattering" presses.[2]

The squalor and misery Pound describes in Canto XIV echo Dante not only in the way punishments fit sins but also in direct allusions to passages in the *Inferno*. Dante's sinners suffer in ways that reenact or exaggerate their earthly sins. Pound's do too. Priests and politicians who might colloquially be said to "talk out of their asses" are made literally to do so, and those who "perverted" the press during their lives operate "perverted" presses, while those who profited from the sale of scarce goods during the war endure steel wire lashes laid on by the financiers who backed them. More than this, though, Pound's punishments refer directly to related passages in the *Inferno*. Like Dante, who locates "sodomites" at the bottom of the Seventh Circle, perched at the precipice of the canyon of Fraud, Pound closely juxtaposes "perverts" and "perverters of language." And just as Dante first introduces punitive devils in the Eighth Circle, where they beat the shades of liars, Pound shows devil financiers wielding steel wires as whips against the backs of profiteers.

Pound had, of course, read Dante carefully and for some time when he came to write these "Hell Cantos" in the early 1920s. I want, however, to suggest another possible influence before moving on to show how Pound condemns specific elements of European, especially

English, society in these cantos, for another poem Pound might well have come across in the British Museum would have offered another immediately imitable model for katabatic cultural critique.

James Bronterre O'Brien's "A Vision of Hell or Peep Into the Realms Below, Alias Lord Overgrown's Dream" is not a poem of which most contemporary readers will have heard. Published in London in the early1850s, O'Brien's sixteen-page satirical pamphlet circulated narrowly and then disappeared from view. The British Library's copy is bound with a number of other poetic pamphlets from the 1840s and 1850s, all of which sank promptly after making their small splash with even smaller audiences. O'Brien's mission, though, is quite similar to Pound's. "The object of this light Poem," he writes in a note to the reader, "is to turn the tables on those preachers" who use "hell as a sort of artillery on the side of established power."[3] O'Brien turns the tables by endeavoring "to show from what sources Hell must be presumed to recruit its population," arguing that "if God have ordained eternal punishment for any, it can only be for those enormous sinners" who have committed such crimes as "robbing a people of their land—of their free will—of their self-government—of all means of mental and moral culture…so as to perpetuate their degradation, corruption, and enslavement…"[4] Chief among such sinners, from the perspective of O'Brien's Irish nationalism, is the recently deceased Sir Robert Peel, who had died in 1850 after serving as Prime Minister of England from 1841 to 1846. Peel is named in O'Brien's long subtitle, which begins "DESCRIBING HIS LORDSHIP'S FANCIED REUNION WITH THE LATE SIR ROBERT PEEL IN THE REGIONS BELOW," and his readers' note, which offers Peel as the best representative of the class of "land-usurpers and money-changers" who plunge nations into "poverty, slavery, vice, corruption, sin, and crime."[5]

In this poem, Pound would have found not only a fellow adapter of Dante (O'Brien writes "Oh! for a Dante's muse to sketch / What Peel and Lloyd [Lord Overgrown] that moment felt"[6]), but also a kindred spirit in the condemnation of specific elements of English culture. On first glance, the poems seem dissimilar in this regard. Not only is O'Brien's poem in rhyming doggerel stanzas, but it is also clearly provoked largely by the colonial subjugation of Ireland. Pound's unrhymed and unmetered Modernist lines touch only very briefly on this topic, locating "in the ooze" the "murderers of Pearse and Macdonagh," two leaders of the Irish Republican Easter Rising of 1916, and British Captain J. Bowen-Colthurst, notorious for killing Irish political prisoners in his custody.[7] A crucial set of resemblances, though, are to be found in the poems' castigation of the economic forces seen as dominating English society. O'Brien mentions the British Bank-Charter Acts of 1819 and 1844 in his readers' note and, in the body of the poem, provides a catalogue of those who suffer eternal torment that is worth quoting at length for its similarity with Pound's villains:

> Loan-mongers, landlords, millionaires,
> Contractors, usurers, speculators,
> Stock-jobbers, brokers, bulls, and bears,
> Blacklegs, monopolists, regraters,
> Dealers in spiritual wares.[8]

"Usurers" stands out to the modern reader, of course, since usury and its personification as Usura are central to Pound's project, not only in these cantos ("usurers" are among those condemned in Canto XIV and Usura appears in Canto XV) but also throughout *The Cantos*; the demonic figure of Usura dominates the famous Canto XLV, for example, and the concept motivates many of Pound's angriest lines. O'Brien's "licensed spoliators," who appear a few lines after those quoted above, prefigure Pound's "profiteers" and his "hired reviewers, / And fabricators of false news" resemble Pound's perverters of language. Especially striking, though, is "monopolists," another crucial word for Pound that appears in O'Brien's catalogue. Canto XIV concludes with those sinners who most raise Pound's ire: the "obstructors of knowledge" and the "obstructors of distribution" (*Cantos* 63). Central to Pound's Social Credit economics and to the politics that follow from it is the notion that the world naturally provides sufficient abundance to prevent the scarcity that leads to war. Scarcity results, then, only when abundance is hoarded (when the naturally equitable distribution of goods is obstructed). Since monopoly, the exclusive control of a commodity, enables the manipulation of a commodity's price through artificial controls on its availability, it is by definition the sort of hoarding Pound condemns. The last lines of Canto XIV set "obstructors of knowledge" between the apposite "monopolists" and "obstructors of distribution" because those who artificially control the circulation of information (as language) enable the malign control of the circulation of goods. O'Brien's poem links these as well; the stanza that condemns merchants and bankers moves to "fabricators" just a few lines later.

Whether Pound had read O'Brien's poem or not, he certainly pursues a purpose consonant with the earlier poet's. In letters from the early and mid-1920s, he writes again and again that Cantos XIV and

XV were intended as cultural critique. To Wyndham Lewis, for example, he wrote that his " 'hell' is a portrait of contemporary England,"[9] and to John Drummond that "the hell cantos are specifically LONDON, the state of English mind in 1919 and 1920."[10] In 1925, after the publication of *A Draft of XVI Cantos* by William Bird's Three Mountains Press, Pound wrote to his father that he "intended to give an accurate picture of the spiritual state of England in the years 1919 and following."[11] That London is the target of Pound's critique is clear within the poem as well; describing the "utter decrepitude" above the "hell-rot" so evocatively sketched, Pound compares "the great arse-hole, / broken with piles" to the "sky over Westminster," and he emphasizes that this hell is populated by "many English." But the specific focus of his critique, indicated by the crimes and punishments Pound names, are, first, the elements of English and European society of the 1910s that he blames for the Great War (profiteering, monopolistic hoarding) and, even more vehemently, the forces that produced cultural stultification after the war: censorship (especially of artistically adventurous discourse), literary envy, Christian conformity, conservative scholarship, debased politics, the whole "bog of stupidities, / malevolent stupidities, and stupidities" (*Cantos* 63).[12] These, Pound shows, render the potentially productive soil of culture corrupt. His strong implication is that corrupt culture will yield a disastrous historical crop. (He makes this more explicit in Canto XVI's purgatorial rehearsal of the run-up to the First World War.)

Canto XV begins by establishing continuities with XIV but then proceeds to narrate the arduous way back up to the world of light. Themes, images, and persons repeated from XIV enforce the continuous habitation of a single space in these two cantos. The "arse-hole" of London recurs in the fourth line of XV as "the great scabrous arse-hole, sh-tting flies," the image of a "condom full of black beetles" recurs along with the figure of "...Episcopus." The sinful continue to suffer their fitting punishments, and their sins continue to refer to obstruction of the free flow of information and natural abundance. Two additions in the first half of this canto are noteworthy. First, Pound consigns to his Hell those who work within the political system to effect change and, just as important, includes both ends of the mainstream political spectrum by naming "fabians" (bourgeois socialists) and their Conservative counterparts. The only difference between the two is that while the Fabians want a nicely decorated, newly designed conduit to move the excrement in which they stand, the Conservatives seem content to stand in the "sh-t" as long as they wear the hides of the poor their policies have skinned. In addition, Pound provides a specific monstrous embodiment of the overarching sin he condemns in this canto's reference (the first in the poem) to "USURA," described as "the beast with a hundred legs" (64). Taken together, these additions in Canto XV suggest the intractable character of the Hell London has become. The various agents of obstruction—profiteers, the press, censors, and clergymen—might be defeated, but the monstrous principle behind their actions, an embodied abstraction, seems immortal. Moreover, political action is not only shown to be inefficacious but is itself a sin meriting punishment in Pound's Hell.

The second half of Canto XV shows the way out of this Underworld. Pound begins by introducing yet another addition, a first-person narrator accompanied by a tutelary figure from the philosophical past. The guide turns out to be Plotinus and he is armed not only with such wisdom as "Close the pores of your feet!" but also with the shield of Perseus, whose continual reflection of the slain Medusa's head solidifies the muck so that the two can walk on it and make their way toward the light. Pound's Dantean narrator is accompanied by a Neo-Platonic philosopher dedicated to the proposition that embodied being is an inferior reflection of a universal and ideal Mind.[13] Plotinus's philosophical wisdom alone does not suffice to rescue the narrator. Instead, it is when the "mirror" takes the form of Perseus's mythological shield that it is able to harden "the track" and hammer "the souse into hardness." The shield is a doubly significant metonym. On one level, it figures the legacy of story that Pound inherits from classical culture (via Ovid); on another, it figures the ideal of the artwork as a transformative reflection of the world.

It is important to note, though, that Pound's ascription of solidifying power to the mirror / shield constitutes a revision of his mythological source, and this revision is key to understanding the way out of hell that Pound envisions. In the fourth book of Ovid's *Metamorphoses*, it is only the head of the gorgon itself that turns things to stone; the fact that the reflection of the head in Perseus's bronze shield does not have this power is precisely what enables him to kill Medusa.[14] Here Pound attributes the power to the reflection, which somehow persists in the shield. It is, then, neither the thought of Plotinus alone, nor the thought of Plotinus condensed with classical narrative in the allusion to Perseus that enables the speaker to leave the Underworld. It is, instead, these *combined* in the peculiarly *revisionary* synthesis of the poet-hero, a synthesis similar the one Pound achieves in the first canto's simultaneous translation and foregrounding of transmission of Odysseus's *nekuia*. The hell of "LONDON, the state of English mind in 1919 and 1920" is to be escaped only by the poet who can reflect on that place, that state, through the literary and philosophical traditions as synthesized by his own heroic intelligence and creative will.

*   *   *

The Hell Cantos establish a pattern that recurs throughout the twentieth century, especially the first half of the century. Poets who set out to condemn some elements of their culture often do so by suggesting an analogy between their culture and Hell. Pound's poem demonstrates some of the gains and losses entailed by this katabatic approach. On one hand, the analogy provides a good deal of rhetorical force. Pound's condemnation of obstructors and perverters is unforgettable, and as I write I am mindful of his implication that "pets-de-loup" (wolfish scholars) are often to be found "obscuring texts with philology" as they sit on (punning) "piles of stone books." On the other hand, though, for all its violence, Pound's katabatic mode of critique grants the forces he condemns even greater power. If Hell is eternal, and if the awful London against which Pound reacts is Hell, then that London too is eternal, unalterable, insusceptible to social change. Pound's tactic runs the risk of rendering his critical energies impotent.

This difficulty is often found in poems that deploy Hell for the purpose of cultural critique. Countee Cullen's "Yet Do I Marvel," for example, implies that the condition of the black poet bid by God to sing is hellish when he adduces the torments of Sisyphus and Tantalus as illustrations of the similar sort of thing he imagines God might explain. The analogy powerfully suggests the experience of desperate desire confronted with the impossibility of success. Just as Tantalus reaches for the fruit and water that always recede beyond his grasp, and just as Sisyphus labors in vain to push his stone permanently to the top of the hill, the black poet will never reach his goal of poetic recognition (of recognition *as* poet), will never shift the stone of literary prejudice. The injustice of the black poet's situation is exacerbated by the fact that, unlike these two mythological figures, he has done nothing to deserve his plight. The sonnet's couplet lays the responsibility in God's hands: "Yet do I marvel at this wondrous thing: / To make a poet black and bid him sing."[15] Just as important, though, the poem offers no hint that change is possible, and the Hell references cinch the bargain. If the poet's torment is divinely designed and if it shares the eternal and relentless character of Tantalus's and Sisyphus's, then the poet grants an undeserved omnipotence to precisely the cultural forces his poem most poignantly addresses. (The implicit solution to this eternal impasse, of course, is the existence of Cullen's poem itself; this perfectly turned sonnet performs what it deems impossible, and the suppressed rage and anguish of the couplet suggest the existence of energy that could challenge the status quo.) Like many such poems, though, Cullen's does not imagine a connection between that rage and any sort of action that might alter the circumstances that render the speaker's position hellish.

Hart Crane's *The Bridge* narrates a similar descent in its "Tunnel" section (first published independently in 1927, then as the seventh and penultimate section of *The Bridge* in 1929). In the long poem, "The Tunnel" follows the materialist nadir of "Quaker Hill" and carries out that section's concluding command to "descend" even as it sets the stage for the triumphant ascent of the poem's final "Ave Maria" section. From the garishly lit and hectic "Circle," at once Columbus Circle and the first circle of an infernal urban space, the speaker descends into the subway. Crane first imagines this space in terms that recall "The River" (in the "Powhatan's Daughter" section of the poem), in which he fuses space and time and traverses the span of American history and the American continent. In the "subways, rivered under streets / and rivers," though, we find only enclosure, repetition, and fragmentation.[16] Crane quotes snatches of overheard conversation, unfinished ideas and disconnected phrases that emphasize desire ("what do you want?") and objectification. This is the dissolution of community, the degradation of history, the replacement of vibrant humanity with signs of wear, exposure, and exhaustion. Crane captures the dehumanized character of these subterranean urban voices when the "monotone of sound" in the subway becomes "phonographs of hades."

Crane presents a case in which the intertwining of literary and political concerns is especially acute; in "The Tunnel," he confronts not only the failure of contemporary society to measure up to the ideals embodied for Crane in the linked figures of Walt Whitman and the Brooklyn Bridge but also the failure of his own poem to realize his initial ambitions. Susan Schultz persuasively argues that the poem's late sections ("Cape Hatteras" and "The Tunnel") "deal very directly with poetic ambition and failure," and she goes on to write that "Cape Hatteras" confronts both "the failure of Whitman's myth in the destruction caused by World War I" and Crane's own poetic failure.[17] The insufficiency of Whitman's vision does not, however, lead Crane to accept the strong alternative posed to that vision by Eliot in *The Waste Land*; as Schultz writes, Eliot's "negative vision" represented, to Crane, "modern failure."[18] As a katabatic descent, "The

Tunnel" embodies a forceful critique of elements of Crane's culture. At the same time, the poem grapples with the Eliotic influence— palpable in its own diction and imagery—in order to redeem the Whitmanian influence that governs *The Bridge* as a whole. In working out its anxieties of influence, "The Tunnel" also imagines a way out of the cultural Hell it sketches as its speaker rides that perfect metonym of contemporary urban anomie: the subway.

Edward Brunner suggestively notes that the confrontation Crane conducts with Eliot takes place in the pages of the elder poet's own magazine; "The Tunnel" was first published in *The Criterion*'s November, 1927 issue.[19] In 1926, though, Crane writes not only against *The Waste Land* but also against the horizon of at least a decade's worth of poems that implicitly imagine the Underworld in terms of the Underground and that do so in order to criticize the poet's culture. Pound's "In a Station of the Metro," first published in *Poetry* (1913) and then in *Blast* (1914), famously locates its shade-like "apparition of these faces in the crowd" in a Parisian subway station. Closer to home, Edna St. Vincent Millay, in her 1917 sonnet "If I should learn in some quite casual way," imagines learning of the addressee's death by reading of it in another passenger's news-paper while riding the subway.[20] Both of these poems represent the urban Underworld as a space of anomie. Pound's "faces" are anony-mous and insubstantial as a consequence of their appearance in the crowd. Even when naturalized or rendered aesthetic by the metaphor of "petals on a wet black bough," they remain at once an undiffer-entiated mass and a set of constituents separated from the whole that grants them meaning; petals torn or fallen from their flowers, these shades are fragments, incapable of participating in the repro-duction of a whole social organism. While less evocative of mytho-logical models and more straightforwardly representative of a space devoted to commerce and commuting, Millay's subway also draws its infernal character from the fact of isolation within the crowd. While the surface world of this society is deadly, the subterranean space of the subway is deadening. The speaker avers that she would not weep or wring her hands "in such a place" and that, more than this, she "could not" indulge in such displays of grief. Surrounded but alone, stuck but in inescapable motion, she can only compose an outwardly careful expression and stare at the lights that pass (they have agency while she endures a forced passivity) and read the advertisements on the train. The sonnet concludes both with an emphasis on surfaces— the speaker attends to her appearance, the ads are for "where to store furs and how to treat the hair"—and a recognition of the mediated character of loss and mourning in the contemporary city. Furs are stored carefully and hair is treated in order to preserve the appearance of vitality in dead remnants. Instead of experiencing the grief at the loss she imagines (the poem unfolds in the conditional mood of its opening "If"), the speaker recognizes that she could only hold on to the dead through the discourse of advertising. That Millay casts this proleptic experience of modern loss in a sonnet, a form saturated at its roots with the tonic of poetic preservation against the onslaughts of mortality and sluttish time, is a hell of an irony.

Advertisements surround Crane's speaker too; indeed, the "toothpaste and the dandruff ads" under which he meets a tutelary shade seem almost direct echoes of Millay's well-chosen examples. It is not, however, only ads and anomie that render the subway infernal for Crane. Where Pound leaves his faces as floral fragments, Crane reports their fragmented speech, evidence of fragmented consciousnesses. The bodies of the subway riders, too, are represented as fragmentary: tongues, hair, bone. Where Millay worries about the death of a possible lover, Crane confronts the death of love itself. Desire is both rampant and mediated (through popular song evoked by the repetition of "why did you / swing on it, why *didja* / swing on it"). In its aftermath the speaker finds "love / A burnt match skating in a urinal," love, that is to say, exhausted, extinguished, discarded into and with and as bodily waste. And all of this occurs within a frame of repetition, and the whole infernal passage plays out in present-progressive verbs, simultaneous motion and stasis, and a sense of deja-vu ("Why do I often meet your visage here").

The hellish aspects of Crane's journey underground climax in a horrifying vision that condenses urban anonymity, violence, and fragmentation: "Whose head is swinging from the swollen strap? / Whose body smokes along the bitten rails" (99). It comes as no surprise that the prophetic figure encountered in these depths is the shade of Edgar Allan Poe, an infernal counterpart to Walt Whitman, the poetic spirit who hovers over *The Bridge*. Where Whitman, elsewhere in the poem, is the speaker's "*Panis Angelicus*," the bread of Heaven who offers salvation through expansive love and who is symbolically associated with the bridge that connects individuals and communities across space and time ("that great Bridge, our Myth, whereof I sing"), Poe represents death and descent, drunkenness and illness ("they dragged your retching flesh through Baltimore"), partisan divisiveness and political dissolution ("That last night on the ballot rounds"), and, finally, despair. The poet of isolation and madness, Poe sings the body electrocuted, the death of love and the obsessive love of death.

Crane asks "why do I often meet your visage here," suggesting (as does the way Poe's eyes are seen "on and on / Below the…ads") that both Poe and this moment of encounter are caught up in the repetition that is part of what makes Hell hellish. And while Crane questions the shade (as Aeneas questions Anchises), Poe never answers. Instead, he simply stands as a conduit for "Death" as it sweeps toward the poet. The closest thing to Poe's own speech we might find in this encounter is an echo of his most famous poem: "O evermore!" Here, Crane seems to name the shade, but he does so in a way that recalls the raven (and "The Raven"), whose repeated "Nevermore" propels that poem's speaker to madness. When Crane's speaker questions the shade of Poe (*again*, as the "often" suggests), he repeats the "Raven" scenario; seeking surcease from sorrow for the lost New York, he asks questions that, at some level, he knows will receive no helpful answer.

I began this discussion of Crane by noting the especially tight intertwining of cultural critique and poetic crisis. It is not going too far, I think, to say that it is precisely through solving his problem of poetic inheritance that Crane imagines a solution to the social problems encountered in their most pressing form in "The Tunnel." Like Pound in Canto XV, Crane depicts a culture wallowing in its own depravity. Also like Pound, he narrates salvation not through any imagined political action committed to social change but through a specific set of aesthetic commitments. After his confrontation with Poe, the speaker in "The Tunnel" begins, "like Lazarus, to feel the slope" and rise from the city's Underworld, but there is no suggestion that Poe has given the speaker resources or wisdom necessary to ascend. Rather than Poe, the poem strongly suggests that it is Whitman who brings about this resurrection. The nature and identity of the saving "Word that will not die" is given not in "The Tunnel" itself but in this section's concluding structural and verbal echoes of the closing moments of the earlier "Ave Maria" and "Cape Hatteras" sections. All three end with lines stair-stepped across the page; "The Tunnel" concludes:

> Kiss of our agony Thou gatherest,
>   O Hand of Fire
>   gatherest—(101)

The repeated "gatherest" here resembles Eliot's repetition of "pluckest" in "The Fire Sermon" and, with the capitalized "Thou," suggests a divine presence positioned to redeem the speaker. In this final Eliotic echo, though, Crane takes his leave of *The Waste Land*; instead of the "Lord" called upon in Eliot's poem, the repeated image of the hand links the saving Word to Whitman, so that the deity praised and present in the flames is the poet who sings and celebrates himself. That this flaming hand not only pulls the speaker from the subway but also enables his ascent is suggested by the way the concluding lines of "The Tunnel" do not conclude a sentence; the dash that ends this section leads directly to the opening lines of "Atlantis," the triumphant last section of *The Bridge*, so that we might read the sentence as: "Thou gatherest / O Hand of Fire / gatherest— // Through the bound cable strands, the arching path / Upward" (101–5). More than this, the poetic resolution stands for the broader social solution required for the problems sketched on the subway. It is not any act on the part of the speaker (or any other person described in the subway) that brings about the resurrection and the reference to Lazarus ascribes the responsibility for it to a supernatural, divine presence. Twice, however, the ascent from the subway is linked to song; directly after the confrontation with the shade of Poe, Crane has an escalator lift "a serenade," and immediately before the Lazarus-like rise he describes the riders' nerves as "Impassioned with some song." Crane's descent into the tunnel (and into "The Tunnel"), into worldly lust, commerce, drunkenness, and despair, into the Hell that is beneath but at the same time somehow *is* New York, can only be redeemed by Whitman's poetic "Hand of Fire."

In "Burnt Norton" (1936), originally published alone and only later as the first of *Four Quartets*, T.S. Eliot deploys the subway as a similar figure for the fallen world dependent for its redemption on something beyond our power to conceive. The third of the poem's five movements is set in "a place of disaffection," where past and future coexist in artificial light. This subterranean space resembles the subways of Pound, Millay, and Crane. Under flickering lights, the "time-strained, time-ridden faces" of commuters are "Distracted from distraction by distraction," the constant motion and omnipresent advertisements filling them with "fancies." Subtly Dantean imagery adds to the infernal atmosphere as "men and bits of paper" are "whirled by the cold wind / That blows before and after time."[21] Eliot echoes himself here, the subway commuters of 1936 resembling as they replace the commuters on their Dantesque and deathlike march across London Bridge in the first section of *The Waste Land*: "So many, I had not thought death had undone so many," a translation of lines from Canto III of Dante's *Inferno*. That echo is important, for the fundamental problem of this "place of disaffection" is that its artificial timelessness grants neither the "transient beauty" that results from natural temporal progression nor "darkness to purify the soul." In this regard, the subway in 1936 is like the London of 1922; the inhabitants of both are trapped in a state of living death and so are incapable of either living in time or fully dying out of it. In *The Waste Land*, Eliot alludes to the legends of the Holy Grail to suggest that this static and liminal suspension prevents the absolute death necessary for renewal of land and society. In "Burnt Norton," he represents the suspended state as constant motion in the flicker of artificial light. The motion derives not only from the wind, an "Eructation of unhealthy souls" that has been at its belching since before time, but also from the pursuit of desire and satisfaction. The tracks of the subway are the emblem of this motion: "the world moves / In appetency, on its metalled ways" (18).

Where *The Waste Land* resolved on the irresolution of shoring the ruins of culture with that culture's own fragments, and where Pound's Canto XV resolves the infernal situation of late 1910s London culture with an appeal to Plotinus's Neoplatonism, and where Crane reaches for the flaming hand of Whitman to pull him from the hellish space of the urban subway, Eliot in "Burnt Norton" offers radical ascesis as "the one way" out of the Underground-as-Underworld. The "still point of the turning world," he writes, must instead be sought by a deeper descent: "Descend lower." In the series of nominalized verbs that follows this imperative, Eliot at once specifies the sacrifice required and enacts the being-out-of-time the sacrifice might enable: "deprivation," "destitution," "Desiccation," "Evacuation," "Inoperancy"(18). The way out of all that the subway represents is a way *down* into self-denial and self-abnegation, a way of loss and absence and, finally, stillness, which stands in opposition to the world's movement in "appetency."

While it offers no way out per se, Charles Olson's "In Cold Hell, in Thicket" (1953) similarly emphasizes form and pattern in its exploration of an Underworld. Imagery of "traceries" and "markings" recurs throughout the poem, though, as I will argue, Olson proffers neither these patterns themselves nor an ability to read them as a solution to a hellish world (or way of being in the world) in which "all things are bitter, words even / are made to taste like paper."[22] Unlike the *katabases* I have so far discussed in this chapter, Olson's "cold hell" is located within rather than around the poet/speaker. The poem nevertheless at least implies a critique of its culture; where Hell for Pound and Crane is other people and Hell for Eliot is the metalled way of worldly appetency, Hell in Olson's poem is the psyche of what Thomas Merrill calls the "non-projective man," a space constructed

in and by one's culture, and into which one is driven by that culture.[23] "In Cold Hell" performs a "cultural critique of the contemporary social field" similar to the one Walter Kalaidjian finds in the
Maximus poems, a rigorous attention to and subversion of "ideological narratives, whether Eliot's version of Christian humanism or the
foundational story of bourgeois individualism."[24] As Kalaidjian suggests here, and as critics like Robert von Hallberg and Andrew Ross
have argued, the means of social change for Olson is the same as his
mode of cultural critique: poetry itself.[25]

Olson's poem opens "In cold hell" and with a question: when confronted with the discursively produced enervation of the world, how
sufficient is the intellect alone for finding some source of renewal?
The prelude section of the poem begins to answer the question indirectly by realizing the necessity of action and by specifying the mode
of that action, for this speaker at any rate, as speech: "if it is me,
what / he has to say" (15). In his setting out of the problem and the
necessity of speech-as-action, Olson's poem echoes both the descriptive and prescriptive pronouncements of his 1950 essay "Projective
Verse." In that essay, published in *Poetry New York*, Olson posits mere
intellect ("the mind alone") as the grounds for T.S. Eliot's failure as
a dramatist, his failure to go "down through the workings of his own
throat to that place where breath comes from," which is necessary for
the development of a poetry or drama that effectively communicates
energy from poet to reader rather than dissipating energy. While he
does not make such a claim explicitly, Olson implies that the poetic
revolution he describes and advocates is necessary precisely because
poetry as practiced in the print age has at once suffered and contrib-
uted to a broad cultural exhaustion.[26]

To recognize that action is necessary, though, is not to suggest
that the necessary action is easy; as both Thomas Merrill and Robert
von Hallberg have written, the poem registers "suffering" and "stumbling" in its efforts to overcome what Merrill characterizes as a "linguistic anemia...which has severed man from nature's energies."[27] In
"Projective Verse" Olson emphasizes both the spiritual anxiety and
the physical labor involved in "composition by field," and in "In Cold
Hell in Thicket" he admits the difficulty of the required speech act, a
difficulty related to the prior difficulty of reading the place: "In hell
it is not easy / to know the traceries, the markings." Not only does
Olson describe the difficulty; his recursive treatment of it enacts the
difficulty of knowing what is to be done or said (they are the same
thing in the poem). The place is illegible and its illegibility deprives
the poem's protagonist of ease and pleasure; indeed, the impossibility

of reading the space is what makes it "a sort of hell." What is required, then, is a creative act whose precise character is unknown because it is cast as a question: "how / shall be convert this underbrush, how turn this unbidden place / how trace and arch again" (16).

The setting in which this questioning is carried out merits some attention since it not only echoes both Dante and Pound but also introduces a historical component to the speaker's unfolding question. The poem characterizes the speaker's hell as an illegible thicket, a muddy place where the speaker fears that he will "trespass on his own dissolving bones." This slough resembles the bog in which Pound's speaker finds himself in Canto XV and the muck in which Dante sees spirits mired in the fifth canto of the *Inferno*. Where Merrill argues that this imagery points to "an obsession with time" (as opposed to space) as the constitutive problem of "cold hell," I would argue that the mud and dissolving bone strongly suggest not only time but also history;[28] the place "where the mud is" is also the place "where there is altogether too much remembrance," and what is remembered seems, in several places in the poem, to be past military conflicts.

These references continue a thread of imagery from the beginning of the poem, where Olson refers to lead soldiers and a "spit-hardened fort." As von Hallberg argues, such images, in 1951, against the backdrop of the Korean conflict, strongly suggest "a historical context where...political conflicts...were becoming contrived and manipulated like toy soldiers in a toy fort."[29] The battlefield here, though, with its "rotted" condition indicating the passage of some time, seems also to take in a longer sweep of American history. The historical character of the poem's "cold hell" suggests that even though it is internal ("not external, not to be got out of"), it is nevertheless shaped and situated by aspects of the self's culture. The historical facts of battlefields with their dissolving bones and the recognition that the ground on which one steps contains one's own (one's ancestors'?) dissolving bones lead to the conclusion that the sociohistorical fact of violence ("that men killed, do kill") is also "part...of his question" (19).

Just like the other realizations at which the poem's voice arrives, the realization that Hell is internal does not make it easier to address or amend the hell's hellishness. The facts are "simple," but that simplicity does nothing to ease "this unhappy man's / obscurities." Any action taken by the one who endures the poem's cold Hell is characterized as not only difficult but also dangerous. More than this, any step he takes will lead only to "a later wilderness." In spite of this, Olson writes, "He shall step." The nature of that stepping, the nature of the action the self takes to read the traceries, to move onto different soil, to effect the necessary confrontations, is cast in terms that echo Olson's writing about writing. When he asserts that "he" will "cross," he adds in parentheses that "there is always a field / for the strong." The word "field" names the dangerously revealed space the self must traverse, of course, but it also suggests Olson's "composition by field," the poetic practice that transfers the energy of the writer's vision to the reader through an emotional and physical engagement with language and the space of the page. The risky entry into the field, which is, in the poem, what Merrill calls "humiliation" of the ego and von Hallberg describes as the self-as-manifested-in-action, is at the same time an entry into what Olson calls in "Projective Verse" the "large area of the whole poem," the place "where all the syllables and all the lines must be managed in their relations to each other."[30] It is only in this entry into the whole poem that "he" can become a "participant in the larger force" and, hearing through himself, gain access to "secrets objects share." Instead of the escape from self that Eliot advocated, then, Olson suggests a risky commitment to the enacted self as an intersection with the world, as the locus of one's "relation to nature."

That the means of escape from (or, perhaps more accurately, the transformation of) Hell are specifically poetic is made clear not only by these echoes of "Projective Verse" but also by the emphasis on language and making in the final gestures of "In Cold Hell." The bulk of the poem's final section elaborates on the protagonist's resolution to act. This action will occur on the grounds of the body and its spatial, historical, social location, but it most importantly comprises the crossing of a field (the phrase "he will cross" is not only repeated twice, it is set off and stressed by its distance from other lines; Olson surrounds the phrase with white space both by double-spacing before and after it and by setting it on the page's left margin and indenting the lines that precede and follow it). That is, the self's action is poetic action. The reading, raising, and making described and prescribed in earlier sections take on this specific form as the poem ends; each is reinvoked in the concluding stanzas in either a verbal or an imagistic echo, and all are set under the aegis of the self's response to the "questions" the poem has so far posed, the "demand" it has made. Olson notes the care "he" will take in doing "what he now does" and, in the poem's final stanza, links through this precision the physical body in which the self resides and the verbal body it constructs: "precise as hell is, precise / as any words, or wagon, / can be made" (21). "Wagon" in this stanza recalls the poem's earlier image for the body and here it is alliteratively and conceptually connected to "words." In language, then, the self as hell is constructed, that the self as paradise might be imagined and wrought.

*   *   *

The way indicated by Pound, Crane, and Eliot—the way of Art, Poetry, the Tradition, the Word—is, in Eliot's phrase, "the one way," but in the range of katabatic poems of the early twentieth century, there is at least one other way and it is not at all "the same." Vergil famously has the Cumaean Sybil say in *Aeneid* VI that the way down to the Underworld is easy but that getting back up, reentering history after the sojourn into myth, is tougher. The way up that is indicated by Pound, Crane, Eliot, and even Olson—the way of Art, Poetry, the Tradition, the Word—might suggest that while the infernalizing of a culture can sharpen a critique, it blunts the edge of any tool that might effect social change. Some voices, though, alloy their katabatic cultural critiques with political diagnoses for contemporary cultural ills and, among these, a few go as far as to imagine political cures.

Perhaps the most entertaining and powerful political diagnosis is the one Sterling Brown offers in the katabatic descent of "Slim in Hell." Sent to Hell as a spy for St. Peter, Slim the trickster encounters Dixie analogues for infernal allusions: for Cerberus, the three-headed dog who guards the Greek Underworld, a "big bloodhound" that comes "aroarin' / Like Niagry Falls," and in a brilliant condensation of Dante and dialect, a sign reading "DIS IS IT."[31] These exemplify what John Edgar Tidwell describes as Brown's synthesis of the tradition of literary satire from Moliere to Twain and the oral folk culture he absorbed in "barbershops, 'jook joints,' and isolated farms" after earning his MA at Harvard in 1923.[32] Joanne Gabbin has described the poem as "a synthesis of two viable traditions," a "fusion of the black folk ballad" and "allusion as a means of reinforcing the idea of a descent into Hell."[33] Where Gabbin sees Brown alluding to the story of Orpheus and Eurydice, however, I am arguing that Vergil and Dante are his models. St. Peter's injunction echoes the divine assistance Aeneas receives from Venus more than the permission Orpheus receives to seek his lost beloved (for whom there is no analogous figure in Brown's poem), and the catalogue of sinners and punishments much more strongly echoes the *Inferno* than Ovid's account of the Orphic myth.

It is through the sights Slim sees on his tour of Hell that Brown effects his cultural critique. After a cordial exchange of greetings, the Devil shows Slim around and points out "people / Raisin' hell" (90). The fighting and gambling and whoring he sees remind Slim of New Orleans and Memphis in the first of three explicit comparisons Slim makes between Hell and home. Here, though, what is striking is the pleasure on offer in this Underworld. The place is full of roulette wheels, "bawdy houses," cabarets, and stills. A couple of stanzas later, though, Slim sees how this pleasure palace is heated. When the Devil takes him to the furnace, Slim witnesses "White devils wid pitchforks" throwing "black devils on" the fire (91). The pleasurably infernal enterprise is fueled by the literal consumption of black bodies. When he sees how things really are in Hell, Slim makes his second comparison to the American South (with Brown repeating his Dantean pun): " 'Dis makes / Me think of home," Slim says, "Vicksburg, Little Rock, Jackson, / Waco, and Rome" (91). Where Memphis and New Orleans would be obvious figures for the hell-raising Slim first sees, this second set is hardly the group of southern towns that come most immediately to mind. Brown's Southern metonyms here are well chosen, though, each referring to the site of a lynching or a "race riot" (a euphemism for white-led massacres of African Americans) sometime between the 1890s and the 1920s. (Waco, for example, was infamous after the 1916 lynching there of seventeen-year-old Jesse Hall, a mentally retarded African American man who was tortured, hanged, and burned on the town square in front of ten–fifteen thousand cheering white citizens.)[34]

Upon his return to Heaven, Slim reports to St. Peter, who asks what new tricks the Devil is up to. His reply makes the third and most explicit connection between Hell and the American south; where the others function as similes, though, this last comparison strengthens to metaphoric status: "De place was Dixie / Dat I took for Hell" (92). In what Tidwell describes as the "snapper climax or exposure at the end" typical of tall tales, St. Peter retorts "Where'n hell dja think Hell *was* / Anyhow?"[35] What Slim has discovered, in other words, is what Brown's African American readers in 1933 already knew: "Dixie" was constructed for the pleasure of whites, was fueled by the destructive consumption of black bodies, and was policed by satanic "crackers" wearing sheriff's stars.

We might ask what cultural work could be performed by Brown's poetic belaboring of the obvious. In his analysis of the Slim Greer poems, Mark Sanders argues that Brown demonstrates the political limitations of the trickster figure by dramatizing Slim's failure even to recognize the infernal that has surrounded him all his life: "Simply put, Greer exists in a historical vacuum, employing only ad hoc measures of resistance; therefore, as the result of an extremely truncated view of his own condition, Greer's talents remain equally limited."[36] Sanders's conclusion might be at least partly right, but it depends on reading "Slim in Hell" as the culmination of the sequence of Slim Greer poems, the concluding climax of a fragmentary narrative in which Slim's tricksterish selfishness has sometimes had negative consequences for his fellow African Americans (I am thinking here especially of "Slim in Atlanta," in which Slim monopolizes the "telefoam booth" that is the only place African Americans can legally laugh in order to laugh at this law; when others line up for their turn, this only increases Slim's mirth). "Slim in Hell," however, did not appear along with the other Slim Greer poems until the publication of Brown's *Collected Poems* in 1980. We might, then, want to consider it in a couple of other important contexts when seeking to determine its cultural work. We might, for example, read "Slim in Hell" against the backdrop B.A. Botkin's regional miscellany *Folk Say*, in which it first appeared in 1932. There, "Slim in Hell" is the first of a group of Brown's poems (including "Call Boy," "Long Track Blues," "Rent Day Blues," "A Bad, Bad Man," and "Puttin' on Dog") under the general title (apparently assigned by Botkin) "The Devil and the Black Man." In the context of *Folk Say*, "Slim in Hell" provides the African American view of the contemporary South and also the African American folk voice to complement the various other voices included in the anthology. The poem provides the backdrop against which readers would go on to encounter, in Scrappy of "Puttin' on Dog," a trickster figure very much like Slim meeting the sort of fate we might imagine Slim meeting upon his return from Heaven (shot by a bad man and "a-puttin' on dog in a pinewood box").[37] All the other Brown poems appear, then, not only under the rubric of "The Devil and the Black Man" but also under the specific vision, elaborated in Brown's *katabasis*, of an infernal South fueled by burning black bodies.

Reading the poem in the broader context of the poems included in Brown's first book, *Southern Road*, and of the poems written around the same time but not included in that volume, we can see in Slim's combination of strengths and weaknesses an example of what James Smethurst describes as Brown's self-conscious attempt to demonstrate the value (and limitations) of the indigenous folk culture of the African American South. Where such contemporaries as Langston Hughes elaborated "a vision of liberation through progress," Smethurst writes, Brown advocates and models "the cultural forms of expression and resistance that developed in the intense racial opposition of

the South."[38] More than this, we can read the poem as translating
into folk idiom a radical political vision that incorporates not only
tricksterish subversion but also the Communist Party's economic
analyses of American racial oppression. In his vision of the South as
a hellish pleasure palace for whites whose furnace consumes "black
devils," Brown proves correct Smethurst's contention that the poet's
work resembles the slogan of "the CPUSA-led League of Struggle for
Negro Rights, 'Promote Negro Culture in Its Original Form with
Proletarian Content.'"[39] This is precisely what we might expect from
a poet lauded on the Left, from William L. Patterson's 1928 appre-
ciation in *New Masses* to the magazine's presentation of an award to
Brown for "Contributing toward a Democratic America" in 1945.[40]

Finally, though, the poem's cultural work is inseparable from its
katabatic structure. This makes it far from clear that Slim is guilty of
what Sanders describes as a failure "to perceive the literally cosmic
implications of racial oppression."[41] The return from the Underworld
to the world has been, from the beginning, a key component of the
katabasis. Aeneas leaves the embrace of Anchises and makes his arduous way back to the world above in order to complete his task; Dante
is enjoined to return and write the *Commedia*. The return in the
katabatic tradition is also a *turn*, away from the myth for which the
Underworld is a metonym and to the history unfolding in the world.
Read in this light, Slim's forced return to earth is not only a punishment for being "too dumb" to stay in Heaven. It is also a reentry into
history. While Brown stops there, the katabatic conventions suggest
that Slim returns to the world changed by what he has witnessed. It
would be going too far to imagine that he takes up activism back in
Dixie, working like Brown's poet-intellectual to reveal the foundations of the system in which his community is enmeshed. In sending
Slim back to earth, however, Brown invokes the tradition that makes
his poem do so in Slim's place.

Like Crane's "Tunnel," Louis Zukofsky's 1934 poems "'Mantis'
and 'Mantis,' an Interpretation" suggest the by now familiar analogy
between the subway and the mythological Underworld. Unlike Crane
(and Pound and Eliot), Zukofsky's poem offers a political (rather than
literary, philosophical, or religious) vision as the mode and means of
salvation.[42] The sestina ("Mantis") narrates and meditates upon the
speaker's surprise discovery of the title insect in the urban and subterranean space of the New York subway; the "Interpretation" lays
bare the devices of the sestina, denaturalizing the form and revealing
the labor involved in the production of the poem-as-artifact. Both
elaborate a way of seeing that is necessary for the building of a "new

world" antithetical to the "oppression of the poor" that is, Zukofsky writes, "the situation most pertinent to us" in the Underworld of the present.[43]

While the Underworld analogy is only suggested in Zukofsky's poem(s) and while the Dante quoted and alluded to in the interpretation of the sestina is *La Vita Nuova* rather than *The Divine Comedy*, the space of the subway is at least implicitly infernal. It is inhabited by the poor, who ride on seats of stone as if to endure some punishment. Moreover, the anthropomorphized mantis (*man*-tis?) takes on the properties of a seer ("prophetess") or, perhaps, the Cumaean sybil (aged to an insect-like appearance) who enables Aeneas's descent. Over the course of the sestina, the mantis becomes the locus of a vision that, like Aeneas's gift from Anchises, offers an exit from the Underworld and into history.

The poem's two central problems are introduced in the sestina's opening apostrophe: the consociation of mantis and the poor and the problem of seeing. The mantis and the poor are brought together first by the description of the insect's eyes, which are "poor" and which, like some of the poor, "Beg," and then by the embedding of these two ("poor" and "you") in the end-words that will obsessively repeat over the sestina's six stanzas and envoi. At the same time, an inability or unwillingness to look or see characterizes both insect and speaker. The "poor" eyes of the mantis "beg" rather than seeing, while the speaker "can't bear to look" and the others who surround the tableau are blind to it ("no one sees"). Over the course of the sestina, blindness becomes sight, though the shift from sight to effective vision is slow. In the third stanza, a newsboy sees the mantis; he dismisses any significance, however, knowing it is "no use" and finding the lone insect "harmless" to the system in which he operates as a cog whose function is to enrich others: "papers make money, makes stone, stone / Banks." A stanza later, though, the poor "see it." The pronoun's reference is unclear; "it" could be the mantis or the speaker's "fright" when it lands on his chest or it could be the "shame" shared by the speaker and the poor. In any case, the poor's newfound ability to see introduces the insect's folkloric role as a leader of lost children and men to safety.

If the mantis and poor are somehow the same, though, how can the insect lead the poor from their subterranean existence? The fourth stanza admits that though it is a "prophetess" the mantis will, in this space of stone, "die, touch, beg, of the poor" (74). The content of the vision that expands over the course of the poem is precisely the similarity in the situations of the mantis and the poor. Evoked together in the first stanza's figurative language, both insect and poor are trapped underground, brought there by forces beyond their control or understanding. Both are "harmless" to the system, both are left with no one to feed or save them, and both are subject to trampling. The penultimate stanza reinforces the unity of these two terms when the mantis is addressed in an apostrophe as "Android, loving beggar." From the Greek *andros*, or man, the mantis is here characterized at once as "man-like" and as a beggar; it shares the situation of the poor. It does so, though, in a sympathetic mode ("loving"), and is imagined, finally, speaking to the poor. Where it begins as an object in need of salvation, its eyes pleading for someone to "save it," the mantis becomes by the end of the poem an agent of salvation, no longer speaking the words "save it" but appealed to as the agent who can "build the new world in [its] eyes."

A related progression through the poem is the mechanization of both setting and denizens. The second stanza asks "what wind-up brought" the mantis to this place, the strange hyphenate condensing natural forces ("wind-up" as storm) and mechanical ones ("wind-up" as the operating principle of a toy or machine). The sixth stanza figures the mantis in mechanical terms: "Graze like machined wheels." We might read this figurative strain as opposed to the other logics I have traced through the poem, but it is in fact a central component of the necessary vision Zukofsky sketches in the sestina. It is in the apprehension of their current mechanical state (an embodiment of the reification against which Zukofsky is working) that insect and poor alike will find the means to "arise like leaves," to become once again organic and to find strength as "armies of the poor," strength with which to "build the new world" and "Save it."

As Michael Davidson argues, the sestina on its own might run the risk of aestheticizing (and thereby occluding) social tensions, but "'Mantis,' an Interpretation" challenges "the totalizing gesture implied by the [sestina's] form and manifested in its utopian apostrophe."[44] The "Interpretation" therefore completes the elaboration of a politicized vision necessary for emergence from the urban Underworld. As its subtitle—in both Latin and English—suggests, "names are sequent to the things named," or language is rooted in reality. While this notion itself might be rooted in William Carlos Williams's dictum "No ideas but in things," the specific charge it carries in Zukofsky's hands is the foundation of the sestina's vision in the social realities it at once names and sets out to transform. The interpretation does this by revealing the labor that went into the construction of the sestina. Zukofsky gives the initial version of the poem's opening, he rehearses his process of thinking through the insect's significance and of finding the form most fitting for a moment of insight. Indeed, form—as "experiment," which Zukofsky criticizes and rejects, and as "force," which he affirms—is central to the poet's meditations. The sestina suits the situation neither because it testifies to the poet's virtuosity nor because it asserts the poet's relationship with the troubadour tradition from which the form descends, nor even because it performs kinship with a modernist like Pound (who wrote several sestinas during his own "troubadour" phase in the 1910s), but because it enacts what Zukofsky's own sestina calls "thoughts' torsion" and what his gloss on that phrase in the interpretation calls "The actual twisting / Of many and diverse thoughts" (75) and, at the same time, with the "repeated end words / Of the lines' winding around themselves" reinforces the continuity (in "the Head") of experience, reading, observation, and interpretation.[45] While the *fact* of Zukofsky's achieved sestina might be a Yeatsian "artifice of eternity," the *act* of its composition, recorded in the "Interpretation," exposes the continual process of which the sestina is but a frozen moment, and that exposure reactivates the obsessive continuity the form performs.[46]

In a similar way, the "Interpretation" accounts for the equation of mantis and poor and the utopian results of vision that might, in the sestina alone, draw fire as aestheticizing gestures. Zukofsky writes that the mantis does not symbolize (thereby displacing and objectifying) the poor. Rather, the two are linked by the poet's experience of "repulsion." The poet sees both as untouchable, similar in (and, as a consequence, repulsive for) their "helplessness," "separateness," and "ungainliness." The repulsion, though, is a starting point rather than a conclusion; Zukofsky's reaction to the mantis and the poor provokes "self-disgust" and the shock into seeing that the sestina dramatizes. The content of the vision thus provoked is the machinery of capitalism that at once exploits the labor of the poor and maintains them in exploited isolation. The newsboy's dismissal of the mantis as "harmless" in the sestina, Zukofsky shows in the "Interpretation," results from "the economics of the very poor" and the ideological common sense that keeps the boy from thinking beyond subsistence to the circular logic of commodity exchange, that transforms rags into paper into money into banks into loans into poverty so that, finally, "poverty makes rags" (79). The defamiliarizing sight of the mantis out of its expected place provokes a shareable realization that, like the mantis, the poor have been driven by forces beyond their comprehension into unnatural (though ideologically natural*ized*) spaces and processes. The defamiliarizing sight of Marxist analysis in a sestina might perform a similar function.

The "Interpretation," then, renders explicit much of what remains implicit in the sestina, setting out both the poem's raw material and the processes by which that material was fashioned into an artifact. In the interdependence of "Mantis" and "'Mantis,' an Interpretation," we see the crucial difference between Zukofsky's *katabasis* and those I have so far sketched in this chapter (even Olson's, which most closely resembles it). Where the way out of the Underworld, however arduous it might be, is somehow immanent in the poems of Pound, Crane, and others, it is situated *outside* Zukofsky's sestina. It is political action rather than the poem itself, rather even than the political imagination embodied *in* the poem itself, which will enable an ascent from the poem's Underworld.

As in "Mantis," politics rather than poetry, philosophy, or religion is offered as the way out of the Underworld in the katabatic episodes of two long poems of the later 1930s, Muriel Rukeyser's *The Book of the Dead* and Louis MacNeice's *Autumn Journal*. When she wrote *The Book of the Dead* (the poem was published in 1938 as the first half of Rukeyser's second volume, *U.S. 1*), Rukeyser was six years younger than MacNeice and had published only one book of poems (*Theory of Flight* in 1935, chosen by Stephen Vincent Benet for the Yale Younger Poets series). Rukeyser, a writer clearly on the political Left (assumed by the FBI to have been a member of the Communist Party),[47] set out in *The Book of the Dead* (and in the other poems in *U.S. 1*) to "extend the document" (as her "Note" at the end of the volume puts it).[48] Her experimental mix of documentary, myth, and modernist poetic strategies is intended to reveal the complicity of various institutions (including the American House of Representatives) in the murderously exploitative behavior of corporations. By 1937, when he undertook *Autumn Journal*, MacNeice was a highly regarded poet in England, his books published by Faber and Faber, his membership in the dominant poetic scene confirmed in the right-wing poet Roy Campbell's mocking coinage of the composite "MacSpaunday."[49] In the "Note" that precedes *Autumn Journal*, MacNeice makes clear his own aims. Rather than a "didactic poem proper," in which he would have corrected what he calls "overstatements and inconsistencies" in the poem, MacNeice offers a journal in which "a man writes what he feels at the moment."[50] His poem is an impressionistic account of life in London (with excursions to Oxford and Spain as well as trips into the poet's past) during the autumn of Barcelona, the Sudetenland, and Munich.[51] The katabatic episodes in these two poems are conditioned by their contexts, both within and surrounding the poems, and by the poets' divergent positions and purposes. They share, though, the role of crystallizing political realization for their poet-speakers.

As its title suggests, Rukeyser's poetic sequence is structured around death and the modes of memory, the rituals of remembrance, which will enable the dead to live on. The "otherworld," then, is an allusive presence throughout, and a dynamic of burial and resurrection governs the progression of the sequence as a whole. Within that broader structure, however, Rukeyser reenacts the *katabasis*. She narrates a descent whose climax is a dialectical vision important for the sequence's political imaginary. The inspiration for Rukeyser's sequence is not the metaphysics of Egyptian mortuary practice but is instead the biggest industrial disaster in American history, the silicosis deaths of hundreds of West Virginia miners who worked on the Hawk's Nest tunnel project during the late 1920s. Originally a project intended to divert water from the New River to a hydroelectric dam, the tunnel became a mining operation when a large deposit of silica was discovered. Silica was used in the electro-processing of steel and if cheaply obtained would enhance the profits of the Electro-Metallurgical Company, a subsidiary of Union Carbide. The Dennis and Rhinehart company, another subsidiary, undertook the extraction of the silica. Because silica dust is essentially tiny glass particles and damages the lungs when inhaled, the U.S. Bureau of Mines recommended a set of safety procedures for its mining; a wet-drilling method was to be used to minimize dust in the air, mines were to be well ventilated, and miners were to wear protective masks. These procedures added to costs in various ways (wet-drilling and ventilation were expensive, the filters in masks had to be rinsed out frequently) so they were, for the most part, neglected in the Hawk's Nest tunnel. As a consequence, hundreds of miners breathed large amounts of the dust, which lacerated their lung tissue and caused scarring, a fatal condition known as silicosis. In order to minimize their liability, the tunnel contractors paid local officials to attribute deaths to other causes (pneumonia, pleurisy), had bodies buried before they could be examined, and even paid the local undertaker to bury bodies in a cornfield instead of the cemetery. When they sought compensation for the deaths, miners' families were stonewalled and outmaneuvered by corporate attorneys. What money they finally won in judgments was largely owed to lawyers. Media attention prompted an investigation by a subcommittee of the House of Representatives' Committee on Labor. The subcommittee recommended a broader Congressional investigation into mining practices and statutory limits on corporate liability, but the full Committee declined to pursue the investigation.[52]

After reading about the case, traveling to West Virginia, inspecting the sites and interviewing numerous individuals involved, Rukeyser wrote her poem sequence as an attempt to understand the political forces at work and to derive some possibility for effective political action. In effect, Rukeyser set out to perform what the U.S. Congress had decided not to do, to "extend the document" beyond the subcommittee's report and to bring the issues at the heart of the disaster to the attention of a broader audience. As Robert Shulman has argued, the mythic structure of the Egyptian *Book of the Dead* guides Rukeyser's handling of the Hawk's Nest tragedy, imposing a burial and resurrection, or a dispersal and recollection, plot onto the sequence.[53] In the penultimate poem, after the Congressional subcommittee impotently "subcommits," Rukeyser writes that "dead John Brown's body" walks out of the Hawk's Nest tunnel "to break the armored and concluded mind," and the sequence's concluding, title poem imagines the dead of the disaster as "planted in our flesh," "seeds of unending love" that will germinate in a radicalized memory and consciousness willing to "strike against history" (65).[54]

Within this structure, in the poem entitled "Power," Rukeyser narrates a descent into the Underworld that conforms to the katabatic structure I have traced so far in this chapter. The poem opens with a description of the landscape—both natural and synthetic—whose erotic terms render the production of hydroelectric power in almost orgasmic terms. Accompanied by a tutelary figure analogous to Dante's Vergil—the engineer who designed the power plant—Rukeyser's speaker tours the New Kanawha Power Company's dam and power plant, the result of the tunnel workers' labor. Rukeyser augments the scene's echoes of the katabatic tradition with repeated imagery of circles; the light from the engineer's flashlight is reflected in circles around the empty plant, the speaker points out wheels and dials on the control panels and calls the turbine pit a "scroll" and "volute case" (50–51). The two descend a spiral staircase, pause at "the second circle," a "world of inner shade" whose diction invokes the Underworld tradition, and then "Go down" another spiral staircase, "and still go down" insistently descending until even "the last light in shaft" disappears and they are in utter darkness. Jones, the engineer, complains that "some fools call this the Black Hole of Calcutta," unaware of the dam's production of "brilliance," which Jones refracts through Miltonic quotation ("Hail, holy light, offspring of Heav'n first-born"). At this nadir of her descent, in this space of absolute darkness, the speaker encounters a figure that embodies the prophetic wisdom sought by Underworld travelers from

Odysseus and Aeneas on. This poem's Tiresias or Anchises is a welder in whom Rukeyser condenses the poem's political way of seeing. The welder is dehumanized in and by his labor; "masked for work," he is unrecognizable, his hands covered and his face imprisoned in "a cage of steel" (52). At the same time, though, he is endowed with creative capacities. The welding torch is figured as a tool for writing that is capable at once of "brightening" the welder and "marrying steel." It enables illumination and vision, then, and brings about strong, elemental unions.

The welder is an emblem for Rukeyser's dialectical understanding of labor and power, two key terms in *The Book of the Dead*. While John Wheelwright spent his review of *U.S. 1* (published in *Partisan Review*) castigating Rukeyser for her emphasis only on this capitalist excrescence and her failure to explore the broader economic conditions that would drive workers to endure the tunnel's conditions, *The Book of the Dead* actually unfolds a sophisticated vision that sees labor and power achieving their value not in spite of but simultaneously with their exploitation in a capitalist framework.[55] The silicosis that kills tunnel workers by blocking their lungs with scar tissue is a figure for the various blockages with which efforts toward social change are beset: the corporation's attempts to block investigations by hiding or explaining away miners' deaths, the company doctors' testimony aimed at blocking a court's decision to grant compensation to miners' families, the Congress's blockage of the broader investigation urged by the subcommittee. The alteration of the landscape (by a dam that blocks the river's flow) is associated with the alteration of workers' bodies (by the scar tissue that blocks their lungs). In both cases, the results of labor are rendered in terms of illness and suffering, whether the sickness of miners with lungs full of glass particles or the sickness of the landscape described in "Alloy": "Crystalline hill: a blinded field of white / murdering snow" (47). At the same time, though, the alterations produce enormous power. The tunnel dug by the men diverts water to the obstacle that converts its rushing to electricity, and that electricity brings light to the country, as Rukeyser writes in "Praise of the Committee" and elsewhere in the sequence. Rukeyser, however, never loses sight of ownership of the means of production and the sequence has as one of its primary aims the conversion of the literal light produced by the workers' labor and suffering into a metaphorical illumination that not only grants them the "answer" that "they demand" (23), but also transforms their buried bodies into what the sequence's final phrase calls revolutionary "seeds of unending love" (72).

In a 22 November 1938 statement written for his publisher to use as catalogue copy, MacNeice describes *Autumn Journal* this way:

> It is written in sections averaging about 80 lines in length. This division gives it a *dramatic* quality, as different parts of myself (e.g. the anarchist, the defeatist, the sensual man, the philosopher, the would-be good citizen) can be given their say in turn.
>
> It contains rapportage [*sic*], metaphysics, lyrical emotion, autobiography, nightmare.[56]

The chief drama of MacNeice's poem is the inexorable intrusion of the public, political, and historical into the private spaces, thoughts, and activities of the poet. Nowhere is this more clear and pressing than in the sections dealing with Czechoslovakia and the Munich Agreement. In his apartment across the street from Regents Park, MacNeice listens as "Hitler yells on the wireless" and as trees are cut down on nearby Primrose Hill ("they want the crest of this hill for anti-aircraft" [22–23]). The falling trees are likened to "the roast flesh of chicken," evoking, as Robyn Marsack has written, the traditional British Sunday dinner and so illustrating the vulnerability of home to history.[57] MacNeice imagines that vulnerability in more intimate terms when he wonders whether to bother choosing fabric for curtains or to "stop the cracks for gas or dig a trench." This seventh of the poem's twenty-four numbered sections is saturated with the dread of a war seen as inescapable. Events in Europe and the analysis of those events in the English press (as well as the response to them by the English Army and the government's emergency preparedness agencies) certainly seem to justify the poet's anxiety. The *Times* of London's front pages throughout these weeks of September are filled with the twists and turns of Prime Minister Neville Chamberlain's negotiations with Germany and with accounts of domestic preparations for the air attack that officials expected as the first stage of war with Germany, while broadcasts on the BBC emphasized the mobilization of the British Fleet and Territorial units and the digging of trenches in London parks. The very walls of London buildings were a text of war preparation, plastered with posters calling for volunteers to become Air Raid Precaution (ARP) wardens and advertising the agency's recommendations for preparedness.

One section (and a few days) later, Neville Chamberlain, the British Prime Minister, has concluded negotiations with Germany and signed the Munich Agreement, thereby averting war for the moment. The poet's relief is palpable ("once again / The crisis is put off and things look better") but so is his guilt over this relief. It is this guilt that drives MacNeice, in section XIV, to travel to Oxford for the Parliamentary by-election, the journey that he casts in katabatic terms. The Oxford by-election was the first after Munich and was therefore seen by many in England as something of a referendum on the government's agreement with Germany. Quentin Hogg, the Conservative candidate, ran in support of Chamberlain and Munich. His opponent, Master of Balliol College A.D. Lindsay, did not represent a party but spoke out against the agreement. By late October (the election was held on 27), MacNeice had come to regret his relief and had become critical of the government, the agreement, and the policy of appeasement that both were seen to embody. He was enlisted by his mentor E.R. Dodds to travel to Oxford for the election and drive Lindsay voters to the polls.[58] The trip is cast as an Underworld descent, at first subtly, through the insistent repetition of circular imagery (the "North Circular" road, the "semi-circles of petrol pumps," the road "like a lassoo" [*sic*]), and then more openly (the countryside is "damp and dark and evil"), and finally explicitly:

> And coming over the Chilterns the dead leaves leap
> Charging the windscreen like a barrage of angry
> Birds as I take the steep
> Plunge to Henley or Hades. (45)

The road to Oxford even takes on malign agency; it "solicits" MacNeice's "irresponsible tyres" into an accident.

MacNeice makes it to Oxford in spite of all this and puts in his day driving voters to the polls in spite of his doubts about the efficacy of this political activity and in spite of his recognition that he is acting "for a half-believed-in / Principle." At the end of the day, the katabatic resonances come once more to the foreground: "the streets resounded / To the triumphant cheers of the lost souls— / the profiteers, the dunderheads, the smarties" (47). Supporting Hogg, the Chamberlain government, and Munich, the majority of Oxford voters have at least momentarily turned their city into what is, from MacNeice's point of view, a Hell of souls lost in their own self-interest, ignorance, or calculation. While "profiteers" interestingly echoes Pound's Canto XIV, the shape of MacNeice's cultural critique is of course quite different from Pound's. Ashamed of his own earlier fear for his own skin (expressed in section VIII's relieved "Save my skin and damn my conscience" [28]), MacNeice castigates those in whom he sees that aspect of himself as well as those who do not realize what he has come to realize: that at this historical moment, even the skeptics like himself, even "the nicest people in England," who are predisposed against "solidarity and alignment," must come together (47).[59] Now, war seems the necessary step to keep a rough beast at bay; as Edna Longley writes, MacNeice realizes at this point that "the current crisis *de facto* has politicized everyone."[60]

Where Pound's Hell offered only a synthesis of philosophy and poetry itself as a way out of the Inferno of contemporary English society, MacNeice concludes his katabatic episode with a resolution to engage in mundane political activity, however depressing, difficult, or dull: "Each occasion must be used, however trivial" (47). While MacNeice does not dramatize a sudden and total shift from skepticism to commitment, the revelation he experiences in the Oxford *katabasis* does propel a reentry into history (one MacNeice the classicist would almost certainly, if not entirely consciously, have modeled on Aeneas's ascent from Avernus). In his life outside the poem, MacNeice energetically took to activism in the late fall of 1938, joining the Association of Writers for Intellectual Liberty (a group whose stated purpose was "to alert the public to the threat of fascism"), participating in marches to demand British intervention in support of the Spanish Republic, and, that December, traveling to Barcelona, then under attack by Nationalist forces.[61] In Barcelona, MacNeice visited refugee shelters and makeshift air-raid shelters in the Metro and helped to deliver food and supplies to Tarragona (enduring the bombardment of the convoy as it returned to Barcelona).[62] In the poem, as Margot Heinemann writes, the speaker, "haunted by nightmare corpse-like figures from the concentration camps and battlefields," travels to "the heroic city."[63] The Barcelona episode doubles and revises the trip to Spain MacNeice recalls earlier in the poem. That visit was the touristic expedition of a "tripper" bothered by the rain and believing that the low standard of living "was not our business" (19). Now, though, the poet identifies and makes common cause with those who suffer in Catalonia for "human values" and adds his voice to those of other *propagandistas*. MacNeice resolves to "make amends" for his own past tendency to abstract and analyze, he recognizes that "when doing nothing we find we have gained nothing," and he commits to "the truth" embodied in the Republic.

Events soon overtook MacNeice (as well as Rukeyser and their audiences). Barcelona fell, Germany continued its armed expansion, and soon the world was at war. While cities like London and Coventry (and Warsaw and Berlin and Dresden and Stalingrad) quickly became hellish, the deployment of the infernal for purposes of cultural critique came less readily to poets' hands. Instead, the early 1940s saw poets turn to the Underworld descent less to attack their societies than to wonder about the worth of their own pursuit during such a moment. In "The Walls Do Not Fall," the first installment of her wartime *Trilogy*, for example, H.D. compares the present-day ruins of bombed-out London buildings to the ruined temple at Luxor into which she had descended on her visit to Egypt some years before. Doing so in loosely rhyming terza rima, as she does in the poem's first numbered section, she casts a stroll by revealed cellar walls as a gesture toward the katabatic tradition, and against the backdrop of that tradition (as well as the Egyptian mythology and Christian mysticism that inform much of *Trilogy*) she explores the powers of the artist in the face of history, finding, later in the poem, grounds for confidence in the way language can renew one's bond with the world and, perhaps, renew the world itself. Both terza rima and *katabasis* fall quickly away in *Trilogy*, though, and H.D.'s spiritual optimism manifests in her references to the cyclical life of Osiris and "Zadkiel, the righteousness of God."[64] It is for another poet who had absorbed Osiris and other traditions into his individual talent to reenact the encounter with the dead in a more sustained way, and to do so as an exercise not in poetic confidence but in poetic self-critique.

3

IN *NEKUIA* BEGINS RESPONSIBILITY: "LITTLE GIDDING" AND THE POSTWAR NECROMANTIC TRADITION

It is almost dawn, "the uncertain hour before the morning / Near the ending of interminable night," and the air-raid fire warden is walking the Blitzed city streets. The hour is a time of beginning situated in the "ending" of the night, a night in this case made interminable by the fire-bombing of the warden's adopted city and, perhaps, by the elemental deaths he has sung in the three lyrical stanzas that precede his early-morning walk: "This is the death of water and fire."[1] The moment's setting is characterized by death and destruction; it emphasizes ending. But in it, the poet finds a beginning in his confrontation with another: "I met one walking, loitering and unhurried" (LG 86–88). The other met here "between three districts" is not just any other. He is, first, another Poet, "some dead master" (LG 92–93). Moreover, he is multiple, "Both one and many," a "familiar compound ghost." And, as that last noun indicates, he is that most other of all possible Others, one of the dead. A colloquy ensues, and it takes place not on the bombed streets of London but "nowhere," as if at an intersection of the world and the Underworld, that place where those whose lives have ended find their eternal beginnings.

This famous passage in T.S. Eliot's "Little Gidding" (1942) performs an important set of endings and beginnings within the narrative, thematic, and philosophical logics of the *Four Quartets* (1943).[2] In this chapter, though, I want to suggest another ending and beginning performed in, or perhaps by, this strange episode, for in "Little Gidding," Eliot revises the necromantic tradition in which this episode participates and, by so doing, sets in motion a new tradition that becomes central in mainstream English language poetry of the later twentieth century. In the next chapters, I will offer readings of some major post-Eliotic necromantic poems: James Merrill's "Book of

Ephraim," Derek Walcott's *Omeros,* Tony Harrison's *v.,* and Seamus Heaney's "Station Island." Here, though, I will first describe the revision Eliot undertakes—the change he effects in the cultural work performed by reenactments of the classical *nekuia*—and then sketch the line of descent that this episode in "Little Gidding" launches by examining Walcott's "Hotel Normandie Pool" and Eavan Boland's "The Journey" in light of the "familiar compound ghost" episode of "Little Gidding." In short, Eliot inaugurates a specific strain within the twentieth-century necromantic tradition, one that stages through its central episode of encounter a chastisement of the poet and a chastening of poetry itself.

*   *   *

In the first two chapters, I argued that the *nekuia* has largely been deployed by poets who need to face up to (and stage a face-off with) literary history while *katabasis* has typically been deployed by poets whose chief motive is cultural critique. Pound's Cantos XIV and XV, for example, use their detailed depictions of the Underworld and its inhabitants to attack contemporary cultural and political targets, while his Canto I translates Odysseus's invocation of Tiresias to work through the modern poet's relationship to his poetic predecessors. In their *nekuiae* of the 1920s, of course, Eliot and Pound enact critiques of their cultures even as they undertake their engagements with literary history, but in both cases the primary purpose of the Underworld encounter is the meeting of tradition and individual talent. In "Little Gidding," this changes; Tradition chastises individual talent, and not only for specifically literary failures. The change is by no means absolute. Eliot's "compound ghost" *is* a poetic master (or a collection of poetic masters), and a central subject of the shade's speech is speech itself ("the dialect of the tribe"). At the same time, though, the wisdom passed by the spirit to the poem's speaker concerns poetry not in relationship with itself (with new poetry, or Eliot's poetry, or the poetry of predecessors) but, rather, poetry and its relationship with the broader concerns of "the tribe" whose dialect it purifies. In "Little Gidding," those concerns are summed up in the ideas of penitence and "redemption," notions central at once to *Four Quartets* and to Eliot as an explicitly Christian poet writing in and for a fallen age, but these ideas themselves condense concerns that are historical, political, and ethical as well as spiritual.[3]

The "uncertain hour" passage begins with a long sentence that unfolds over eleven lines. As many critics have pointed out, Eliot establishes a formal relationship with terza rima here (however attenuated) and so invokes Dante and the *Commedia* from the beginning (before the more obvious allusions to the poet's encounter with Brunetto Latini in *Inferno* XV). Eliot's diction emphasizes the paradoxical stillness within motion that recurs as a theme throughout *Four Quartets* but also contributes to the strange timelessness of this encounter. The "uncertain hour" is "near the ending" of a night that is "unending." A long series of prepositional phrases defers predication (the sentence's verb does not appear until the ninth line), and when he appears the walking figure is "loitering," continuing a pattern of participial verb forms—"unending," "flickering," "walking"—that render the moment static. The pattern of paradox established here shapes the whole preface to the shade's speech: the "familiar compound ghost" is "both one and many," "intimate and unidentifiable" (LG 94, 96); the speaker describes "Knowing myself yet being someone other" (LG 100); the two are "Too strange to each other for misunderstanding" (LG 104); they find each other "at this intersection time / Of meeting nowhere" (LG 105–6). The result is an atmosphere continuous both with the poetry that precedes this moment in *Four Quartets* and with the long tradition of Underworld descents and invocations of the dead.

At the same time, Eliot is up to something new in his elaboration of this Underworld/Unreal City. That last phrase, of course, recalls *The Waste Land*, and I want to note how this "uncertain hour" resembles "the violet hour" during which Tiresias sees the typist home at teatime in the earlier poem. The passages are linked not only by these strange hours—"violet" and "uncertain," crepuscular and predawn—but also by long sentences with numerous modifying phrases that defer predication (in *The Waste Land* this is, if anything, even more interestingly accomplished, with repeated "when" phrases putting off the appearance of Tiresias, the sentence's subject, for four lines, descriptive phrases deferring the verb for another two lines, and three more phrases delaying the arrival of the direct object for two lines).[4] The later poem's echo of terza rima is reminiscent of the earlier poem's fragmentary gestures toward the sonnet. The earlier poem's tutelary spirit, Tiresias, has his counterpart in the ghost of "some dead master" (LG 92).

A number of critics have remarked on the structural resemblance between each *Quartet* and *The Waste Land*, and some have argued that these structural echoes contribute to Eliot's rewriting, replacing, or renouncing of his earlier work and worldview.[5] Among the most interesting of these is Peter Middleton's recent essay, "The masculinity behind the ghosts of modernism in *Four Quartets*," in which he argues that the last three *Quartets* erase the modernist poetics of "Burnt Norton" (and *The Waste Land*) with increasing thoroughness, their "refining fire" sacrificing Eliot's earlier poetry's "masculine ideals and desires" so that "only compound ghosts are left from the auto-da-fe of this poetry of war."[6] An important part of the earlier poetry that "Little Gidding" revises, of course, is its relationship to the poetic tradition that stands behind (or looms over) Eliot. Middleton emphasizes the presence of "the tradition" (or such figures for it as Dante and Yeats) as representative "unmourned homoerotic objects," foci for Eliot's vocational and sexual identification.[7] To read the compound ghost as Eliot's melancholic refusal to mourn lost loves (lost because destroyed in war or lost because ideologically unavailable), though, is to miss the chastisement Eliot stages for his poetic persona and, in it, both his contemplation of poetic responsibility and his revision of the ancient topos at the center of this study. Middleton sets "Little Gidding" alongside "Burnt Norton," the poem he argues it progressively "unwrites"; I want to set it alongside *The Waste Land* for a moment, for in the "uncertain hour" episode's revision of the "violet hour" passage in "The Fire Sermon" this revision of the *nekuia* is precisely the project Eliot undertakes.

As I have shown, the two passages have a good deal in common: each describes and enacts liminality; each echoes traditional stanzas; each narrates an encounter with a figure for tradition. They differ from each other, however, in two crucial ways. First, where Tiresias represents the Western literary tradition in *The Waste Land*, the "familiar compound ghost" in "Little Gidding" embodies that tradition's multiplicity. The individual constituent standing for a larger whole fits with the fragmentary nature of *The Waste Land*, a poem in which metonymy does a good deal of work, while the synthetic "compound" figure epitomizes the mystical, metaphorical, and accretive character of *Four Quartets*.[8] Second, and more important, the poet's stance toward tradition differs radically between the two passages. In *The Waste Land*, Tiresias is, at best, a figure to be pitied; though a seer, his self-descriptions emphasize his age, his blindness, his frailty, and passivity. Moreover, his prophetic vision contains Eliot's attack on a cultural heritage figured in the sonnet and the amatory situation with which that form is conventionally associated. In "Little Gidding," though, the ghost is a "master," indeed a host of masters,[9] and the poet's attitude is almost obsequiously respectful. Where it seems unsurprising to find Tiresias in the wasteland, the speaker in "Little Gidding" is (allusively—the line paraphrases Dante's reaction to finding Brunetto Latini in the Inferno) shocked: "What! are *you* here?" (LG 98). Where Tiresias is simply observed observing and heard speaking, the compound ghost is joined by the speaker; together they tread "the pavement in a dead patrol" (LG 107). Finally, the speaker in "Little Gidding" invites the master to speak, admitting that he "may not comprehend" (LG 110).

What Eliot is up to becomes clearer if we attend to some of the obvious allusions that frame and compose the ghost's speech. The episode echoes Dante's meeting with the shade of Brunetto Latini, with the specific diction of "brown baked features" and the speaker's surprised reaction very nearly quoting that passage in the *Inferno*.[10] The ghost's speech quotes Stéphane Mallarmé's "Le Tombeau d'Edgar Poe," rendering *"Donner un sense plus pur aux mot de la tribu"* as "To purify the dialect of the tribe" (LG 127).[11] William Butler Yeats is present throughout the ghost's speech (about which more below), but the clearest instance of his own verse here is in "the laceration / Of laughter," which echoes the way "Savage indignation there / Cannot lacerate his breast" in "Swift's Epitaph."[12] Each of these allusions is to a poem in which the poet engages "some dead master" and, taken together, they make this episode stage not only Eliot's engagement with the literary tradition (which is what the "violet hour" passage of *The Waste Land* does) but also Eliot's engagement with the literary tradition of staging engagements with the literary tradition. In the earlier poem, Eliot sets up a synecdoche for that tradition and finds it deplorable. Here, though, he sets himself down at the feet of the tradition (figuratively), as Dante, Mallarmé, and Yeats all have done before him.

This change in the poet's stance toward the tradition revises Eliot's earlier deployment of the *nekuia*; the content of the shade's speech in "Little Gidding" revises the tradition of the *nekuia* itself. As David Pike argues and as I have noted, the topos has typically been used to stage a poet's encounter with literary history, an encounter that enables the poet to synthesize and supersede the tradition he sees himself as joining (and thereby altering). Relations between the living and dead poets tend to be cordial; the burden of these scenes is often the interdependence of the new poet and his predecessors, his need for their models as a foundation for his innovation balanced by their need for his innovative voice as a means of keeping their models in circulation. Such, certainly, is the kind of relationship we find in the three poems to which Eliot alludes here. Dante and Brunetto are touchingly solicitous of each other, Mallarmé is clearly indebted to and defensive of Poe, and Yeats both preserves Swift's voice by translating the dead poet's Latin epitaph and includes a warning to future generations (and himself): "Imitate him if you dare."[13]

We might expect something similar in "Little Gidding," since the compound ghost episode is so obviously patterned on Dante's meeting with Brunetto, since Eliot explicitly set out to write "the nearest equivalent to a canto of the Inferno or the Purgatorio, in style as well as content, that I could achieve," and since Eliot's speaker is so respectful, poised for a reassuring tete-a-tete with the dead master.[14] We (and the speaker) might understandably be surprised, then, when the compound ghost casually dismisses our expectation: "I am not eager to rehearse / My thought and theory" (LG 113–15). In lieu of conventional advice or assurance, the compound ghost delivers a chastising lecture. Since the two participants in the colloquy are poets, whose "concern was speech," those words might address this shared work. The ghost abjures shop talk, though, and instead concerns his speech with "the gifts reserved for age" (LG 129–30). What follows is a three-part meditation on old age and death. First your senses go, the spirit says, and then comes crankiness ("the conscious impotence of rage / At human folly"). Finally, the shade describes the twilight processes of self-examination and recrimination, the "rending pain of re-enactment" that reveals "harm / Which once you took for exercise of virtue" (LG 138–42). This subjects the poetic career to the glaring light of ethical judgment. As part of "all that you have done," and perhaps especially as part of that "Which once you took for virtue," the poet-speaker's poetry is prey to "the shame / Of motives late revealed." Maturity holds for the poet the dubious opportunity to examine his career for its ethics and threatens that the process will transform the "approval" the poems once found to "stings," and to "stains" the "honour" they once garnered (LG 143).

In this regard, the colloquy in "Little Gidding" is reminiscent of the late-career reckonings of Yeats. Critics beyond counting have found Yeats's shade lurking in the compound ghost. This is partly because Eliot's earlier drafts more explicitly indicated Yeats, as Helen Gardner shows in her tracking of changes over the course of the poem's composition and revision, and partly because, in a letter to John Hayward, Eliot anticipates that the "visionary figure...will no doubt be identified by some readers with Yeats though I do not mean anything so precise as that."[15] The lines themselves suggest Yeats too. The body left on another shore echoes Yeats's death in France, the images of dancer and fire echo such poems as "Sailing to Byzantium," "Among School Children," and "Byzantium," and the preoccupation with aging echoes many of Yeats's later poems like "The Spur." To this list, Jonathan Nauman adds "Ego Dominus Tuus," which seems to have offered Eliot a model for a speaker's encounter with a figure at once "doppelganger" and Other.[16] But with its ghostly echoes of terza rima and the chastising tone of the interlocutor, the "uncertain hour" passage also evokes Yeats's very late poem, "Cuchulainn Comforted," which deploys a more straightforward version of Dante's stanza in its elaboration of an Otherworld.

Cuchulainn, of course, is the Irish hero who, in various earlier Yeats poems, stands for the heroic Irish past, the heroic poet, and perhaps for Yeats himself. In "Cuchulainn Comforted," composed during the last year of his life, Yeats narrates the hero's entry into the afterlife.[17] There he is confronted by shrouded, birdlike creatures, the spirits of those who were cowardly during their lives, and is invited to join in their collective labor—the sewing of shrouds. To find peace, the individual hero must join those whom he despised in life. He must renounce individual renown and become an anonymous one among the many. He must lay aside his sword (a figure for the powerful poet's pen) and take up the needle (certainly a diminished phallic symbol, and more importantly a figure for domestic rather than heroic labor), performing the devalued collective work reserved for women instead of the valorized individual labor of the warrior. Coming on the heels of "The Circus Animals' Desertion," "Cuchulainn Comforted" performs, even as it thematizes, what Eliot's shade calls the "rending pain of re-enactment." The birdlike creatures that inhabit Yeats's Otherworld refer to "The Wild Swans at Coole" or to the mechanical bird "of hammered gold and gold enameling" of "Sailing to Byzantium." In those earlier poems, the birds symbolize other worlds, realities to which the speaker has no access except the partial and problematic way revealed by art. Here, they populate the Otherworld, but instead of keeping awake the drowsy emperor of Byzantium or flying off in pairs, they sew shrouds, and here the poem's protagonist does indeed join them (though in penitential labor, not exactly the esoteric knowledge the younger Yeats imagined the swans possessing). When he submits his hero to this treatment, Yeats seems to see the error of his ways (or to see his ways as having been erroneous). He seems, that is, to find a life devoted to poetry and the renown of a literary career less valuable than a life that might have been lived for different ends. Like "The Circus Animals' Desertion," "Cuchulainn Comforted" revalues Yeats's career-long values; both poems evince regret for having passed up communal life and relationships for the quest for individual and national expression and recognition.

While Cuchulainn's afterlife has a component of chastisement, though, its purgatorial character affords a "sweeter" life (as the leader of the birdlike creatures has it) and the "comfort" promised by the poem's title. Eliot's encounter with the compound ghost offers neither sweetness nor comfort, but only the "refining fire" (LG 148) that might transform the dross of worldly success into something like moral or spiritual gold. We can see how Eliot locates those purifications outside poetry by noting how he imagines the descent of the Holy Spirit. In the *Acts of the Apostles*, the Spirit appears above the heads of Christ's disciples as tongues of flame that endow the disciples with the gift of language. Touched by this fire, each can speak the Truth in a way some human society can understand. Eliot reimagines this moment as the flight of an enemy dive-bomber; linguistic manifestations of the Spirit and its Truth become the history that "is now and England" (LG 239).

While the figures of fire and dance occur in poetry, their poetic existence is, like poetry itself, of the world and therefore transient and fallen. Rather than serving as redemption, then, poetry is responsible to the real means of redemption. As the concluding movement of this concluding "Quartet" has it, poetry as language purified, as language "that is right where every word is at home" (LG 219), offers an end ("Every poem is an epitaph") which is a beginning (the recognition that "We die with the dying"). But poetry is *only* a beginning, as the compound ghost makes clear; while it might bring us to the "refining fire," it is not *itself* that fire. Poetry is an act in the world, part of "All that [we] have done," and to purify the language of the tribe is only to catalyze an awareness that more profound purifications are required.

Several things distinguish the necromantic moment of "Little Gidding" from the *nekuiae* of *The Waste Land* and Canto I. First, where the reader's encounter with Tiresias in *The Waste Land* is implicit, "Little Gidding" stages an *explicit* encounter between identifiable principals (the poet and the master) and has the dialogue between them at its center. Second, the encounter occurs in a liminal space that is at the same time historically and geographically specific. Third, the conversation between speaker and Shade has poetry as its explicit subject, but, fourth, the talk is of poetry as it relates to extra-literary concerns (the spiritual, the political, the ethical). Finally, those concerns arise within and from specific historical conjunctures that are suggested by the setting in which the encounter occurs. Where the necromantic moments in, say, Pound's opening Canto and in Eliot's own earlier work perform poetry's self-referential means of purification, Eliot here finds poetry and the poet answerable to a nonliterary refinement: the penitential, purgatorial, and Pentecostal flame condensed in the image of the dive-bomber, a transformation effected in history but to which we must be directed by poetry.

* * *

Eliot's use of the necromantic scenario to think through the relationship between poetry and realms of responsibility establishes a template numerous poets have since adapted. For the remainder of this chapter, I will examine two examples written almost half a century after Eliot's uncertain hour: Eavan Boland's "The Journey" and Derek Walcott's "Hotel Normandie Pool." Each develops the innovation Eliot undertakes in "Little Gidding" and performs a chastisement (or at least a mild chastening) of the poet. In so doing, both Walcott and Boland work through the relationship of poetry to such extra-literary discourses as politics and ethics. Each poem's development of the Eliotic donnée, though, answers to its own historical moment and the imperatives of its author's biography, career, and aesthetic (as well as political or ethical) commitments so that, taken together, these two poems suggest how the "compound ghost" scenario, this wrinkle in the fabric of the necromantic tradition, has been deployed in the later twentieth century.[18]

Walcott's and Boland's poems are products of the early 1980s, composed and published almost exactly forty years after "Little Gidding," produced in and for a dramatically different historical context. Moreover, these two poems (published within two years of each other) are produced by quite different poets writing out of distinct situations. By the early 1980s, Walcott had established a global reputation as both poet and playwright, as well as a powerful voice intervening in debates about the (post)colonial writer, language, and history. While not yet as well known outside Ireland, Boland had developed a reputation within Irish literary circles for her feminist revisions of Irish poetic pieties (especially the tendency to represent women as muses or objects of desire or figures for the nation but not as agents with voices and desires of their own).[19] Nevertheless, "The Journey" and "Hotel Normandie Pool" share the key dramatic situation of a poet encountering an important predecessor and being led by that predecessor through a consideration of poetry's responsibility to, for, and in its context, as well as the limits of poetry's capacity to respond. More than this, each poet emerges from the encounter with a chastened sense of poetry's power. Each poem articulates that chastened sense to a different aspect of poetry; Boland emphasizes limits to poetry's efficacy to affect the world, while Walcott is troubled by the ethical questions that arise from poetry's involvement in the world.

Boland's "Journey" announces both its narrative roots and the revisionist work intended by its necromantic encounter in its epigraph from *Aeneid* VI:

> Immediately cries were heard. These were the loud wailing of infant souls weeping at the very entrance-way; never had they had their share of life's sweetness for the dark day had stolen them from their mothers' breasts and plunged them to a death before their time.[20]

Here, Aeneas has crossed the Lethe and is on the threshold of the Underworld; he brushes by these shades of children on his way to the central and necessary conversation with Anchises, to the patrilineal passing of patriarchal authority. In its opening stanzas, Boland announces her dissatisfaction with this episode and the poetics she sees it underwriting. Echoing epic conventions, the poem begins *in medias res* (and mid-sentence): "And then the dark fell and 'there has never,' / I said, "been a poem to an antibiotic" (182). While poets, male ones according to the single pronominal reference to them, waste their time dreaming up "hyssop dipped / in the wild blood of the unblemished lamb," the merits of sulpha go unsung. These poets' Vergilian rush past realities in their search for "the obvious // emblem" has dire consequences both for poetry and for its ability to respond to its world: "every day the language gets less // for the task and we are less with the language" (182).

Boland resolves the opposition structured by epigraph and opening by crafting a hybrid. She grafts onto the classical descent topos the culturally specific form of the *aisling*, the (often nationalist) Irish dream vision poem; she maintains the narrative structure in which a poetic "master" appears as a guide, but replaces Dante's Vergil or Eliot's familiar compound ghost with Sappho; within the conventional narrative of Underworld descent, she refocuses the attention of protagonist and reader alike, putting the "infant-souls" who are at the margins of Aeneas's quest at the center of her own; and just as Eliot evokes without actually conforming to Dante's terza rima, Boland echoes without actually deploying standard lyric stanzas, gathering unmetered lines into quatrains and tightening the poem's relaxed diction with occasional rhyme and frequent aural repetition. This thoughtful generic and formal blending suggests that Boland's project is not a simple attempt to displace or replace "the patriarchal tradition." Rather, she establishes a dialogue with that tradition and, like Eliot, uses that dialogue to think through questions of poetic responsibility.

"Little Gidding" is not, I suspect, the antecedent poem that first leaps to the mind of a reader first encountering "The Journey," but scene and situation as well as theme place the poem firmly in the wake of the compound ghost episode. Boland's speaker inhabits a setting as specific as Eliot's London dawn, a cluttered room, comfortably inhabited, which becomes similarly liminal and in which the speaker encounters a ghostly Other with similar aplomb, "calm and unsurprised / when she came and stood beside me" (183). "She" is Sappho, suggested to the speaker by the page at which her book has been left open, and the poetic predecessor leads the speaker on a descent that, though it unfolds over three stanzas and repeats the word "down" five times, still arrives at a place that seems at once the speaker's world and the Underworld of myth. There, the speaker is claimed by Sappho and absorbs a complex lesson, not, as Eliot's speaker does, on the rewards of age and the responsibility of poetry to the means of redemption, but on poetry's duty to "the silences in which are our beginnings" (184).

Where the compound ghost lectures Eliot, Sappho at first simply reveals a vision to Boland's persona: "Behold the children of the plague" (183). Across the river, the speaker sees shadowy women and children, victims of those diseases that once "racketed / in every backstreet and alley of old Europe" but have been tamed (at least in old Europe) by the antibiotics that male poets have failed to celebrate. When the speaker recoils from the vision, Sappho urges her to overcome the distancing, historicizing view that would define the women by their work or class or dress and to identify instead with their shared motherhood, their shared participation in the mundane tasks of childrearing, the picking up after children that Sappho calls "love's archaeology" (184). The phrase suggests a critique of other influential "archaeological" poetic projects (the bog poems in Seamus Heaney's 1975 volume *North*, for example), in which the dug-up remnants of ancient cultures appear to rationalize contemporary sectarian violence as human nature. While the archaeological evidence turned up in Heaney's digging finds betrayal and murder and division all the way down, Boland's archaeology uncovers an alternative midden, the scattered evidence of familial relationships. The imagery's anachronistic character (the women of "old Europe" might have picked up rag dolls but they certainly did not pick up tricycles) grants motherhood a timelessness and universality that competes with the continuity of violence posited in *North*.[21]

This vision of an alternative, silenced history resonates with the poetry whose silencing incensed the speaker at the beginning of "The Journey" and suggests the alternative poetic project she might undertake, a poetry that would bear witness to this history of women's suffering. Patricia Haberstroh has written that this is exactly what happens. Boland's speaker, she argues, "identifies with the anxiety of grieving women who must confront the terror of their children's death," and when the speaker whispers "let me at least be their witness" Sappho encourages her.[22] This reading nicely aligns the poem at once with much contemporary poetry on themes of history and suffering and with certain projects Boland has outlined for her work in her published prose,[23] but Sappho's response seems less to encourage a poetry of witness than to indicate limits to poetry's witnessing capacity. "What you have seen is beyond speech," she says, "beyond song" (184), which is to say that the vision Sappho has revealed to the speaker is beyond *poetry*, even a poetry whose primary aim is to "be their witness."

What follows, though, is not an abdication of poetic responsibility (Sappho has, after all, shown the poet this vision for a reason, and she goes on in the next stanza to "adopt" the speaker as her poetic descendant) but is instead a chastened and precise sense of poetic responsibility within poetry's limited capacities to respond. The compound ghost shows Eliot's speaker that poetry is an act in the fallen world and is thus limited in its power to effect redemption, but that it is responsible to the real means of redemption. Sappho similarly shows Boland that poetry is limited in its capacity to respond to untold generations of maternal and familial suffering, but that poetry must act within those limits. If the suffering that brought women and children to this threshold of the Underworld is unspeakable, this is nevertheless a generative silence, one in which women poets from Sappho to Boland "have an origin like water" (184). While this vision of suffering is beyond poetry, it is, Sappho says, "not beyond love." While it cannot be contained in the verbal construct that would bear witness, then, it can be remembered ("remember it, you will remember it," Sappho tells the speaker) in the practices of "love's archaeology," in actions of caring that reenact these mothers' love.

The full character of Boland's revisionist treatment of the *nekuia* becomes apparent when we compare Sappho's revelation to the one Aeneas receives from Anchises in Book VI. There, Anchises narrates a proleptic parade of what will become Roman history, a parade rich in heroes and martial splendor. Boland's Sappho shows women rather than men, suffering and loss rather than military gain, passivity rather than conquest. Just as Anchises' revelations serve to propel Aeneas from the Underworld of myth back into the history he must make, though, Sappho's words urge Boland's speaker out of the allusive dream and back into the world of antibiotics and the quotidian domestic practices that lie "outside history" (as the title of Boland's 1990 poetic sequence has it) but that have profound effects on how history is lived.

* * *

In "Hotel Normandie Pool," Walcott conjures the shade of Ovid while he sits writing beside a swimming pool and uses the encounter to test and critique his own sense of poetry's value. The occasion of the encounter is fraught with personal significance for the poet. It is New Year's morning, a time of beginnings, but the poet is in his fiftieth year, in the middle of his life and, with the poem's publication in *The Fortunate Traveler* (1981), around the middle of his career. One's fiftieth year is a time of reflection, of course, and reflection is one key strand of imagery in the first of the poem's three numbered sections. At the time of the poem's composition, Walcott had already lived a largely nomadic life for several years. He had resigned from the Trinidad Theatre Workshop after directing it for sixteen years, he had begun to spend more and more time in the United States (*The Fortunate Traveler* is his first collection published after moving to the U.S. semipermanently in 1980, and the poem was first published in the *New Yorker* in January, 1981), and he had recently ended his sixteen-year-long second marriage.[24] This situation suggests Dante's "*mezzo del cammin di nostra vita*," and the number nine (the speaker chooses "one of nine / cast-iron umbrellas set in iron tables" and the poem is in stanzas of nine iambic pentameter lines) strengthens the allusive echo (it suggests the nine circles in the *Inferno*, but Walcott's stanza might also refer obliquely—by tripling its length—to Dante's terza rima).[25] The necromantic encounter stages a mid-career assessment, and it does so by foregrounding issues at the heart of Walcott's career: empire, exile, and the ethical questions arising from a politically invested poetic practice. Where Boland, like Eliot, has her poetic predecessor explicitly point out poetry's limitations, though, Walcott's Ovid largely endorses the poet's stated poetics. It is the poem's imagery and diction that perform the problem that besets poetry: constructed in language, poetry is prey to the same perversions that plague political speech so that even when it sets out to build an alternative to the world, it cannot help but replicate the violence it seeks to escape.

The first section of the poem finds Walcott reflecting on his divorce as he seeks a further separation from the world in the "mirror" of the page, seeks an escape into the "fetid and familiar atmosphere of work."[26] Poetry, then, is offered as a consolatory activity, a means of escape from the pain of lived experience. The poem's second section introduces Ovid in ways that recall the timeless time and placeless space of "Little Gidding." Walcott transforms the scene from the quotidian setting of a hotel poolside complete with sun, umbrellas, and palm trees, to the symbolic terrain of the Underworld (or, as in Eliot's poem, a liminal space between the two). Walcott renders the pool "seamless," the placidity of the water suggesting an unnatural (or supernatural?) stillness, and has the palm across the pool "burn." When a figure appears, he has "Roman graveness"; the pun imbues him with the suggestion of death as well as classical gravitas. Walcott describes the mundane act of smearing on tanning lotion as "mummy-oiling" so that this "petty businessman" becomes a precious and preserved body. Appropriately, Ovid's appearance involves a series of metamorphoses. The preservative shifts from Egyptian to Roman, from unguent to numismatic, when the figure is imaged as "negotiable bronze" in a "toga-slung" towel. The figure shifts shape another and final time when the "lines of his sun-dazzled squint" take textual form so that the speaker reads there: *"Quis te misit, Magister?"*

The shape-shifting in these first couple of stanzas performs three intertwined tasks. First, Walcott echoes Eliot (and, through him, Dante) in his evocation of a space at once recognizably terrestrial and suggestively otherworldly. In addition, the metamorphoses of these stanzas allusively enact the metamorphoses (or *Metamorphoses*) that are best-known work of this ghostly interlocutor. Finally, the oscillation Walcott establishes between the present-day hotel poolside and the setting of Ovid's life in exile introduces a set of analogies the poet will extend over the next four stanzas, suggestive comparisons between his subject position as postcolonial poet and that of the exiled Roman imperial poet.[27]

The burden of the analogy is the danger political intrigue poses both to poets and to poetry itself. It is this danger the poet seeks to evade by positing the page as a world apart, and it is this evasiveness that the encounter with Ovid tests and seems to affirm, but with which the poem's language wrestles. Walcott works down from the big similarities to the individual analogy between himself and his Roman predecessor. The pool is like the "thunder of surf between the Baltic pines" of Ovid's exile. The light that shone on "Rome's squares and palaces" now "splashes a palm's shadow at your foot" (the pun here makes clear that it is in the space of the poem that this temporal lamination occurs). Contemporary Caribbean "house slaves" pine for just what slaves might have during the Empire, a "calm proconsul with a voice / as just and level as this Roman pool" (67). Instead they get the "corruption, censorship and arrogance" that, like those of Rome, "make exile seem a happier thought than home." This treatment of setting through analogy shows the poet's Caribbean home to be as hazardous as Ovid's Rome: "[E]ach idea has become suspicious / of its shadow." Where Rei Terada reads this line as evidence of the poet's Platonic suspicion of the referential or representational, it more directly refers to the political situation from which the poet hopes to escape at once into and for the sake of poetry: the Caribbean is paranoid, its population resentful and afraid, because "ideas / with guns divide the islands," their threat made palpable and present in the form of militias (68).[28]

The threat to poetry and poets is not simply that they might be silenced (like the friend who whispers even in his own home for fear of being arrested), but that they might be implicated in the corruption and violence that govern. Walcott's speaker recognizes that he embodies this danger of imperial implication; he is one "whose ancestors were slave and Roman," the speaker has a face that has "held negro Neroes, chalk Caligulas" (67).[29] One function of this line is to set up the next stanza's recognition that the islands have their own indigenous tyranny. We might therefore be tempted to read this line as simply saying the speaker has seen, has *be*held, tyrants of all races, emperors on "both sides of the imperial foam." Walcott's language, though, clearly locates the imperial presences in himself. He is implicated in empire because the empire is *in* him. The fear here, however, is not just that poets are inescapably implicated in the political world, but that poetry itself is too. While the ideas and their armies divide the islands, Walcott writes that *poems*, as opposed to poets, gather in dark squares "like conspirators." This threat to poetry's purity as a space apart drives Walcott's speaker to choose exile in order to write poetry (he is leaving Trinidad and the Theatre Workshop) and also to choose poetry as exile. Far from the threat of political implication, the poet might still escape into the safe space of the aesthetic.

Much of what Ovid says to the poet after he appears seems to confirm this consolatory understanding of poetry and poetic space. When first exiled, Ovid tells the poet, he too suffered the absence of his language, he too imagined his absent child, and he too felt alienated from the world. Only when he wrote, did he find his "place" (68). Creating a world of words returned him to an unalienated relationship with the world around him. In an image that recalls Yeats's birdlike apparitions in the afterlife, Ovid recalls that he was "pricked" by "needling birds" to "learn their tribal tongue" and that he joined them with the parted beak of his pen, "till we chirped one song" (68).

More than rejoining the world, though, poetry written in exile, far from conflicts into which it might have been conscripted, provided Ovid—as it has the poem's speaker—his own alternative world, an empire he himself could demarcate, expand, and rule. While the Roman legions "enlarged our frontiers like clouds," the poet's "own government" was the table on which he "hammer[ed] out lines…to fit [himself] for the horse" (69). Especially noteworthy in his account are the military and imperial diction and imagery: the poet's work fits him for a position in an imagined or created military elite; his solitude is "tyrannous," his tabletop a "government." Ovid's language unsurprisingly echoes that of Walcott's speaker in the poem's first part, where he engages in a "war," coughs a "fusillade," and imagines himself inhabiting a novel's chapter set "during the war," when "the prince comes home" (63).[30] On the foundation of this power to create and rule an alternative empire, the poet outlasts his critics: "And where are those detractors now…?" (69).

Of the four stanzas of his speech, then, Ovid devotes three and a half to testifying for a position much like the speaker's, so that, unlike Eliot and Boland, Walcott seems to be affirmed by the shade he encounters. When chastisement comes in this encounter, it is brief: "Romans"—he smiled—"will mock your slavish rhyme, / the slaves your love of Roman structures" (69). As Terada writes, this is an offer of "stoic comfort," a "Dantean 'prophecy'-which-has-already-happened."[31] At the same time, though, these lines are the master poet's admission that the creation of a world apart does not spare the poet from the world in which he continues to live. The created world might outlive critical "detractors," but it will do so (if it does so) only after the poet has suffered that world's mockery. The poet committed to poetry's "own order," the poet who, as Paula Burnett has it, "rejects both the literature of recrimination (of the descendents of the slave) and the literature of remorse (of the descendents of the colonizer)," will be shot by both the margins and the metropole.[32]

Still more troubling is Ovid's offhand concluding salvo. After his departure, amidst reflective imagery that recalls Narcissus, the master poet answers the living poet's unasked question about why he should appear here: "Because to make my image flatters you" (69). This remark, delivered by the echo of a shade, admits the fictional construction of all that has preceded it, including the apparent Ovidian sanction for the poet's notion of poetry as an empire of one's own. Like the apparition of the "*Magister*" himself, the substance of his speech "flatters" the poet who fancies such traditional support for his notion of poetry and its relationship with the historical and political realms. If part of the condition the poet seeks to escape is the way "each idea" has become "suspicious of its shadow," this parting word by the dead poet (or his "echo") suggests that the speaker, too, suffers this ineradicable condition. Indeed, the language he invents for Ovid in order to flatter himself, its very way of demarcating the poet's world-away-from-the-world through military and imperial diction, recalls precisely the threat Walcott's speaker has limned: the implication of "poems...like conspirators" in the clash of ignorant armies and armed ideas. Even when inventing a necromantic encounter to justify poetry's separation from the world of politicized language, the poet cannot help but use the very language he would escape. This is the hard lesson hammered out in the poem.

The shade of Ovid departs and the poem ends: the darkness drops again and now the poet knows dusk and blackening, the flattening of signifying difference as trees come to resemble poolside umbrellas. The opening section's imagery of reflection is replaced here by the "Suspension of every image and its voice" (70). The speaker strikes correspondingly chastened notes. While the last two lines enact compelling metaphors, they present images of falling light ("mangoes pitch...like meteors") and, finally, speechlessness: a fruit bat figured as a "tongueless bell." It is as if the poet, recognizing that the world's intrigues and divisions, whether familial or political, are inescapable for poet and poetry alike, has reached a resolution Seamus Heaney has encapsulated in the famous phrase "whatever you say, say nothing."[33]

I have set out in this chapter to sketch the new shape taken by the necromantic poem in Eliot's "Little Gidding" and to chart the trajectory of poems that fall into that poem's powerful orbit. The issues Eliot deals with so forcefully—the implication of even purified poetic language in the merely worldly, the anxiety over poetry's political efficacy, its capacity to act in or to affect the world beyond the text, and the concomitant anxiety over poets' ethics, the question of whether they *should* seek to intervene through poems in the world beyond their poems—all weigh upon the poets to whose works I turn in this book's remaining chapters. The specific combinations and proportions change from poet to poet, of course, just as we have seen Boland emphasize questions of efficacy while Walcott emphasizes questions of ethics. Different poets differently dramatize the encounter with the shades, as well, with some (Merrill, Heaney) seeking them while others (Harrison, Walcott) find themselves involuntarily summoned. What the poets share, though, is the tangle of intertwined concerns that motivate Eliot in "Little Gidding" and that drive Boland and Walcott to their own similar dramas. They share a set of problems, that is, that require them to go to Hell in search of solutions.

PART 2

4

James Merrill's "Book of Ephraim"

Unlike Odysseus or even Eliot's speaker in "Little Gidding," the necromancers in James Merrill's *Changing Light at Sandover*—JM and DJ—need not leave their home to seek wisdom from beyond. Instead, they sit together in their Stonington, Connecticut dining room and use a makeshift Ouija board. The parlor game becomes serious when they catch the attention of (or are sought out by) Ephraim, a spirit who becomes their guide. Much of the poem is offered as Merrill's (JM's) transcript of the pair's sessions with Ephraim and, especially in the later volumes, other spirits (whose speech is rendered in capital letters). At over five hundred pages, recounting and transcribing thirty years' worth of revelations from the spirit world, and encompassing not only multiple histories but also an entire cosmology, *The Changing Light at Sandover* (1982) is perhaps the most sustained project of poetic necromancy produced during the twentieth century.[1] Like Pound's *Cantos* and Eliot's *Waste Land*, it deals at length with poetic inspiration and indebtedness. Like the *katabases* surveyed in chapter 2, Merrill's poem conducts a forceful critique of the poet's society: the United States of the 1950s, 1960s, and 1970s. And, like "Little Gidding," "Hotel Normandie Pool," and "The Journey," *Sandover* often foregrounds questions of the poet's relationship with the historical world, of poetry's capacity to affect that world, and of the ethical obligations such power entails. Merrill braids these strands throughout the poem. The trilogy's second installment, *Mirabell: Books of Number* (1978), for example, contains both lengthy worries—among spirits and humans alike—about such historical concerns as nuclear war, overpopulation, and environmental destruction but also the poet's nagging need to assure himself that his work is his own and not simply the product of poetic predecessors and the bat-shaped spirits with which they hang around. In this chapter, though, I will focus only on the first part of the trilogy, "The Book of Ephraim," originally published in Merrill's 1976 volume, *Divine Comedies*. I draw this limit in part because the length of "Ephraim" is similar to those of the other post-Eliotic necromantic poems I will be discussing for the rest of this book, partly because, as Richard Saez has written, it is "the most personal" of the three parts and "the infinite finiteness of the alphabet results in better sound and sense than the finite infinity of numbers (*Mirabell*) or the *hemiola* of pivoted opposites (*Scripts*),"[2] and partly because, as what we might call the "Inferno" of Merrill's Divine Comedy, "The Book of Ephraim" best fits this study.[3] My decision to examine "The Book of Ephraim" rather than the entire trilogy is most powerfully influenced, though, by the prominence Merrill there grants to the problematic with which I am most concerned: the writer's responsibility in and to his society.

In chapter 1, I argued that the structure of the *nekuia* tends to foreground concerns about poetry itself and about the poet's relationship to his medium and its past practitioners. Readings of Merrill's trilogy (and of its constituent parts) have often emphasized its participation in these dynamics, with numerous critics reading the Ouija board as a figure for poetic language and / or the poetic tradition. Helen Sword, for example, argues that the board "provides a spirited, provocative means...to explore the paradoxes of poetic authority and the vicissitudes of poetic language," and that it is a "symbol for the metaphoric and metamorphic capacities" of poetic language.[4] In a similar vein, Ann Keniston writes that Ephraim, the tutelary spirit who instructs JM and DJ, represents "a kind of protolanguage" because he is "always bodiless, making his presence known only by the planchette's movement from letter to letter,"[5] while both Mutlu Konuk Blasing and Timothy Materer link the Ouija board to what Materer calls the "play of language for its own sake."[6] Blasing also finds Merrill engaging the tradition in *Sandover*, writing that he "pits history as tradition against history as a disruptive, irrepressible force at work in language itself,"[7] a point also made by Rachel Jacoff and Peter Sacks.[8] This connection is amplified by Brian McHale, who argues that Merrill uses the Ouija board as a "metaphor for tradition, whether in Eliot's sense of 'Tradition and the Individual Talent,' or in the more agonistic and melodramatic sense of Harold Bloom's 'influence'" and works throughout the trilogy "to insinuate himself into this tradition by engaging its representatives in dialogue, but also by struggling, in Bloom's sense, with his poetic precursors."[9] The critics disagree on just what Merrill is up to with all of this linguistic play and literary self-reference. On one hand, readers find Merrill attempting to resolve such fundamental problems as theodicy (Saez), mortality (Sacks), and humanity's need to control its own destructive capacities (Materer). On the other hand, some readers argue that

Merrill is attempting to subvert idealism and metaphysics (Blasing), conduct a political assault on science and "mystified representations of the divine" (Kaldaidjian),[10] or reveal poetry's "basis in mechanical procedures...rather than in the poet's 'heart' or 'psyche' or 'subconscious'" (McHale).[11]

While it has often been compared to or read in light of Dante's *Divine Comedy*, Merrill's poem has not been discussed in the terms Eliot establishes in "Little Gidding." This Eliotic context is useful, though, for it helps us to see Merrill's struggle to articulate poetry's public capacities. Like Eliot's speaker, JM is approached in and through poetic language and the tradition (the Ouija board compares to Eliot's loose terza rima and the tissue of allusion that is the familiar compound ghost's speech). Like Eliot's speaker, JM is forced to reconsider his career to date, and like Eliot's speaker he is compelled to recognize a new calling. It is no longer enough to purify language; the poet instead must use his gifts to make some otherworldly "teaching" available to the world.[12] While that teaching involved the real means of spiritual salvation in "Little Gidding," it involves the real danger of physical and spiritual annihilation in *Sandover*. Ephraim tells his interlocutors that "NO SOULS CAME FROM HIROSHIMA" and that in the aftermath of the atomic explosion the earth was surrounded by a cloud made up of "SMASHED ATOMS OF THE DEAD."[13] The human capacity to annihilate not only the planet but also the spirit world, and the parlous state of political affairs and American political morality throughout the period during which the Ouija sessions took place (the 1950s through 1970s—a time during that, as Materer puts it, the doomsday clock kept by the *Bulletin of the Atomic Scientists* moved from fifteen minutes before midnight to just four minutes before midnight[14]), lead Merrill to an unaccustomed urgency. "Time...was running out," he writes in the poem's opening lines, and so he initially considered "the baldest prose / Reportage" so that he could "reach / The widest public in the shortest time" (3). As a result, according to Charles Berger, "the trilogy's center of anxious concern, its deep origin, however clouded by mythic analogue and autobiographical excursus, is the development of the atomic bomb."[15] Or as McHale puts it, *Sandover* is "nothing less than a jeremiad against the threats of nuclear war and destruction of the environment."[16] It is precisely this urgency, though, that brings both Eliot and Merrill (especially in "The Book of Ephraim") to question poetry's capacity to do the work required of it. Where the familiar compound ghost poses these challenges in "Little Gidding," JM himself does so in "The Book of Ephraim."

Nevertheless, both poems show the poets working through these concerns. The key difference between Merrill's poem and Eliot's is tonal. As if directly *against* Eliot's prophetic and philosophical voice, Merrill loads every rift of his poem with the ore of witty wordplay. Though it predates "Ephraim" by almost a decade, an exchange in an interview with Donald Sheehan is apposite here:

> Sheehan: Can the joke control the sort of oracular voice of Eliot and Pound, tone it down, make it more human?
> Merrill: That is my fond illusion.[17]

Even before Ephraim is introduced, the setting of the Ouija encounters is imbued, in Merrill's description, with punning and allusive "wit": "Walls of ready-mixed matte 'flame' (a witty / Shade") (5). As Nick Halpern has written, "wit does a tremendous amount of work in the trilogy. It puts and keeps things in relation."[18] Or, as Merrill (through Ephraim) more, well, wittily, puts it in the poem, "Must *everything* be witty? AH MY DEARS / I AM NOT LAUGHING   I WILL SIMPLY NOT SHED TEARS" (17). While Merrill himself once dismissed the poem's tone as coating on a pill, suggesting that readers ought to focus on the pill itself—the poem's political message— even as he sympathizes with those who might choke on it, critics like Halpern and Lee Zimmerman have persuasively argued that the tone *is* the poem's political message.[19] Halpern calls wit Merrill's "hybrid speech genre," and this seems right at least inasmuch as it names the "doubleness" that is a crucial component of Merrill's poetic practice. In interview after interview, Merrill emphasizes the need to "be always of two minds."[20] Like Rachel Jacoff, Halpern sees the poem's politics enacted by the ways wit and conversation deny the poet "peculiar authority" and establish a sense of equality between audience and poet.[21] Zimmerman argues that the "vision of interdependence" created by the poem's tone and its conversational dynamic is "perhaps more deeply political than even the poem's explicitly posed warning and challenge" because it "stands up against the oppositional thinking that has made the arms race possible."[22] He concludes that "conversation, indeed, may model a way of containing the dark forces," the "narcissistic denial of the Other basic to absolutist world views," and that Merrill's trilogy "locates authority or truth precisely in this interplay."[23] These arguments seem to me to capture the poem's way of being. In what follows, I want to lay out what these and other readings have not

yet focused on: the way Merrill thinks through poetic responsibility so as to justify the poem's way of being vis-à-vis the historical and political. More specifically, I will argue that Merrill does
so by adapting (though in a revisionist spirit) the conventions of
the *nekuia*, especially as Eliot has already revised them in "Little
Gidding."

* * *

For all of its stenographic pretensions, "The Book of Ephraim" is
an obviously (and elaborately) designed text. It is divided into twenty-
six abecedarian sections (to allude to the letters laid out on a Ouija
board). The second section of the poem describes "backdrop" and
"properties" and the fourth sets out the "Dramatis Personae" to
emphasize its theatrical aspects. The poem announces its necromantic identity through allusions to Dante and also through details of
setting (the dining room is faintly infernal with its "flame" paint, a
"witty shade"). Merrill also foregrounds form throughout the poem,
writing in rhyming couplets when talking about Pope, concluding
several sections with sonnets (in which the subject is the sonnet
itself, or the sonneteer), and casting one crucial section in terza rima.
Indeed, the poem begins with an explicit meditation on literary form
and the relationship between form and content or purpose. Only after
a page or so of wondering whether a novel might be the best form for
the subject matter he is treating, does Merrill resolve upon the form
his book will finally take: "In verse, the feet went bare. / Measures,
furthermore, had been defined / As what emergency required" (4).
Merrill makes clear from the very beginning, then, that this is a poem
about what poems are good for.

The question returns and is at the heart of the poem's most obviously Dantean section. In "W," JM recounts his meeting and conversation with Wendell, a (fictional) nephew who also happens to be
Ephraim's earthly representative. Merrill alerts readers to the section's
Dantean ancestry through stanza, language, and allusion, as well as
theme. Where some other crucial moments in the poem draw attention to themselves by appearing as sonnets (I address some of these
below), "W" is in terza rima, the stanza of the *Divine Comedy* and
the one subtly performed by Eliot in the compound ghost passage of
"Little Gidding." The stanzaic allusion is matched, early in "W," by
imagery and language. Merrill emphasizes the liminality of the place
and time of Wendell's appearance: it is sunset (like the "violet hour"
of Eliot's Tiresias episode, and similar to the dawn during which

Eliot meets the ghost in "Little Gidding"); Wendell is on the stairs of a bridge, both of these architectural features suggestive of passage, "betweenness," and becoming. He is also marked as one in transition (Merrill calls him a "pilgrim" and gives him a "pack and staff"), and as amphibious (his hair is "merman-blonde"). At first, JM does not recognize his nephew; he notices a resemblance between the pilgrim's gaze and his own and says the young man "compares // With one met in some other sphere" (78). The sphere hearkens to Dante's rings and circles, while the sense of familiarity but the inability quite to recognize the figure echoes both Dante (as in *Inferno* XV, when he does not immediately know Brunetto) and Eliot, whose speaker cannot precisely identify the familiar compound ghost.

Within this heavily allusive texture, though, JM resists and revises the burden of the typical necromantic encounter. When they finally recognize each other, JM and Wendell have dinner together and, as we might expect from earlier necromantic poems, this dinner becomes a symposium on the artist's responsibility to his historical moment. Where Eliot is set straight by the familiar compound ghost, though, JM is unconvinced by this representative of his spirit guide. Every aspect of the characters establishes the contrast between their views. Where JM is an indulgent gourmand, Wendell "rather looks down on the scene." Indeed, Wendell looks "through" the meal, even as he seems to enjoy it. His artist's eye is always aware of the suffering behind or beneath the laden plates. We see this especially clearly when the conversation turns to art. Wendell "proffers a sketchbook," whose contents illustrate the gulf between his artistic vision and JM's. While Wendell's facility and painstaking composition please his uncle, the subject matter ("pain and panic and old age") so carefully rendered jars him. Wendell defends his work in terms of cultural critique. While others "talk about how decent, how refined" humanity is, Wendell finds this to be a sham. Art that represents "mankind" as anything other than "Doomed, sick, selfish, [and] dumb" is simply a dodge, a way "To watch what's happening and not to mind" (79). An artistic vision that sees what JM suggests ("Our famous human dignity," the self as "a great, great / Glory") is, to Wendell, dishonest; it simply enables the suffering Wendell's art preserves.

Against Wendell's implicit argument for art's responsibility to represent (in hopes of alleviating) human suffering, JM argues for art as timeless tonic. He sets out this competing vision in the pair's postprandial stroll through Venice, privileging the aesthetic over the historical, the designs of creative imagination over the means of production and the concomitant miseries that underlay their realization.

Pointing to a building, for example, he says "'The Renaissance / Needn't be judged by its aristocrats.'" This focus on surfaces explicitly opposes Wendell's way of looking through the scene and it reiterates a resolution JM recalls in "V": "Never again / To overlook a subject for its image, / To labor images till they yield a subject" (76). Wendell's compositions derive not from what is visible on the surface but from his tendency to look both down on and through surfaces. He is guilty of precisely what JM claims in "V" to have given up: he overlooks a subject for its image, the framed and composed and therefore motivated product of the artist's way of seeing rather than the thing itself seen; he labors images until they yield a vision "subject" to his own predispositions and interpretive schema. Against this, JM poses a willingness to keep his attention on the surfaces, to bracket all that, in Benjamin's famous formulation, makes a monument of civilization at the same time a monument of barbarism. He, therefore, is the one who sees and shows things simply as they are, or at least contests Wendell's implicit claim that *he* is the more straightforwardly mimetic artist.

Merrill's conduct here marks a divergence from the necromantic tradition on which the episode clearly draws. Where figures who either invoke or unexpectedly encounter shades (from Odysseus to Eliot to Walcott and Boland) take the position of petitioner or pupil, JM here seeks to instruct Wendell even when the younger man bears all the typical and traditional marks of the tutelary spirit and even though (JM forgets this until after their encounter), Wendell is the earthly representative of Ephraim, JM's guide to the spirit world. While the early tercets of "W" allude to the tradition, the encounter Merrill stages dramatically revises it. JM not only positions himself as instructor to the figure from whom he would conventionally set out to learn but also rejects the potential guide's wisdom and concludes by confirming himself in the position he has, in earlier sections, constructed, challenged, and come back to. Rather than questioning it, "W" consolidates JM's resistance to a political role for poetry, to the idea that the poet's vocation entails a responsibility to criticize, warn, or try to alter his society. Belatedly realizing that Wendell is Ephraim's earthly representative, JM does not regret his failure to yoke the young man's talent to the specific message he has himself received from Ephraim. Instead, he seems simply to wish that meeting the young man had sparked the same sense of connection JM has felt with the disembodied voice of Wendell's patron. In the Venetian dawn, JM decides that, despite the mission handed on to him via the Ouija board, his "sunset years" are not the time to try "Mending my ways, breaking myself of rhyme / To speak to multitudes and make it matter" (81). Rhyme, as a metonym for the resources of JM's chosen form, encloses history; in the section's penultimate tercet, it rhymes with "Time," the two conjoined ideas bracketing "matter" or the possibility of moving "multitudes." JM's poetry subjects historic time to a reversible syntax in which "near turns far, and former latter," in which, in other words, history can be rewritten.

* * *

Just as Eliot, when chastised by the compound ghost, is forced to think through language's limitations, to recognize that only in its brokenness can it point the way to the ineffable, Merrill, working under Ephraim's imperative to "SET MY TEACHINGS DOWN," must determine the extent of poetry's power in and around the political realm. Where the conclusion of "W" suggests a choice between clear alternatives, though, the much more typical and powerful gesture of the poem is a "both/and" move consonant with Merrill's insistence in interviews on "remaining of two minds." This is best seen by tracing Merrill's visions and revisions of the relationship between poetic and political power in the poem's middle sections, where we find Merrill at one moment suggesting that the aesthetic can contain or restrain power exercised in the political world and at the next, or, more effectively, within the same verbal gesture, reversing the polarity of the opposition's terms and acknowledging the power of earthly movers and shakers.

In the crucial section "P," for example, Merrill makes clear just how important the historical and political are, and he does so in a way that locates them *within* rather than in opposition to the aesthetic / cosmological system represented by Ephraim. More than this, he links them in a constant dance of interdependence. The theme of "P" is power; the section begins and ends with an invocation to "Powers of lightness, darkness, powers that be," and it includes some banter between JM and Ephraim about both aesthetic and political power, banter that lightly plays on art's containment of political power and the terrifying reality of the uncontainable. Aesthetic power is embodied in Mozart, who is able to skip the stages of purification normally endured by a soul before it is reborn on earth. When JM asks "Is this permitted?" Ephraim's answer suggests the absolute character of aesthetic power: "WHEN U ARE MOZART YES" (54). Political power wielded during an earthly lifetime carries no such posthumous rewards; indeed, "Power's worst abusers," men like Hitler or Caligula, Merrill writes, are forcefully contained, held, in Ephraim's words, "INCOMMUNICADO / CYSTS IN THE TISSUE OF ETERNITY" (55). The suggestion here is that the political can be contained while the aesthetic cannot. (Indeed, since the cosmological system that contains Caligula and Hitler like cysts is the product of Merrill's poetic imagination, or of that imagination inspired—like Dante's—by the spirit world, Merrill here enacts the containment of toxic power even as he describes it.)

This superiority of aesthetic power has hardly been suggested, however, when it is canceled by worries over atomic power, whose threat exists in both the terrestrial and celestial planes. Merrill first sneaks this topic in as part of a catalogue of failed efforts at containment, but the possibility of nuclear annihilation quickly takes over the verse paragraph in which it appears. He thus enacts the way fear of nuclear destruction similarly overwhelms his consciousness. The elemental and absolute nature of destruction (souls as well as bodies are incinerated in atomic explosions) frightens the spirit world as well as the one in which JM and DJ live. Indeed, Ephraim suggests when JM tries to shrug off the world's destruction as simply the will of the "Cosmic Mind," Heaven, too, "would up and vanish" (56).

Merrill tries to establish some bulwarks against the destruction he dreads; he does so, suggestively, in two stanzas cast as sonnets, two stanzas that again stage the tension between poetry and history, aesthetic and political power. In the first, Merrill recalls seeing Wagner's *Götterdämerung* as a boy, the opera's destruction of both Heaven and Earth (Valhalla and the Rhine) a spark that landed on an understanding as yet too "green" to be ignited. Ephraim's breath has now, years later, kindled a blazing fire from that spark. In the glow of this fire (the mature poet's imagination of destruction beyond Wagner's capacity to represent), JM sees the destruction of loved ones and companions. The stanza ends with the key question: "How to rid Earth, for Heaven's sake, of power / Without both turning to a funeral pyre?" Read this way, with an emphasis on the movement of ideas and images, the stanza poses but does not offer any solution to the problem. Merrill's manipulation of poetic form, however, does at least imply both a strategy for approaching power and a sense of the poet's responsibility to take up this strategy. I have called this stanza one of two sonnets in "P," but it is really only gesturally a sonnet. The stanza comprises fourteen lines of fairly regular iambic pentameter, but neither syntax nor rhyme scheme matches any classical model of the form. Indeed, the stanza only begins to rhyme at all at its halfway point (lines seven and eight rhyme as a couplet). It is at this point, though, that Merrill marshals the resources of his medium to suggestively contain the nuclear threat: "(While heavy water nymphs, fettered in chain / Reaction, sang their soft refrain *Refrain*)" (56). The threat lingers in diction and figurative language, the heavy water and chain reaction of nuclear power. Merrill establishes, though, a set of mechanisms to bind and contain the threat. Both "heavy water" and "chain / Reaction," for example, are bound by puns to other terms (nymphs and fetters). That the nymphs' "refrain" is "*Refrain*" emphasizes the imperative to resist an impulse to use nuclear power; the immediate repetition of the word enacts the repetition denoted by the word itself (in the sense of a poetic refrain) and both sorts of repetition (along with the italics and the rhyme on "chain") force-fully command restraint and containment.[24] At the moment when this "sonnet" starts to act like a sonnet, then, when Merrill fore-grounds poetic form, the elements of form work in concert to enact (in an enclosing parenthesis) an answer to the question posed in the sonnet's last lines.

Though its octave is dominated by anxious questions, the son-net that closes "P" more confidently suggests the capacity of aes-thetic power to contain historic and, perhaps, even atomic power. "Powers of lightness, darkness, powers that be," the sonnet begins, repeating the invocation with which the section opened, "Come, go." The possibility of total annihilation still troubles the poet. Might the whole cosmic system of refinement, renewal, and rebirth come to an end? Will the Heaven Ephraim elsewhere describes as "A GREAT WHITE WAY OF NAMES IN LIGHTS" still be there to wel-come JM and DJ upon their deaths? The sonnet's second quatrain offers Montezuma and Mallarmé as metonyms for both Heaven and "figures of authority;" the first is an emblem of historic, politi-cal power and the second of aesthetic power, and the sestet of this sonnet stages a comparison between the two. (Merrill formally alerts us to the comparison by devoting three lines, or half of the sestet, to each figure and by linking them in the sestet's rhyme scheme; the rhymes pointedly embody the contrasts between the two, with Montezuma's decorative "plume," for example, matched by Mallarmé's "slim volume.") Montezuma, Merrill writes, "we picture garlanded / With afterimages, fire-sheer / Solar plume on plume" (57). The monarch known as a god to his people is imag-ined in terms of the sun in such a way as to suggest the scale of his power. Mallarmé, on the other hand, is imagined in less graphically compelling terms and, as is appropriate for a poet, is remembered for a bon mot: "with having said / The world was made to end ('pour aboutir') / In a slim volume" (57).

Neither of these metonyms is accidental. Though neither Merrill
nor we discover it until *Scripts for the Pageant*, Montezuma is not only
the last emperor of the Aztecs but is also one of "the Five," a group
of immortal spirits described by different speakers as angels or gods.[25]
He therefore represents not only earthly and historical power but also
the manifestation of the celestial in earthly form. While Mallarmé
has no such claim to cosmic significance, he does carry a good deal
of importance both for Merrill himself and for the work that is at the
heart of "P." On one level, Mallarmé is a figure for a poetics by which
Merrill was influenced early on:

> Because I didn't know what I felt, it seemed to me that what was
> obscurely said had a kind of resonance that charmed me and led me
> at least down that dangerous path toward the impenetrable quatrains
> of Mallarmé, trying deliberately to create a surface of impenetrability
> and, at the same time, such beauty that it wouldn't yield up a meaning
> easily, if at all. Maybe eventually one gets tired of that kind of thing,
> though in my weak moments I still find myself drawn to it.[26]

Merrill here at once claims and disclaims Mallarmé as an influence,
and the "impenetrability" to which Merrill twice refers might explain
the authority he is granted in "P," where JM says he lives "far above"
his "subjects." More important, I think, is the way we can read
Mallarmé as an allusion to Eliot's allusive grappling with the problem
of poetic responsibility in "Little Gidding." For Eliot, as we saw in
chapter 3, the French poet's words are part of the compound ghost's
speech. Moreover, Mallarmé's mission—to purify the language of the
tribe—is the one the ghost disavows as the mistake he (they) made in
life. He represents art for its own sake, a poetry that neither refers to
nor bears any responsibility to the historical world, a poetry, perhaps,
something like that to which Merrill remains dedicated after his dinner with Wendell in "W."

It might at first appear that Montezuma comes out on top in
this comparison, but by addressing the source of JM's anxiety, it
is Mallarmé who quietly demonstrates power equal not only to
Montezuma but also to the atomic energy that drives Merrill's concern. Mallarmé claims that the world will end in the proverbial "slim
volume" of poetry; that is to say that the world and its ending will
be contained in the poet's creative imagination. While the Aztec
king/god's power is expansive (the shape of a plume fans out from
its originating point, the plume is doubled, or perhaps squared, by
the repetition of "plume on plume," and the adjective "solar" grants

Montezuma the radiating power of the sun), the poet's is intensive (yielding just the "slim volume") and contained, not only by the size of the poetic product but by the formal constraints constitutive of the genre. This intensive power, though, is seen as capable of containing the end of the world (and, in a punning alternative meaning of "made to end," as the ordained telos implied in the world's beginning); it is granted a worldly power, while the historical power of the king/god is rendered aesthetic or literary by those plumes (metonymically linked to the pen and, through the pen, poetry) and is therefore contained within the Mallarméan or Merrillian discourse. More than this, the whole set of issues is contained within Merrill's sonnet, an effective figure for the "slim volume" in which "the world was made to end." Historical power and even historical catastrophe are assumed into the aesthetic system at once described and demonstrated by the sonnet itself.

Merrill questions this answer and reopens the issue almost immediately—section "R" opens with his injunction to himself to "Rewrite P." The provocation for this revision is the death of DJ and JM's friend, the avant-garde filmmaker Maya Deren, which has occurred since the time narrated in "P." Deren is the central figure in section "M," which recounts a dream she has (which, it turns out, is actually her spirit's visit to the otherworld, during which she meets Ephraim). That section emphasized the spirit world's power to provide creative inspiration; Deren's vision (which results in her 1946 film, "Ritual in Transfigured Time") is compared to Dante's similar view of the spirit world (Ephraim says her dream is "a low-budget / Remake...of the *Paradiso*" [45]) and compares such inspired work favorably with the more worldly (and political) work (*Inferno* and *Purgatorio*) in which sides are taken and scores settled. In "P," after briefly describing Deren's death and the world-altering sadness it occasions, Merrill turns the poem over to her, speaking through the Ouija board: "DAVID JIMMY I AM YOUNG AT LAST" (64). The crucial component of her communication is another explanation for dreams, one that touches on the poem's concern with artistic power as it intersects with worldly, historic, or political power. Deren tells JM and DJ that she has been put to work. St. Lucy has employed her to "DIRECT SOME AVANTGARDE HALLUCI- // NATIONS ETC FOR HEADS OF STATE." The relationship between dreams and artworks that Merrill elaborates in "M" is strengthened here; not only do some dreams inspire artistic works that bear cosmic truths, but some are themselves artworks that affect the course of worldly events. Merrill's typically witty breaking of a word at the end of a line (and, here, a stanza), implies the power of "halluci" (the wandering of the mind in the word's Latin root) over the "nation."[27] This power is explicitly described in the next lines: "U SHD HEAR THEM MOAN & FEEL THEM SWEATING / WE GIRLS HAVE STOPPED A WAR WITH CUBA." Given the analogy Merrill has established between dreams, film, and poetry (especially in "M"), Deren's claim here strongly suggests the absolute power of the aesthetic to intervene in history. It is not Kennedy's diplomacy or Khrushchev's brinksmanship but artistic dreams that resolve the Cuban missile crisis. In such dreams begin the notion of poetic responsibility (though the tone here also bears a whiff of parody).

The conclusion of "R" fulfills the section's opening promise to rewrite "P," and in so doing it redefines the poet's responsibility. Like the earlier section, "R" ends with a sonnet. Indeed, the two sonnets share an identical and unorthodox rhyme scheme (the octaves rhyme abcd abcd). In "R," though, Merrill casts aspersion on the aesthetic intervention in (or containment of) history upon which the end of "P" resolved. The octave is a series of abdications or resignations: "Leave," "Let," "Let" (65). These add up to an apparent acceptance of the passage of time and all that it entails: age, change, mortality. The way things will pass the test of time is by submitting to time's passing, and two independent clauses that conjoin the annual and the diurnal, the momentary and the monumental, flesh out the senses and scales in which Merrill registers this acceptance.

Up to this point, Merrill has focused on poetry's power. At this point, his attention turns to the responsibility such power entails. Hearing the cheers of fans in the "Sunday stadium," the "Twenty thousand throats" shouting as if with "one single throat," Merrill imagines a mob, driven by instinct and "blood calling to blood." Such a mob's potential for violence is distilled in the imagery of a sharpening blade, the striking spondaic assonance of "deep shriek," and the slant-rhyme of "throat" and "threat." The roar of the mob calls to the poet's mind "the good gray medium / Blankly uttering someone else's threat." While the meanings here are certainly multiple—that punning "good gray medium" might be the television that carries the crowd's cry regardless of its content—Merrill's phrasing implicates poetry itself. The "good gray poet" is, of course, a famous nickname for Walt Whitman, who stands, perhaps, for the tradition of poets speaking for or as a broader community. But this is also clearly a reference to Merrill himself, the middle-aged poet passing on the frightening message Ephraim dictates from the spirit world. That this is the sestet of a (sort-of) sonnet suggests a logical or causal link with the octave, and taken together the parts of the sonnet-stanza indicate the bind in which the poet finds himself. On one hand, poetry cannot resist the tides of time, change, and death. On the other hand, if poetry *could* marshal those forces, its power might unleash other uncontrollable forces.

* * *

Only when the poem concludes does JM accept the burden of responsibility entailed by his communications with the other world. At the opening of section "Z," some time has passed since those communications took place ("Years have gone by," according to section "Y" [87]). Indeed, Merrill writes that "the affair / Has ended" (91). Boxes containing the transcripts of the Ouija board sessions have been set down "by the fire." The cold of a New England winter with a broken furnace is exacerbated by the absence of messages from beyond; Merrill writes of "Mercury dropping," referring, of course, to the thermometer that registers falling temperatures but also to the messenger of the gods who is now failing to deliver. The cold is also made worse, it seems, by the contrast with the summer warmth in which both the Ouija sessions and "The Book of Ephraim" began. Where section "B" emphasized the "witty shade," "Z" emphasizes the closed-up and closed-off qualities of the house in winter. The evocative "shade" is replaced here by a "blind," the house that had been open to the breeze now has its "windows and sliding doors...wadded shut" (90). In place of the Ouija board's letters, we find house plants scattering "Leaflets advocating euthanasia."

The broken furnace threatens the "old love-letters from the other world" with destruction. DJ says that "It's them or the piano" that will have to be burned for heat. In this joke, Merrill wryly poses a question of evaluative hierarchy. Which is more valuable, the piano (music, art, creativity) or the Ouija transcripts, with their concerns over the possibility of nuclear destruction both of this world and the other? As I hope to have shown is typical of the poem as a whole, Merrill does not decide so much as compellingly stage this question. In this case, as in the moments I have so far examined, a key means for that staging is a reference to Wagner's *Ring*. The allusion functions as the vehicle of a simile through which JM imagines burning a page of the transcripts:

> Take this one.
> Limp, chill, it shivers in the glow, as when
> The tenor having braved orchestral fog
> First sees Brünnhilde sleeping like a log. (91)

This passage reprises a set of connections that have been established by earlier moments in the poem. Many of Ephraim's most important messages have had to do with burning, especially the burning of Hiroshima and of the souls that did not escape atomic destruction. Here, those messages themselves face the prospect of burning. As they do so, JM alludes again to the *Ring*, which has, earlier in the poem, represented the absorption of history into art or the interpretation of history and life through art. The allusion-in-a-simile (whose vehicle includes a "tenor") likens the paper's trembling to a moment of clarity and illumination, but both the final simile of the sentence and the personification of the next sentence suggest immolation instead.

Typically, just when Merrill forces the moment to its crisis, an interruption resolves the issue by suspending and displacing it. The telephone rings—"Bad connection; babble of distant talk"—and into or against that static Merrill articulates a multivalent imperative: "We must improve the line / In every sense, for life" (91). Positioning "line" on the line break, Merrill emphasizes the self-reference (as he does with "feet" and "measures" in section "A"). Poetry, then, must be improved. The line (and "the line") also refers, though, to the means of communication generally, and if that "line" leads ultimately to language (and "sense" suggests that it does) then perhaps one crucial component of Merrill's mission is in fact to purify the dialect of the tribe. A crucial but neither lone nor even primary component, though, for as the next line completes the sentence it names a purpose beyond poetic self-reference: "for life." And life speaks up, in the form of "Bob, the furnace man," to help JM realize that the carton of communiqués must be spared; "Too much / Already, here below, has met its match" and gone up in flames.

Part of the theme JM claims for himself, one of the earliest spirit utterances quoted (in section "C") is "PEACE FROM REPRESENTATION," which JM likens to a "motto for abstract art" (10). We might read Merrill's struggle in "The Book of Ephraim," as, at least in part, the negotiation of a responsible course between power and peace, between the world's truths and otherworldly pleasure. This is a version of the negotiation conducted in necromantic poems after "Little Gidding," and while Merrill does not definitively plot that course in "Z," he does conclude the first installment of his necromantic opus by reporting to the helm and accepting some sense in which his art must answer to the world: "For here we are" (92).

5

DEREK WALCOTT'S *OMEROS*

In his reading of the figure of the wound in Derek Walcott's *Omeros*, Jahan Ramazani finds Eliotic echoes in the character of Philoctete, a Saint Lucian fisherman who, like his Greek namesake, suffers an incurable leg wound. "Like the Fisher King in Eliot's *Waste Land*," Ramazani writes, "Philoctete is a synecdoche for a general loss, injury, and impotence that must be healed for the (is)lands to be set in order."[1] Since Philoctete's wound, at least in his own mind, is caused by the manacles of his enslaved ancestors, the "general...injury" for which he stands is the wound of enslavement and exploitation at the center of Caribbean history. And if Philoctete is a Fisher King, Ramazani reasons, then his fellow fisherman, the poem's protagonist Achille, must be the "questing knight" who journeys to Africa—"site of ancestral enslavement" and locus of historical identity—in order to bring about healing of fisherman and land alike.[2] The gulfs and fissures in which Ramazani hears Eliotic echoes are crucial for his elaboration of *Omeros*'s cultural work: Walcott's demonstration of poetry's value in a postcolonial context that more often prizes prose fiction for its clearer performance of nationalist allegory and for the way it cleaves to "racial, regional, national, and gender loyalties."[3] For Ramazani, poetry's intricate metaphoricity enacts the dialectical coidentity of wound and cure and thereby enables textual healing.[4]

While *The Waste Land* taints Philoctete's wound, another Eliotic episode is at work elsewhere in the poem, for *Omeros* includes several distinct and recognizable katabatic episodes that hearken to "Little Gidding"'s compound ghost passage both in their structure and in the cultural work they perform. Early on, Walcott's unnamed narrator meets the shade of his father. Later, the poem's islander protagonist, Achille, suffering sunstroke, undergoes an out-of-body pilgrimage to the African village of his ancestors, where he encounters his own father, learns his African identity, and witnesses a wide span of colonial as well as tribal history. Finally, the poem reaches its conclusion through a descent in which the Narrator, led by an animated bust of Homer, finds the poets enduring eternal torment but also finds the possibility of salvation. Taken together, these episodes, like the wound Ramazani debrides, touch on a tangle of intertwined issues much on Walcott's mind throughout his long career: the relationship of Caribbean poetry and culture to Africa; the colonial subject's relationship with the colonizer's culture; and the task of the poet with respect to the wounds that compose History.

Much of the criticism on *Omeros* deals with the poem's status as an epic.[5] For my purposes the poem's generic classification matters less than its clear deployment of the epic's *nekuia* and *katabasis* topoi.[6] Walcott's loose rendering of terza rima and his occasional direct allusion to *Inferno* are obvious evidence of that influence. More important, though, is the way Walcott, like Eliot in "Little Gidding," thinks through the question of poetic responsibility by restaging both Homeric/Vergilian and Dantean necromantic encounters.[7] Like Heaney's "Station Island," the subject of chapter 7, Walcott's poem includes both explicitly vocational dialogues (between the narrator and his father and between the narrator and Homer) and others whose explicit subject is not poetry but whose contents and outcomes bear powerfully on the poem's developing ideas about what poetry might be responsible to and for (such as Achille's long sojourn in Africa). Through the episodes of descent and encounter in *Omeros*, Walcott elaborates and justifies a poetics responsive to but not enslaved by History (and literary history); he enacts a poetry whose aim is neither to evade nor to intervene in politics but is instead to heal the wounds left in its wake.

The necromantic colloquies experienced by the poem's Narrator and its main protagonist map neatly onto two of what John Van Sickle has described as the poem's three main plots. Achille's journey to Africa enables the resolution of the "village plot" focused on the triangular relationship between Achille, his rival Hector, and Helen, the object of both men's desire.[8] Meanwhile, the Narrator's encounters with his father and his journeys to Europe and to Soufriere, the volcano/Underworld, are crucial moments in what Van Sickle calls the "Narrator's plot."[9] The doubled journeys and *nekuiae* are just two among several devices by which Walcott knots the poem's multiple plots together. Narrator and protagonist each begin the book in pain caused by estrangement; each wants somehow to possess Helen, a St. Lucian waitress; each undergoes both a journey into History and an encounter with his father; each achieves a healing resolution through cultural synthesis; and the twinned resolutions achieved by

Achille and the Narrator are set in opposition to the failed resolution of what Van Sickle calls the "farm plot," in which Major Plunkett unsuccessfully seeks a father and son (and a narrative for Helen) in his historical research. All of this suggests that Achille and the Narrator are themselves doubles, that their conflicts and resolutions complement each other to form a whole. While the Narrator's necromantic episodes manage a set of tensions arising from Walcott's relationship to literary history and literary success, the resolution they bring about is incomplete without reference to the dynamics of the "village plot," which manages tensions arising from Achille's (and Philoctete's) relationship to History (as that abstraction is embodied in slavery and colonialism).

* * *

At the climactic conclusion of Book One (in Chapters XII and XIII), Walcott's Narrator is transported to the port city of Castries, where he grew up. The Castries upbringing is one of numerous similarities between the Narrator and Walcott; they also share the fact of a father named Warwick, long sojourns in the United States and Europe, and successful literary careers.[10] In Castries, the Narrator finds first that his childhood home has become a printers' shop and then that it is still inhabited by the ghost of his father. John Van Sickle characterizes the passage as a dialogue with Vergil and argues that "everything about the encounter—its prominent placement, its length occupying two full chapters, above all its theme of inheritance and drama of paternal counsel—give it crucial programmatic significance in the design of the whole work."[11] To be sure, Warwick functions as a kind of Anchises to the Narrator's wandering Aeneas, but much about this episode also resembles Eliot's encounter with the familiar compound ghost: It occurs in a real-world setting transformed by diction and description into a liminal space between world and Underworld; its interlocutor is a poet-figure; its colloquy concerns poetry and poetic responsibility. As the Narrator and Warwick go for a walk through midday Castries, Walcott's description at once realistically represents the setting and imbues it with symbolic significance. The day is so hot its very reality brings an unreal character, the heat of the asphalt creating rippling waves and emptying the street of living inhabitants; it is populated, instead, by "brown phantoms" whose own suits are "rippled by the grille // of shade."[12] In this infernal context, the Narrator's father not only is a poet but also represents poetry itself. He carries the notebook in which he wrote poems. More than this, he is named for "The Bard's county," and narrates aspects of his life and death through Shakespearean allusion: he recalls his wife as Portia, remembers his death from an ear infection in terms of "Hamlet's old man." Critics often read this passage for its bearing on what Ramazani describes in another context as the question of "what it means to love the English language and hate English imperialism,"[13] on Walcott's linguistic lineage ("It's that Will you inherit"), but it also and obviously has to do with the poetic vocation itself and, especially, with the responsibilities such a vocation might entail. Deprived of access to "the foreign machinery known as Literature," Warwick "wrote with the heart / of an amateur" (68). His son, now old enough to be his father, "reverses" the father's poetic practice; he is not only a professional but is also famous.[14] The overwhelming question posed in the episode is what the Narrator will do with that fame.

To pose that question, Warwick leads the Narrator to two local sites that open onto the island's past: the barbershop and the wharf. The former is overseen by the shade of the barber, "the town anarchist" (71–72). There, Warwick says, "toga'd in a pinned sheet, / the curled hairs fell like commas" (71). The father whose work has been "reversed" by his son's calling here effects a nice reversal of his own, reading the barber's collection of literary classics backward in the mirror as he assumes the imperial position of Roman senator in the shop's "revolving Speaker's seat." And where the black bodies of colonial subjects have often been figured as texts (of varying levels of legibility for colonizing readers), Warwick ascribes to them a capacity for authorship, for making rather than being meaning, through the image of diacritical detritus marking a blank sheet. Authorship belongs to the barber, too, since his scissors create the commas, but where Warwick takes ownership of European culture, the barber rages over the island's lack of its own cultural identity: "The rock he lived on was nothing. Not a nation / or a people" (72).[15] Against this curse, the barber appeals to Marcus Garvey, whose iconic photograph "with the braided tricorne and gold-fringed epaulettes" he displays in the frame of one mirror. With no "nation" or "people" on St. Lucia, the barber seeks a solid cultural identity in Africa. Warwick, however, dismisses this ambition, calling the barber's "paradise" a "phantom Africa" and marking him through two allusions to Shakespeare's Shylock, as eternally and irrevocably diasporic. The positions here resonate with comments on Africa in Walcott's earlier work. In his 1974 essay, "The Muse of History," for example, he is harshly critical of Caribbean poets who hearken back to Africa and perform to the beat of the "tom tom" while "ignoring the dynamo."[16] And in his poetic autobiography, *Another Life*, Walcott even condemns to Hell those poets who "nurture the scabs of rusted chains," who "charge" readers for "another free ride on the middle passage," and "explain to the peasant why he is African."[17]

The thesis (Warwick) and antithesis (the barber) sketched in the barbershop are synthesized at the wharf, where Warwick, like Anchises or Tiresias, addresses the Narrator in imperatives. Significantly, these directives focus explicitly on poetic responsibility, the proper use of the Narrator's poetic vocation. The two walkers first see "a liner as white as a mirage, / its hull bright as paper, preening with privilege" (72). Walcott's similes perform a transitive equation here so that the liner is linked at once to authorship and to the unreal. As if he speaks directly against this image, Warwick commands the Narrator:

> Measure the days you have left. Do just that labour
> which marries your heart to your right hand: simplify
> your life to one emblem, a sail leaving harbour. (72)

The sense of this commandment derives from a set of oppositions. Warwick's "one emblem," a sailboat, represents simplicity and work (it resembles the canoes whose construction opens the poem) as opposed to the corrupted luxury of the liner (which Warwick associates with fame). As Charles Pollard writes, "the white liner represents all that is negative in aspiring after poetic fame,"[18] but it is also opposed to the city whose imagery and life might vivify the Narrator's work. That this work is a historically and socially aware poetry Warwick makes clear in metaphors (rather than the similes that figure the liner); the Narrator must "Measure" his remaining days in rhymed and metered lines and stanzas, working to unify emotion and act (heart and right hand). Sound emphasizes the point: where "privilege" is linked with "mirage" to underscore its unreality, "labour" is linked to "harbour" as a source of energy and productivity.

The lesson does not end, but only begins, with this command to pursue a simplified vocation. Warwick goes on to reveal to the Narrator the necessary subject for the labor he demands. Turning from the liner's wake to the hills above Castries, Warwick recalls watching "women climb / like ants," carrying baskets of coal on their heads" (73). Walcott augments the scene's katabatic echoes when he has Warwick say that "Hell was built on those hills," when he has him call the mine an "inferno" where "every labouring soul" climbed and suffered, and when he has Warwick conclude that the "infernal anthracite hills showed you hell, early" (74). More than this, he forges a link between the hellish scene and poetic inspiration. Warwick first almost casually connects the women's work and the Narrator's: "their work, your pose of a question waiting, / as you crouch with a writing lamp over a desk" (75). He goes on, though, to strengthen and temper the link and to bind the Narrator to it with all the resources of poetic form:

> Kneel to your load, then balance your staggering feet
> and walk up that coal ladder as they do in time,
> one bare foot after the next in ancestral rhyme. (75)

The puns on poetic meter ("feet," "foot"), the simultaneous naming and deployment of "rhyme" (emphasized by the disruption of terza rima's sound pattern), and the vigorously figurative language of the tercet all consociate the women's work and the Narrator's vocation. Subsequent stanzas intensify the bond, by figuring rhyme as hands, as language's ambition to embrace, by stating that only the work of rhyme's hands, work like that performed by the women, will enable the Narrator to supersede the "infernal anthracite," and by performing these linkages in some of the most regularly rhymed terza rima stanzas so far in the poem. The women figure not poetry's credibility but poetic responsibility.[19] The Narrator's work must not so much resemble as become the work of these preceding generations: "the couplet of those multiplying feet / made your first rhymes" (75). The chapter and the first of the poem's seven books conclude with Warwick's injunction to the Narrator: "your duty" is "to give those feet a voice" (75–76).

This climax of Book One opens a frame closed by the climactic *katabasis* in Book Seven, a frame that contains what Robert Hamner has called the three "Middle Passages" at the heart of *Omeros*.[20] Like Book One's colloquy with Warwick (and like Eliot's with the compound ghost), Book Seven's long encounter with Omeros/Seven Seas is at once vocational and ethical. Where the Narrator receives a burden from Warwick in Book One, however, he is relieved of a burden by Omeros in Book Seven; the manner and mode of that relief mixes memory and desire, tradition and individual talent, the Aegean and the Caribbean, poetry and responsibility. As I have discussed in previous chapters, the *nekuia* has long been associated with the poet's need to demonstrate his superiority to the literary tradition he receives (and hopes to be received into). In Book Seven, though, Walcott repeatedly demonstrates his *dependence* upon that tradition. Indeed, the key sin the Narrator must repent during his descent into volcano, Soufriere, is precisely his reliance upon the tradition, a reliance that has prevented him from carrying out the charge he received from Warwick's shade in the poem's first encounter. The episode's echoes of Eliot's "familiar compound ghost" passage, which is heavily freighted with self-recrimination, cast this part of Walcott's project into sharp relief.

The tutelary spirit the Narrator encounters at the beginning of Book Seven is every bit as "compound" as Eliot's familiar ghost. Its appearance goes through a protean shifting of shapes—what first seems to be a marble bust of Homer becomes, when the sky darkens and the shallows change "to another dialect," the St. Lucian blind seer Seven Seas.[21] The figure shifts shapes, alternately "marble with a dripping chiton" and a fisherman wearing a modern undershirt (281), but he bears a unity of sorts throughout these changes since "both of them had the look of men / whose skins are preserved in salt, whose accents were born / from guttural shoal" (281). Walcott effects not only a sense of resemblance but also a cultural synthesis here, absorbing (as Pound does in Canto I) the European literary tradition in order to confront it in its ancient grandness even as he grounds that tradition in a salty, sandy archipelago that resembles his own home. Just as importantly, *Omeros* enables the Narrator's own momentary synthesis with the land he has so often (and for so long) left behind, and does so in a way that, in its diction of insubstantiality and liminality, also echoes Eliot. Climbing a steep path in the bust's company (and in a way that echoes the climbing of the women in Book One), the Narrator loses his own substance as he comes to see "the light of St. Lucia at last through her own eyes" (282).[22]

The content of the colloquy also follows the model Eliot establishes in "Little Gidding." Once the heights (and the view they allow) have been achieved, the Narrator converses with Omeros about a range of topics—women, language, "the love of your own people" (284). Their chief topic, though, is poetry itself, especially the bust's own poem. "I never read it," the Narrator admits, "Not all the way through." On its own, this confession would exemplify David Pike's argument that the necromantic confrontation with a figure for the literary tradition hinges on the living poet's implicit claim to synthesize and supersede that tradition. Walcott's cancellation of the admission, though, is more important than the admission itself, for in it he locates poetic inspiration (the Narrator's but also the tradition's) in the voices of the natural world: "I have always heard / your voice in the sea," the Narrator says, "in the *laurier-cannelles*, pages of rustling trees" (283). Since the Narrator is at this point wholly identified with the island (he himself has become transparent and insubstantial), this identification of Omeros with the sea and the trees suggests a common identity for the two poets as well as a grounding of poetry at once in place and in shared traditions that transcend location.

That sense is strengthened when the two board the bust's canoe and are carried out into the bay, where they sing together the praises of the island. Here, the Narrator's subordination to the tradition embodied in the bust of Homer is made inescapably clear. When Omeros says "We will both praise it now," the Narrator cannot make a sound: "My tongue was a stone," he recalls, "my mouth a parted conch // from which nothing sounded" (286). The figurative language works in tension with the Narrator's location of inspiration in the elements of land and sea a few stanzas before; his identification with stone and shell (and, through these, the sea itself) is not enough to enable his praise song. Only when Omeros, Walcott's figure for the tradition, sings (and sings synthetically, in a "Greek calypso"), can the Narrator add his voice. And far from superseding the tradition, the Narrator's voice is "thin," dependent ("riding on his praise"), and subordinate ("under the strength of his voice").

The poetic praise of St. Lucia is only a prelude, though, to the crucial work Walcott undertakes in this episode; the climactic passage takes up the whole of Chapter LVIII, during which the bust of Homer leads the Narrator on a purgative journey through a volcanic entry and into a Dantean Underworld. This "hell in paradise" is Soufriere, St. Lucia's volcano but also an echo of *souffir*, the French verb "to suffer."[23] The name is apt, for here the Narrator encounters various groups and individuals who suffer for having wronged the island, and here he also confronts his own wrongdoing. The punishments endured by the damned resemble the *contrapasso* in Dante's *Inferno* or in Pound's Canto XIV; each suits its sufferer's offense in life. Amid the "foul sulphur" and "scorching light," the Narrator first sees "traitors // who, in elected office, saw the land as views / for hotels" (289) as they boil in the Pool of Speculation. Similarly, Hector, friend and rival of Achille, who abandoned the sea for readier cash as a driver for tourists, must shoulder an oar as a lance and stand as a "road-warrior," his shade punitively "halt in its passage toward a smokeless place" (292). At last the Narrator is brought to a pit of poets, phantoms who "saw only surfaces / in nature and men, and smiled at their similes, // condemned in their pit to weep at their own pages" (293). He recognizes himself in the punished poets, and slides toward "the shit they stewed in."

Where the necromantic moment typically stages the poet's face-off
with the tradition and provides the poet an opportunity to diagnose
its sins as he simultaneously summarizes and supersedes the tradition,
Walcott's Narrator finds *himself* guilty of the poets' selfishness, poor
vision, and self-regard: "And that was where I had come from. Pride
in my craft. / Elevating myself." Walcott inverts the conventional
power relationship Pike finds structuring the descent trope as the
Narrator (a live poet) slips instead of standing superior and is rescued
by the tradition we might expect him to absorb; it is Omeros who
grips his hand and pulls him from the pit. The rescue is only partial,
though; turning away from his fellow poets in contempt, the Narrator
is "gripped" (just as he is by the marble hand of Omeros) by "a fist of
ice," and is brought face to face with his own failures.

This climactic confrontation is rife with paradox. Following
Omeros's "blind feet" up the slope, image and pun both recalling the
working women shown to the Narrator by his father and offered as
the source and focus of his vocation, the Narrator "contemptuously"
turns his head away from the pit of poets. The icy fist grips it and
"wrenched my own head bubbling its half-lies" (293). The line suggests that the Narrator's head is held by the fist, just as it is held by
the boatman's iron grip during the journey to Soufriere, and that
the "half-lies" it bubbles are the Narrator's (perhaps his claims to
difference from the damned poets). As the sentence continues, this
head the Narrator calls "my own" attempts to cry out its name, but
cannot: "each noun stuck in its gorge" (294). In the face of (and
apparently face to face with) this inarticulate defense, the "ice-matted
head" answers with an accusation.

Walcott obscures the identity of his interlocutor. After it hisses
its closing question, the Narrator says "My own head sank in the
black mud of Soufriere, // while it looked back with all the faith it
could summon" (294). Is this the "ice-matted head" sinking back
into its eternal interment, or the Narrator's head, released from the
icy grip, sinking back onto the realistic ground of the volcano? Is the
head twice identified as "my own" simply the head on the Narrator's
shoulders, or is it a double he confronts, the head out of whose mouth
the crucial accusation issues? Is the accusation one the Narrator levels at himself or does it originate in some Other, and if the latter is
the case, which Other? Terada, perhaps too easily, assumes that "it
is Omeros's head that looks back while Walcott sinks."[24] Pollard,
too, assumes the head is "another iteration of Walcott's multi-faceted
tradition."[25] Syntax and pronouns make identification difficult here,
but it seems to me that this head belongs not to Omeros but either

to the shade of Warwick or to (some already-damned part of) the Narrator himself.

Several clues point to Warwick. Filial resemblance and relationship might lead the Narrator to identify the head as his own, of course, and Warwick's appearance in Book Seven would symmetrically complete the frame opened by his appearance in Book One. Most important, the content of the head's utterance ("You tried to render / their lives" but failed) refers to Warwick's imperative in Book One. What better judge of the Narrator's performance than the shade who set the task in the first place?

Walcott's models for this passage—Dante and Eliot—more strongly support the idea that the head belongs to the Narrator himself. If this seems impossible at first glance, the elements are clearly present in the necromantic tradition. Dante provides a precedent for shades suffering in the Inferno while their possessors still live in the world above. He consigns to and finds in Hell (more specifically, in the Ninth Circle, to which Walcott's Soufriere stands as an analogy) Fra Alberigo and Branca Doria, both of whom are still alive when Dante encounters their shades.[26] And in "Little Gidding" Eliot enacts his speaker's self-division: "I assumed a double part and cried / And heard another's voice cry."[27] None of this makes the head's identity certain, of course, and Eliot's model also suggests a composite (or "familiar compound") identity for the shade. The important point is that little in the passage, in Walcott's closest models, or in the necromantic tradition going back to the eleventh book of the *Odyssey,* would lead us to conclude that the Homeric bust who guides the Narrator (and who is indicated by the head's deictic "that sightless stone") is also the speaker who chastises him.

While it does not help to identify the "ice-matted head," Walcott's pattern of allusion here at least makes legible the force behind the head's speech. The way through this volcanic Underworld maps onto the eighth and ninth circles of the Inferno through which Vergil guides Dante. The Pool of Speculation that Omeros and the Narrator pass is located, Walcott writes, in "the lava of the Malebolge" (289). The Malebolge are the "Evil-Pouches" that make up Dante's eighth circle,[28] the spaces devoted to punishing frauds, thieves, swindlers, counterfeiters, and liars. In Walcott's Malebolge, speculators (perpetrators of a kind of fraud) are punished. Dante's eighth pouch holds Ulysses, punished for his wiliness but captivating Dante with his account of the final journey he makes from Ithaca beyond the edge of the known world. In an analogous space, Walcott's Narrator sees Hector. Where Ulysses dies because he leaves his island for the sea, Hector died because he abandoned the sea; he therefore stands as a sort of inverse allusion to Ulysses. The pit of poets, following Hector, seems then to occupy a space Walcott composes by conflating the tenth pouch of the Malebolge (where liars are punished) and the ninth circle of the Inferno (where traitors suffer their torments embedded in ice).

The figure that confronts the Narrator has "a fist of ice" and an "ice-matted head," and so seems to allude to Dante's traitors even as he reaches out of Walcott's pit of poets. If so, then the speech he addresses to the Narrator must be read as the cautionary utterance of one traitor / poet (Warwick or the Narrator himself) to another (or potential) traitor / poet. "You tried to render / their lives as you could," the condemned head says; it continues:

> that is never enough;
> now in the sulphur's stench ask yourself this question,
> whether a love of poverty helped you
> to use other eyes, like those of that sightless stone? (294)

The poets of Soufriere suffer for backbiting, mockery, self-love, and pride. These sins shape the betrayal about which the shade warns the Narrator. While he has obeyed Warwick's injunction to "give them a voice," the Narrator has at the same time betrayed the colliers of Castries (and the native population for whom they stand). Because this speech is so brief, the precise provocation for the shade's chastisement is difficult to pin down, but the scene suggests that a Walcott figure literally grounded in the soil and stone of St. Lucia castigates another Walcott figure who has left the island and has spent much of his career seeing it through the sightless eyes of the tradition.[29]

Prepared by his own synthesis with St. Lucia before the descent into Soufriere and by Omeros / Seven Seas's comment that no matter how far he has traveled he has still seen nothing, the Narrator is now able to understand his own failures and his own complicity in the island's (and the islanders') suffering. This recognition of disease is at the same time its cure; the episode ends quickly, with the Narrator looking back where he had come from (the phrase repeats his earlier recognition that he had come from the pit of poets, but also suggests a new vision of his origins) and then "The nightmare was gone." The bust disappears and the Narrator awakens.

It is clear that Walcott's position on the role of Caribbean history in his poetic vision and in his evolving sense of poetic responsibility changed between the early 1970s (when he wrote both "The Muse of History" and *Another Life*) and 1990 (when he published *Omeros*). While poets still inhabit Hell, they are condemned now not for the sins Walcott found mortal in *Another Life* (nurturing "the scars of rusted chains") but for pride (they are moved by their own verbal constructions), self-love, and mockery. They share the Underworld of Soufriere with exploiters of the island and its people, but are no longer positioned as exploiters themselves. Moreover, in Seven Seas Walcott portrays a poet-figure that, however syncretic, has its roots in both St. Lucia and the African past shared by the island's inhabitants. Finally, in the necromantic episodes of Books One and Seven, Walcott first dramatizes the Caribbean poet's charge to represent the suffering and exploitation of the island's people (past and present) and later dramatizes that poet's chastisement for failing to carry out this charge.

The episode's denouement provides new figures for writing and authorship: a crab with a pen-like pincer, a beach that closes "like a book // behind me with every footmark," and the continually erasing sea. Walcott's description emphasizes impermanence and ignorance: the ocean is "an epic where every line was erased // yet freshly written in sheets of exploding surf" (296). This has led some critics to foreground forgetting as a crucial component of Walcott's healing poetics. Pollard, for example, argues that Walcott renounces the past's importance and that "this renunciation enables him to see and represent what is truly important in the present."[30] Breslin, whose chapter on *Omeros* is titled "Epic Amnesia," argues that "Walcott's way of dealing with the past...encourages a necessary forgetting" of both historical fact and literary antecedent.[31] For both, this forgetting is contingent upon an experience of memory. As Breslin puts it, "one remembers so that the bitterness of the past, no longer evaded, loses its power to encumber the present" and one can then forget (rather than repress).[32] The ocean becomes a "trope of memory-as-forgetting, hoarding the past in its depths but erasing, with each surge of generative energy, the marks of human presence on the shore."[33]

While Breslin and Pollard are right that Walcott models a process of remembering in order to possess rather than be possessed by the past, "forgetting," "amnesia," and "renunciation" seem too strong for what Walcott portrays here. To be sure, the ocean has no memory of cultural epics and is itself a disappearing text, but it is also a text in which every erased line is "freshly written." And while water "commemorates nothing," it does so only "in its stasis" (297). The constantly moving water of the sea remembers. Specifically, it preserves the past of enslavement and exploitation, "that heart-heaving sough // begun in Guinea to fountain to exhaustion here" (296). Under the sea, rather than in "the sea," Walcott finds the image I would argue is the better one for his poetic stance toward memory and the past and for the processes of his own poem: the coral, "branching from the white ribs of each ancestor, // deeper than it seems on the surface" (296). Revising, rather than erasing, coral is "a patient, hybrid organism" that "feeds on its death." Its remains, whether "bones" or "parodic architecture" reminiscent of past societies, "branch into more coral."

This "self-healing" collective figures Walcott's poem and his sense of poetic responsibility because it preserves as it renews and transforms the remains of the past. The problem with "History," as with the therapeutic process of remembering/forgetting that Breslin and Pollard describe, is its linearity, its certain sense of series and sequence. What has clouded the Narrator's vision of the present-day Achille is not the facts of slavery and suffering that make up history but is instead the way Achille is "simplified by History" (297) and reduced to a symbol of wrath by its "elegies." Those elegies have "blinded" the poet "with the temporal lament for a smoky Troy" (297); the poetic genre that sets out to remember the absent dead, the lament for a destroyed city, assumes the pastness of the past when the clear view of Achille shows his coral-like construction on the past's presence (as skeletal remains). Similarly, Walcott's contemporary Caribbean epic renews and transforms (as opposed to forgetting) the remains of its Homeric and Dantean (and Eliotic) forbears when its characters and situations partially and problematically correspond to classical antecedents. Like the history of colonial servitude, the epic conventions are not first remembered and then forgotten in the poem. Rather, memory and forgetting constantly coexist, the latter dependent upon and inextricable from the former and so always carrying it as a condition of possibility.

* * *

I have suggested that "forgetting" is too strong a word for what Walcott represents; I would argue at the same time that "memory" is perhaps too weak a term for the experience of history Walcott represents and implicitly advocates in *Omeros*, for what the poem repeatedly dramatizes is not acts of intellect or affect (and where we do see these, as in Plunkett's researches, we see them in a critical light) but acts of bodily habitation. And here, thematic content and poetic and narrative structure are especially tightly bound, for the physical enactment of encounters with the past that animates both *nekuia* and *katabasis*, that composes the episodes of the necromantic and katabatic traditions, recurs throughout *Omeros*, not only in the explicitly vocational episodes of Books One and Seven, but also in some of the most important episodes at the heart of the poem.

That these episodes are closely linked is apparent when the Narrator awakens from his nightmare not only to the sound of the island but also to the image of Philocfete and to the awareness that the two of them, poet and fisherman, "shared the one wound, the same cure" (295). To understand the nature of the cure (and, through it, the poetry Walcott describes and defends in *Omeros*), I want to turn now to two crucial necromantic moments in the "middle passages" framed by the climactic scenes of Books One and Seven. The middle books of *Omeros* narrate a series of journeys: Achille returns to Africa, the Narrator travels in Europe, and a narrating consciousness travels into both the Caribbean and the North American pasts. While all of these journeys bear some allusive hallmarks of the necromantic and katabatic topoi, two—Achille's dream journey to Africa and Philocfete's healing descent into a brew prepared by Ma Kilman—demand the bulk of our attention. These episodes are linked by structure, imagery, and theme at once to each other and to the Narrator's experiences in Books One and Seven. More than this, these episodes suggest the productive relationship a Caribbean poet of the twentieth century might forge with the history of slavery. Just as Eliot revises some aspects of *The Waste Land* in "Little Gidding" and the rest of *Four Quartets*, Walcott here revises the position he takes on the Caribbean poet's relationship to the pasts of Africa and the Middle Passage in such earlier work as "The Muse of History" and *Another Life*.

Like the Narrator in Book One, Achille returns in Book Three to a "birthplace" and encounters a "father;" like the Narrator, he also meets an avatar of the protean Omeros figure, in this case an African griot; and, like the Narrator, he endures a confrontation with history that is at once wound and cure. From the fairly straightforward narration of the "town plot"—in which the waitress Helen leaves the fisherman Achille for his fellow fisherman, friend, and rival Hector— Book Three shifts rapidly into the strange spatiotemporal dimension of collective memory. In the opening tercet and a half, Walcott transports Achille from St. Lucia to "Africa," the continent in quotation marks both because, as several critics have pointed out, it conforms to Achille's cinematically informed imagination of Africa rather than to any empirical reality and because it seems also to be an Underworld of sorts.[34] When the Charon figure of "a skeletal warrior" stands up behind him in the canoe, clamping Achille's neck "in cold iron" and steering the boat into an unfamiliar river, even God's assurance that he is permitting Achille "to come home," that he is guiding the fisherman with the sea-swift "whose wings is the sign of my cruci- fixion," cannot entirely erase the infernal (or perhaps Elysian) sug- gestion (134), and when Achille sees "two worlds mirrored" in the river, when he sees "himself in his father," when his father greets him with "widening hands" that recall Vergil's description of Anchises greeting Aeneas ("He stretched out both his hands in eagerness"),[35] and when he realizes he is "moving with the dead," the suggestion becomes a certainty.

Once in this Underworld Africa, Achille, like Aeneas, like the Narrator, settles into a conversation with his father (though since they speak different languages, "Time translates" their utterances). Where Anchises foretells the destiny of Aeneas and his line, though, and where Warwick enjoins the Narrator to undertake specific future work, Afolabe, Achille's father, focuses on what his descendant has lost by forgetting. When Achille introduces himself but cannot say what his name means, Afolabe points out that he is made insubstan- tial by his loss of the entire referential basis of his ancestors' language: "if you're content with not knowing what our names mean, // then I am not Afolabe, your father," he says, and, moreover, "you, name- less son, are only the ghost // of a name" (138–39). The conse- quences here are supernaturally severe; the etymological connection between shadow and shade, the literary connection between shade and soul, lends this linguistic erasure an ontological weight. Not only does Achille himself fade into "the ghost // of a name," but Afolabe so completely loses himself that he is not even a shadow. On one hand, this fate contrasts with that attached to the poem's other crucial moment of insubstantiality, when the Narrator fades to invis- ibility on the heights of St. Lucia, because Achille here does not gain sight from the land's vantage point as the Narrator does. On the other hand, though, both moments precede and enable their protagonists' penitential self-reckoning.

For Achille, that self-reckoning begins with a literal habitation of his ancestral culture, which leads to his recognition that his con- temporary culture is rooted in that ancestral soil. He moves into a hut (which he is invited to share with "any woman he chose"), learns to chew kola nut and drink palm wine, listens to the tribe's orally transmitted history and mythology, joins in night-long communal singing, and, finally, takes his place in the "sacred circle of clear ground / where the gods assembled" and recites the names of the tribe's deities (139–40). The somatic and active character of Achille's immersion in this African tribal culture makes his knowledge of its impending end an unbearable nausea; the peace of the river in which he fishes with the tribe is overwhelmed by the roar of the ocean in Achille's head, a figure for the Middle Passage he knows the tribe will endure. When he tries to drink away this knowledge, to forget the future with the help of beer the tribe brews from fermented bark, he weeps and sees a vision of the wounded Philoctete. In a dream within the sunstroke dream that has carried him to Africa and the past, Achille walks across the ocean bottom and through the next three hundred years, back to St. Lucia, where he sees his own canoe before he wakes to find himself back with the tribe.

A simple return to the African past cannot solve the problem that afflicts Achille, not only because it is impossible (his knowledge of what will befall this paradise infects it and prevents him from settling into it) but also because it removes Achille from his home and work and community in St. Lucia. What is required, then, is not return but *recovery*, a lived experience of the past that enables Achille to see *its* presence in *his* present. Walcott briefly and evocatively heals the rupture when the tribe celebrates Achille's feast, wearing the same costumes and dancing the same steps as he and Philoctete do in their St. Lucian Boxing Day celebrations; Africa and St. Lucia are joined in these lingering, syncretically adapted rituals, and Walcott emphasizes the link between Achille's two cultures by repeating the word "same" six times in the last five stanzas of Chapter XXVI, four of these in the final stanza, in which each line ends with "the same" and the last sentence is just that phrase repeated twice.

As soon as Achille achieves this insight, though, things fall apart: his ancestral tribe is captured and sold into slavery by other Africans. Achille must confront his helplessness in the face of this history; he stands "with useless arms" amidst the raid and can only watch as his ancestors become "a chain of men / linked by their wrists with vines," a "line of ants" marching into slavery. Just as his knowledge of his ancestors' culture only becomes complete when Achille lives their folk-ways, though, his knowledge of his incapacity to alter history achieves completeness only when it too is embodied and enacted. Taking an oar from the abandoned village as his weapon, Achille ambushes the end of the raiding party, kills a "grinning laggard," and plans to liberate his ancestors by repeating the ambush. His chase comes to an end, though, when "a cord / of thorned vine" captures and wounds his heel. Like his epic namesake, Achille is undone at once by an unprotected heel, by his own wrath, and by the inevitability of the foreknown and foretold.

The closing stanza of this episode condenses a number of important images into a single sentence that articulates the failure of a strategy dependent upon a return to Africa and the past:

> Ants crawled over Achille
> as his blind eyes stared from the mud, still as the archer
> he had brained, the bow beside him, and the broken oar. (148)

The crawling ants recall the women hauling coal at Castries and foreshadow the ants Ma Kilman will follow to the cure for Philoctete's wound. As Breslin writes, the repeated image of ants becomes a symbol of "anonymously laboring Caribbean people" and of their "persistence and disproportionate strength."[36] The image binds Achille's experience to that of the Narrator, who imagines himself as an ant on an atlas when he awakens from his own nightmare descent into Soufriere. The blind eyes here also link the moment to other persons and episodes; elsewhere in the poem they belong to Homer, to his contemporary Caribbean counterpart, Seven Seas, to St. Lucia's namesake, and, again, to the Narrator. The bow here resonates with Philoctete, whose Sophoclean antecedent is an Achaian bowman. Even the phrase "stared from the mud" seems to look forward to the icy head that speaks to the Narrator in Soufriere. Each of these images is, at some point in the poem, associated with vocation and responsibility. Here, though, they are bundled in a tableau of failure. Walcott's alliteration in the closing line—"brained," "bow," "beside," "broken"—emphasizes the inefficacy of Achille's wrath. The oar that might steer a boat has been rendered useless by its misuse as a weapon. While the descent into the past must be undertaken, then, it must also be completed with a return to the present, just as the easy way down to Avernus (myth) must be followed by the difficult climb back up to the world of the living (history). Achille has failed to change the future because he has tried to act in the irrevocable past. Moreover, he has left himself with no way home, with a broken bow and no golden bough.

On one hand, Achille's journey to this African Underworld confirms the dismissal of Africa familiar not only from Book One, where Warwick criticizes the barber's Garveyist fantasies, but also from "The Muse of History," where Walcott writes of contemporary poets' historical preoccupations as "the malaria of nostalgia and the delirium of revenge," and where he argues that "morbidity is the inevitable result" of poets' myopic focus on "the rusted slave wheel of the sugar factory, cannon, chains, the crusted amphora of cutthroats, all the paraphernalia of degradation and cruelty which we exhibit as history."[37] On the other hand, though, Achille's imagined sojourn in the African past and his imagined experience of the Middle Passage are necessary elements in his healing, his recovery of a sense of his own identity. The self-revision here is enacted not only in the episode's plot but also in its allusive texture, so that Achille's time in Africa is also Walcott's, for the katabatic narrative he writes for his protagonist is shaped not only by the descents of Aeneas and Dante, but also by the otherworldly adventures narrated by Nigerian novelist Amos Tutuola in *My Life in the Bush of Ghosts* (1954) and *The Wild Hunter in the Bush of Ghosts* (published in 1982, though written in 1948). In Tutuola's work, a narrator makes his magical way to the land of the dead and, once there, undergoes various picaresque trials based on Yoruba folk tales of ghosts and gods.[38] The narrator of *The Wild Hunter* finds himself in the Bush of Ghosts after his father's death, while the narrator of *My Life* is able to enter the otherworld after running miles to escape enemies and wild animals because of his precocious understanding of the difference between good and bad. Achille has also lost his father, and his participation in the rituals of his ancestral tribe closely resembles Tutuola's narrator's experience among the river ghosts in *My Life* (he joins in communal singing and becomes intoxicated by the smoke of an enormous pipe filled with ghost tobacco).[39] The Africa to which Achille travels in his sunstroke dream and the communion he experiences with his ancestors there synthesize the cultural legacies of the Western traditions of *nekuia* and *katabasis* and the Yoruba stories retold in works like Tutuola's, performing not the amnesia that Walcott calls the "true history of the New World," but a concerted attempt at recovering—in the episode's plot and its entire textual fabric—the forgotten past.[40]

If an Anchises figure welcomed Achille to this African otherworld, it is a Tiresias figure (and a poet) that provides him the way home. This mode of return enacts the recovery of the past that Walcott implicitly advocates in place of the return to Africa that he rejects. When he makes his way back to the abandoned village after the raid, Achille once again finds the griot and listens to his song, the narrative of slaves' suffering. That suffering includes not only physical pain and privation, but also the loss of culture when the Ashanti, the Mandingo, the Ibo, the Guinea feel "the sea-wind tying them into one nation," and when the hunter feels the loss of his sapling lance, the weaver his unrepaired straw fishpot, and each the loss of his own name and the tribal names for things (150–51). The song is Achille's way home because it traces the line of forgetting along which he descends from Afolabe. With the chapter's closing line, "always the word 'never,' and never the word 'again,'" Walcott brings Achille full circle, back up from his sojourn in the Underworld, ready to be awakened by his mate. And when he awakens, Achille remembers; he has recovered what the generations were forced to forget. In his 1994 poem *Turner*, David Dabydeen offers a striking figure for cultural forgetting, the contrast with which clarifies Walcott's commitment in *Omeros* to recovery rather than forgetting. The tribal shaman, Manu, breaks his jouti necklace, whose beads are the tribe's memories and mores, scattering and disorganizing what had been a pattern handed down "from his father and those before." He tells the children who gather handfuls of the beads that "in the future time each must learn to live / Beadless in a foreign land; or perish."[41] Where the drowned slave in Dabydeen's poem is bereft of any memory that connects him to the past, Achille recovers a pattern that enables him to recognize its lingering presence as one strand of his contemporary culture.

Achille's immersion in Africa is matched a few chapters later by Philoctete's immersion in Ma Kilman's cauldron. The latter episode draws out and makes explicit the possibility for healing left in tatters and implicit upon Achille's awakening; moreover, it strengthens the link between Achille's experience in the African Underworld and the Narrator's in Soufriere and in so doing helps to clarify the historical poetics Walcott explores and enacts in *Omeros*. Before turning to Philoctete's healing, it is useful to see how clearly Walcott links the fisherman's story and the Narrator's. I have mentioned that the Narrator sees that he and Philoctete share the same wound and the same cure. In this episode, when Ma Kilman has found the plant that will heal Philoctete's wound, the Narrator interrupts and sees in her "my mother, my grandmother, my great-great- / grandmother," as well as "their coal-carrying mothers" (245). Sharing a history of "shame" and "self-hate," the Narrator and the St. Lucian fishermen are all wounded. All, then, depend upon the obeah-woman, the syncretic sybil who can understand the language of the ants, recover the knowledge of the ancestors, and find the reeking bloom that blossoms from a transplanted African seed. Philoctete's cure is Achille's cure is the Narrator's cure. And since Philoctete bears a traditional association with the figure of the artist, the metonymic chain between the healing of the fisherman's wound and the healing of poetry itself is strengthened.[42]

Achille's journey and Philoctete's cure are most obviously linked by Africa. Achille travels to a dream version of that continent to meet his ancestors and begin a healing process, while Philoctete descends into Ma Kilman's cauldron and a healing bath whose key ingredient originates in Africa. A sea-swift, or its cruciform shadow, leads Achille to Africa; similarly, a swift "carried the strong seed in its stomach / centuries ago" from Africa to St. Lucia, aiming "to carry the cure / that precedes every wound" (239). After the long and arduous journey, the swift reaches "the horned island" and ejects the seed. While the bird dies soon after, "the vine grew its own wings" and "climbed like the ants, the ancestors of Achille, / the women carrying coals." The final image, of course, connects the episode not only to Achille's African sojourn but also to the Narrator's encounter with Warwick in Book One. The chapter's final line strengthens this link; as the transplanted weed grows stronger, a lizard (referring to the island's creation myth) crawls up it "foot by sallow foot," the pun on meter recalling the similar pun Warwick makes to connect the Narrator's work to the women's walking.

What must be brewed for the bath to heal Philoctete's unclosed wound? The swift-carried seed is not simply a figure for Africa; as Warwick's shade made clear in Book One, as Achille's sojourn makes clear in Book Three, returning to Africa is impossible, not least because the ancestral homeland is, as Warwick says, a "phantom Africa." Recovery of history as lived experience, rather than a doomed attempt to return to or change it, is the necessary act. The seed figures history's wound on African bodies and souls in the Middle Passage. What will heal Philoctete is immersion not in Africa or its history or culture but in "the wound of the flower," in the shame and rage "festering for centuries," in the marked body that "reeked with corrupted blood," and "in the mind / ashamed of its flesh, its hair" (244).[43]

While it is Philoctete who most obviously descends in this episode (into the cauldron to be cured), the story in chapters XLVII and XLVIII belongs to Ma Kilman, as well; she seeks the "sybilline cure"'s crucial plant, and must undertake her own bodily engagement with the land in order to find it. Leaving Mass early in the morning, Ma Kilman is at first frustrated in her search; she cannot recall the healing plant's location. The hat and wig she wears to Mass and the ritual's lingering smell of incense conspire to obscure the path she must take. Though she sees that the ants following her from church signal "a language," she can neither recognize nor understand it. Like Achille, she has lost the names that once bound people to the land and the knowledge of their ancestors. Like the Narrator, she is alienated from her home. The thicket in which she finally finds herself, though, is aswarm with deities "waiting to be known by name." Thinned by the thinning belief in them, these gods distil their rituals and power "in the whorled corolla of that stinking flower," the weed carried from Africa by the sea-swift (242).

As Breslin notes, though, Ma Kilman's Catholicism "competes with her faded ancestral links to African deities."[44] She is able to find the necessary plant only when she removes her hat, with its fake berries and "false beads," only when she takes off her henna wig of horsehair and undertakes a bodily communion not with Christ but with St. Lucia. Walcott's diction joins sybil and soil; Ma Kilman's hair is figured as moss while the "moss in the dark / wood" is figured as "coiled green follicles." When she touches her bare head to the ground, the ants scurry "through the wiry curls" of both moss and hair, "passing each other // the same message" (243). It is a message Ma begins to understand: "her mossed skull heard // the ants talking the language of her great-grandmother" (244). This communion with St. Lucia and recovery of her ancestral language enable Ma to find the distillation of Africa and of slavery's suffering. Like Achille on his way from ancestral Africa back to the present, she follows the chain of exploitation that leads back into the African past.

The transplanted African flower is the crucial ingredient, but the vessel in which Ma Kilman brews the root is also an important component of Philoctete's cure. "One of those cauldrons from the old sugar mill," the pot is a relic of colonial exploitation. Walcott describes it in military terms (it resembles a helmet knocked off during an infantry charge) and calls its mouth "the scream / of centuries" (246). Like the flower, it symbolizes a specific mode of historical suffering. Once it is filled with "seawater and sulphur" (signs of the Middle Passage and the Underworld), once it boils and bubbles, the cauldron comes also to resemble Soufriere; indeed, when Ma Kilman leads Philoctete to enter the bath, Walcott calls the concoction "gurgling lava." To enter this brew is to enter history-as-suffering, history-as-shame. As Achille does during his African sojourn and as the Narrator will during his katabatic descent, Philoctete confronts a distillation of his own dispossession. When he remains immersed in this noxious stew beyond what he feels he can bear (he starts to rise and is "rammed" back in by Ma Kilman), when, in other words, the confrontation is complete, the stubborn poisons bequeathed by that history leach out. Philoctete feels his sore "drain in the seethe," feels the brew "drag / the slime from his shame" (247). His cure is complete.

His cure is also apparently collective. As Philoctete's drained wound closes and heals, historical defeat is undone and forgotten language is recalled. A dead warrior is resurrected, his bow leaping back into his hand as if in a film run backward. The image alludes to the Greek Philoctetes (a bowman who regains his bow and his proficiency with it when his wound is healed and who then uses that bow to effect an intervention into history), but since the bow is also related to the Bight of Benin (the bow that shot the swift like an arrow toward the Caribbean), the image also suggests the recovery of Africa, of all that was lost when the empty-handed slaves were transported. When Philoctete stands up from the bath he is, like the risen Christ, a new Adam. More than this, though, the land itself (as Ramazani suggests) is renewed through the healing of this figure: "And the yard was Eden. And its light the first day's" (248).[45] Most important, this shedding of shame accumulated over centuries generalizes the individual discoveries of Achille and Ma Kilman; the lost language is rediscovered. The resurrected warrior is released from the burden of a "wrong name" and his grasp of an oar is figured by "the ident- // ical closure of a mouth around its name" (248). Philoctete's purged shame is "the shame of the loss of words." His recovery is theirs.

The collective recovery, though, is (always and necessarily) incomplete. In its closing moments, the chapter returns to the Narrator, who is at first apparently healed by Philoctete's performance of the Fisher King's role. His love for the island, though, turns out to be "common as dirt," insufficient, weak, and weeping, because it derives from the Narrator's faulty vision. The fault is not with his vision's clarity; the rain has made it so clear he can count "the barrack-arches on the Morne" (249). Rather, he looks "down from the wrong height, not like Philoctete "limping among his yams." An allusion that foreshadows his eventual *katabasis* suggests the only solution. With his newly clear eyes, the Narrator gazes toward the heights and sees the rain over Soufriere. He imagines it "cooling the bubbling pits of // the Malebolge." The renewal effected by Philoctete's cure, the recovery of lost language and an intimate relationship with both land and history, allows the Narrator to imagine (to see, in his mind) "proof of a self-healing island." It is only when he undertakes his own descent, though, when he loses the clear vision allowed by the wrong height and sees the island through its own eyes (and not the sightless eyes of the tradition) that he will fully share in Philoctete's cure.

And this is the point. The climactic episodes of what Van Sickle calls the Narrator's plot in Books One and Seven, episodes in which the Narrator experiences explicitly necromantic and vocationally focused encounters, frame and highlight these crucial episodes of the "town plot," episodes in which Achille and Philoctete are immersed in the history that brings their ancestors and their culture from

Africa to St. Lucia. The Narrator's descents perform the same work as Achille's and Philoctete's. While Achille's and Philoctete's "exorcisms" (to borrow another word the Narrator uses when he awakens from the nightmare of Soufriere) involve the expulsion of historic shame to enable a richer life on St. Lucia, the Narrator's involves expiation of his *literary* sins as well. Where self-purification is the goal for the fishermen, poetic purgation is the Narrator's burden. The Narrator's necromantic experiences suggest that responsible poetry is inspired by and works to represent or witness the history of slavery and colonial exploitation. Moreover, such poetry must register the simultaneous necessity and insufficiency of literary traditions associated with the colonizers; the women carrying coal in Castries must be seen through eyes other than (as well as through) the sightless eyes of Homer. European trappings—blinding "elegies" and "the temporal lament for a smoky Troy"—must be stripped away and a descent into St. Lucia's unique land, into its inhabitants' unique history, including that history's African roots, must be endured. Only through this process can the suppurating wound of historical shame be healed and the complex cultural legacy of the colony be claimed and celebrated. The wound is its own cure, the poet's weakness his own strength. As Eliot might put it, the fire of shame and the rose of pride, the fire of loss and the rose of reconciliation, are one; only in the recognition and embodiment of this synthesis will all manner of things be well.

As they are, at least for the moment, at the conclusion of Walcott's poem. Philoctete and Achille dress in traditional costumes and dance as women-warriors, renewing by reexperiencing both their African heritage and the pain of its loss. Achille and Helen move in together, Achille having decided to raise the child with which Helen is pregnant (regardless of whether he or Hector is its father) and to postpone the discussion about whether the child should have an African name. "We shall all heal," Ma Kilman says to Seven Seas in the poem's penultimate book (319). Even the Narrator seems provisionally satisfied both with himself and with his work. The sea-swift he has followed has stitched both the poem and the world, reintegrating Africa and the islands, sewing and thereby healing the "rift" or wound of the Atlantic and the history that estranges the cast of contemporary St. Lucians from their cultural roots. At home again, he finds in the island "all I needed of paradise" (320). The quest that drove him into exile, the quest for laurels, those traditional emblems of poetic accomplishment, has ended and the Narrator is satisfied with the native *laurier-cannelles* instead. He can even calmly contemplate his death—even with "so much left unspoken // by [his] chirping nib"—and hope simply that "the deep hymn // of the Caribbean" will perform his eternal "epilogue" (321). When he confronts and is accused of poetic irresponsibility, the Narrator is able to undertake a properly responsible poetry.

6

TONY HARRISON'S *V*

These days, we most commonly encounter the dead in cemeteries, and our colloquies with their shades occur in the spaceless precincts of our minds and memories. Perhaps the most common such scenes involve the silent communion with departed parents, and it is likely that the narratives and rituals that make up the necromantic and katabatic traditions in Western literature derive at least in part from cults of ancestor worship that predate even the ancient pilgrimage to Tiresias's tomb. Parents certainly play important parts in the founding texts of these traditions: Odysseus discovers his mother's death when he sees her among the shades, and the reality of this fact is born in on him when he tries and fails to embrace her, while Anchises takes up the prophetic role for Aeneas so that national destiny and filial piety are tightly intertwined. While the poems from which Eliot draws much of the compound ghost's speech are provoked by the poets' visits to the graves of other poets (Mallarmé on Poe, Yeats on Swift), the more common graveside meditation surely happens in the cemeteries where our ancestors, especially our parents, are interred.

What do the visitors to familial tombs seek? Comfort in the sculpted beauty of the obsequious landscape, perhaps, or a sense of the dead parents' presence. Sometimes the living might even hope for guidance, as if they could conjure the parental voice by standing over the grave. Or, if not advice, maybe they seek a sense of acceptance, a silent benediction from the parents resting in peace. Given the emotional needs that drive the living to their parents' graves, imagine the depth of reaction when one encounters litter and graffiti, the latter not only along the way but actually on the familial gravestone. Imagine the violence that might arise from within when one is accosted by an aggressive and obscene vagrant, an unemployed, beer-drinking ruffian marked by clothing and shaved head as a member of a subculture hostile and utterly disrespectful to all that one holds dear, all that one is. This is the scenario Tony Harrison develops in his 1985 poem *v.*, when the poem's first-person speaker (also named "Harrison") first finds beer cans and graffiti around and on his parents' gravestone and then finds himself in a shouting match with a young skinhead. Setting and stanza have led critics to read *v.* as a variation on Thomas Gray's "Elegy Written in a Country Churchyard" (c. 1750).[1] Both are set in graveyards; both are cast in elegiac quatrains; both ponder mortality, monuments, and memory. Most important, both are poems of vocational inquiry, meditations on the conditions of possibility that underwrite the individual poet and poetry itself in a specific historical moment. Gray famously writes "Some mute inglorious Milton here may rest, Some Cromwell guiltless of his country's blood." In a similar vein, Harrison notes that a Byron and a Wordsworth are buried near his own eventual resting place, but that since Wordsworth was an organ builder and this Byron "tanned / luggage" they are only "peers of a sort."[2] When the spray-painting skinhead appears one-third of the way through his poem, however, Harrison steps more firmly than Gray does into the main stream of the necromantic tradition. Most critics have failed to read Harrison's poem as invoking the *nekuia*; Sandie Byrne briefly mentions that *v.* is "an anti-pastoral elegy" that depicts an "urban Limbo" but does not follow up the implications of his insight.[3] The necromantic tradition is an important interpretive horizon for Harrison's poem, though, for while Gray can peacefully contemplate his elegiac resources in the quiet context of gravestones, Harrison is called on to defend both poetry and his own poetic practice against claims lodged by a spokesman for history's victims. Poetry as transformative Yeatsian gaiety is a hard sell in bleak industrial northern and divided Leeds, though, and the set of easy assumptions about poetry's value and purpose with which Harrison begins *v.* must themselves be transformed, rethought and rearticulated in the context of the social, political, cultural, and generational divisions condensed in the poet's skinhead interlocutor.

In this chapter, I will show how the necromantic encounter on Beeston Hill provokes Harrison to defend poetry against the charge that it is at once implicated in and impotent against injustice. Indeed, the poem mounts two different defenses. Harrison first stands up for the genre in the terms dictated by the skinhead's challenge. Recognizing the inevitable failure of this attempt (though not, I think, registering full awareness of its problems), Harrison retreats from the confrontation and, safe at home, elaborates an alternative defense of poetry. Rather than a weapon or wand to be wielded, poetry comes to be seen in terms of coal: over time, Harrison suggests, it can transform the dead matter of a history constituted in conflict into a source of comfort that ultimately enables love. As it does in the work of Eliot and others, the necromantic narrative here structures a revision of the poet's sense of the medium's role in the world. In *v.*, as he retreats from the skinhead in the cemetery Harrison is also retreating from the aggressive poetics of his own earlier career. I will argue, though, that the kinder, gentler poetry arrived at and implicitly advocated in the poem's second half is itself subverted by Harrison's figurative logic, which erodes even as it articulates the underpinning of this poetry.

Before turning to what I see Harrison's poem doing, though, I need to make clear what I think it is not doing: intervening or imagining poetry's capacity to intervene in the Coal Miners' Strike of 1984–1985. The strike of the National Union of Mineworkers (NUM), in response to a series of mine closures in the early 1980s and the National Coal Board's plans for further closures, quickly proved to be far more than a typical industrial labor action. As Jonathan and Ruth Winterton write, the strike "represented the most important industrial stoppage since the General Strike and coal lock-out of 1926."[4] The two events both "assumed the character of historic battles between labour and capital," with the NUM in the 1980s "attempting to resist unemployment, preserve communities and protect long-term national policy" while the government aimed to "subordinate labour, restructure industry and impose the imperatives of the market."[5] The strike was enormously costly for the Union and its rank and file; because the strike was ruled illegal (it was not based on a secret ballot of the entire Union membership), striking miners had no access to social security payments. As a result, and because the stakes were seen by both sides to be quite high (the Thatcher government was determined not to give in to labor as the Conservative governments of the early 1970s had), the strike was deeply divisive, with pitched battles breaking out between miners and police (the latter sometimes supported by special army units) in Orgreave, Maltby, and other South Yorkshire locations.

Harrison wrote *v.* during the strike and first published the poem in *The London Review of Books* in January, 1985. It reached a broader audience in 1987 when BBC Channel Four broadcast a film version. The controversy over the poem's colorful vocabulary led Bloodaxe, the poem's publisher, to release a second edition in 1989; this edition included photographs of Leeds and of Beeston Hill Cemetery (by Graham Sykes), as well as a selection of reviews, essays, and letters about the poem.[6] The time of the poem's composition, Bloodaxe's blurb for the first edition (which foregrounds the Miners' Strike), and the controversy over its various publications have led some critics to read *v.* as a direct commentary on (or even intervention in) the strike. Luke Spencer, for example, writes that the poem's epigraph from Arthur Scargill (head of the NUM) "seems to align the poem with the mining communities' resistance to [National Coal Board head] Ian MacGregor's programme of pit closures."[7] As Terry Eagleton wrote in his 1986 review of the poem, though, "the actual Miners' Strike impinges on *v.* hardly at all, other than in a moving epigraph taken from Arthur Scargill."[8] Helmut Haberkamm is closer to the mark than most when he calls *v.* "a moving elegy of the decline of the North and the end of a national consensus in Thatcherite England," but I want, in what follows, to complicate Haberkamm's judgment (shared by many readers) that Harrison is therefore "an eminently political and socially committed writer."[9] In his struggle with the skinhead (the revenant spirit of this necromantic encounter), Harrison has real difficulty marking out and defending the sort of poetry-as-praxis Haberkamm leads us to expect. Instead, *v.* arrives at a justification for poetry that relies on its *distance* from the rough and tumble of political conflict.

*   *   *

In the first half of the poem, during which he is accosted by the skinhead, Harrison assumes, and when pressed articulates, a great deal of importance for his chosen medium. Before the skinhead appears, Harrison holds two unquestioned assumptions about poetry. First, poetry is at least as valuable as, and perhaps more valuable than, food and drink. In the first stanza, he metonymically and alliteratively links his work to the work of food providers: "butcher, publican, baker, now me, bard" (3). The gesture is one in a long series throughout Harrison's career. As Sandie Byrne writes, the poet "often reiterates that he has worked hard to become a poet, and earns his living from poetry, and he links it to the occupations of his forebears."[10] Forging such links enables Harrison to claim the position of laborer, his "equal worthiness...to manual workers."[11] More than this, the poet's verbal mastery guarantees a kind of nourishment; coming at the end of the metonymic chain, "bard" implicitly supersedes or subsumes "butcher, publican, baker," offering a metaphoric sustenance more valuable than beef, beer, or bread. Harrison's second assumption regards poetry's power rather than its value; it surfaces when he reads and reinterprets words and signs in the cemetery. This liminal space is a text-rich environment: names, occupations, and fragments of verse (including some in Latin) are carved into tombstones, while obscenities, football team names, and other graffiti are spray-painted on them. Confident in his own "power to master words," Harrison relies upon the "magic wand" of his pen to effect a poetic transformation; his bardic power can turn the painted scrawl on his parents' tombstone—a graffito in support of the Leeds soccer team (UNITED)—into a prayer: "his UNITED means 'in Heaven' for their sake" (7). The poet complacently assumes his ability to "redeem / an act intended as mere desecration" (7).

Easy to hold as he walks alone in the cemetery, these assumptions come to seem weak indeed when vigorously challenged. Interpreting the obscenities he finds spray-painted all over the cemetery as a *"cri de-coeur* because Man dies," Harrison's speaker is brought up short: *"So what's a* cri-de-coeur, *cunt?"* (9). From his very first utterance, the poem's revenant spirit, the poet's skinhead alter ego, deals with complacent assumptions in short order.[12] At the end of a screed about how unemployment will leave him with nothing to have carved on his own stone, he takes Harrison's own earlier assumption that "bard" will be a fit occupation for his epitaph, a fit syntagmatic substitute for "butcher, baker, publican," and throws it in the poet's face: *"They'll chisel fucking poet when they do you / and that, yer cunt, 's a crude four-letter word"*(10; italics in original). The difference of opinion on poetry's value is absolute. Poetry's transformative power comes in for a similarly vicious dismissal. When Harrison shouts at his ghostly interlocutor that his purpose is to "to give some higher meaning to your scrawl," the vandal retorts *"Don't fucking bother, cunt! Don't waste your breath!"* (10; italics in original).

Against the skinhead's claims—not only that poetry is without value or power, but also that Harrison has betrayed his family and class precisely by becoming a poet—Harrison offers the poem's first defense of poetry, arguing for poetry's similarity to the skinhead's vandalism. He begins by appealing to the literary traditions that shape his work, and offers Rimbaud as an example of "skin and poet united" (10). Unconvinced, his interlocutor simply shouts *"no more Greek"* (italics in original). Harrison then adduces his own vandal past, recounting a youthful fire extinguisher attack he carried out against high culture (a soprano singing at a political rally). To Harrison's claim that "'They yelled 'Damn vandal' after me that day," the skinhead retorts *"Ah've 'eard all that from old farts past their prime"* (12; italics in original). The conclusion of this colloquy ought to be evidence of Harrison's success; the skinhead tacitly agrees with Harrison's equation of their work: *"Who needs / yer fucking poufy words. Ah write mi own"* (italics in original). He does so, though, in the context of a strenuous rejection of Harrison's project. The two iterative acts are diametrically opposed: poetry is class betrayal; vandalism is solidarity. This first defense is doomed in part because the speaker himself doesn't buy it. For all his rhetoric of similarity, Harrison shares the skinhead's belief that the two are not at all alike. This is made clear by his appalled reaction when, at the confrontation's climax, Harrison presses the skinhead to sign his work: "He aerosoled his name, and it was mine" (13). Harrison is surprised, but the poem suggests he should not be. Surely the pen he wields is similar to the skinhead's spray-paint can; the fire extinguisher he recalls using in his youth is even more similar. And long before he realizes that they share a name, the poet has shown that he shares the skinhead's language, not only individual slang words but also the wholesale dialect that marks the skinhead's speech: "No, shut yer gob awhile. Ah'll tell yer 'ow' " (11). The poet's surprise springs from his own implicit rejection of the vandal's project. Spray-painting is the poetry of untutored youth, a developmental stage Harrison might once have gone through (both literally, but also in the figurative vandalism staged in such poems as "Them & [uz]," in which he writes "So right, yer buggers then! We'll occupy / your lousy leasehold Poetry") but one he clearly sees himself as having left behind.[13] While the speaker has argued for the similarity of poetry and vandalism, of himself and the skinhead, he has continued to assume their difference; when the poles of each opposition prove to be identical, Harrison is shocked into a reconsideration of his assumptions and into the alternative defense of poetry the last third of the poem mounts.

Before moving on to that defense, however, I want to argue that the failure of the failed defense is due not to its grounding in assumptions about poetry's power and value (which the poem ends up affirming anyway) but to its predication of that power and value on a gendered model of mastery. In other words, Harrison fails to convince the skinhead not because of explicit assumptions the two don't share, but because of implicit assumptions that, like their Loiners dialect, they *do* share. Those shared assumptions equate power with masculine mastery and, as a corollary, they equate passivity with femininity and death. Poet and skinhead share not only these assumed equations but also profound anxiety about their own locations on the gender-power grid they form. Each repeatedly, even obsessively, calls the other "cunt," and while this might exemplify what Haberkamm describes as Harrison's attempt to "guarantee the authenticity and immediacy of his diction" or illustrate lexicographer Jonathon

Green's claim that "in some circumstances cunt…is so frequent and so repetitive as virtually to lose its shock or taboo value and become a neutral synonym for 'person,' " it is also what Spencer calls typical "misogynistic verbal violence," as if the two speakers have agreed in advance that identification with the female (through this reduction to the genitals) is the worst possible insult.[14] But each also worries that he *is* a "cunt"—either actually emasculated or rendered passive in a way he understands to be emasculating. The skinhead rants about the enforced passivity of unemployment, about the nothingness he not only endures but also feels that he *becomes* on the dole: "*When dole-wallahs fuck off to the void / what'll t'mason carve up for* their *jobs?*" (10; italics in original). He lashes out at Harrison, not only calling him a "cunt" but also suggesting that poetry is as unmanned and unmanning as the dole; "*Look at this cunt, Wordsworth*" (10; italics in original). And while poetic labor provides a vocational identity that can be carved on Harrison's stone, the skinhead revalues the honorific "poet": "*that, yer cunt, 's a crude four-letter word*" (italics in original). (Harrison's syntax strongly suggests just which obscenity applies; the crucial phrase can be also read "cunt's a crude four-letter word.") Stung by the skin's insults, the poet suffers similar worries and responds in kind, returning every "cunt" he receives: "Listen, cunt!" (10), "ungrateful cunts like you" (10), "You piss-artist skinhead cunt" (10).

Masculine anxiety marks each speaker's self-defensive gestures as well. The speaker uses a quotation not only to align poetry with vandalism but also to perpetrate an emasculating act of verbal violence. When he mentions Rimbaud, he concludes "the *autre* that *je est* is fucking you" (10). In one reading of the line, "fucking" is a gerund modifying the skinhead (Rimbaud's "other" is, really and truly ["fucking"], "you"); the quotation applies to the skinhead's alienation. At the same time, though, if "fucking" is read as verb rather than gerund, then Harrison is latently (and syntactically) violating his interlocutor ("the other that I is [I] is [am] fucking you"). The skinhead gives as good as he gets (though in his own idiom). He violently replies to Harrison's French "*autre*" and "*je est*," ordering the poet to stop speaking "Greek" and threatening him with bodily injury: "*Ah'll boot yer fucking balls to Kingdom Come*" (11; italics in original). He aims his threat directly at the biological locus of the poet's masculinity (not only his balls but his "fucking balls"), as if to defuse what he perceives as the poet's threatening masculinity. The skin's reaction is motivated by a sense that he is being condescended to, of course, and by his understanding that "language reveals its…nature as a means of power," but the mistaking of French for Greek suggests that he also suspects he's the object of a come-on ("Greek" having long carried the slang connotation of homoeroticism).[15] Harrison responds to being called out as "cunt," "wanker" (masturbatory), and "poufy" (homosexual) by narrating an anecdote in which he aggressively attacks a figure for effeminate high art (the soprano) in retaliation for her artistic "prick-tease of the soul" (11). Threatened by the "wobbly warble" and its "uplift beyond all reason and control," young Tony enhances his phallic authority (by picking up a fire extinguisher) and orgasmically sprays her.

The two male figures' responses—to each other and to their lives' circumstances—coalesce around fear of being rendered passive. Each metaphorically equates passivity with loss of identity, with death and the void of nonbeing. Each also assumes and participates in the cultural gendering of passivity, death, and nonbeing as feminine, the association of the feminine with a loss of masculine authority (and *authority*). This set of assumptions calls from poet and skinhead alike a spasmodic recourse to evidence (or fictions) of compensatory masculine mastery.

When he is forced to realize that the identification he has strategically courted with the skinhead is not only actual but also total, Harrison seems to recognize his enmeshment in an unproductive set of assumptions; he finds that he has lost the transformative power with which he thought his pen-as-magic-wand was endowed: "The UNITED that I'd wished onto the nation," he concedes, is "once more a mindless desecration" (13). Ultimately, wandering around the graveyard, phallus in hand (whether as a pen or as a spray-paint can), is neither magical nor transformative, but simply masturbatory.

*   *   *

Helmut Haberkamm argues that "the poem is meant to serve as a means to achieve representativeness and publicity on behalf of this non-reading 'artless' youth," but that motive is explicitly rejected within the poem itself. The skinhead shouts that *"A book ...'s not worth a fuck"* (10; italics in original), forcefully challenging both poetry's generative capacity and its pleasure. When he sees that the skinhead is himself, Harrison implicitly admits that his antagonist has got a point. *v.* is better read, therefore, as Harrison's attempt to think through the failure of this project (*his* project in earlier work) and to revise his understanding of what poetry can do with respect to the skinhead and all that he represents.

Harrison responds to the skinhead with a long retreat. He walks through the cemetery and through the streets of Leeds, remarking all the way on how things have changed since his childhood—empty houses for sale, storefronts changed from "Co-op" to "Kashmir Muslim Club," empty churches covered with graffiti—and revisiting the changes through the eyes of his father. The poem traces his path away from the cemetery to the domestic space of his home. At the same time, it enacts a retreat from the powerful poetry Harrison at first assumes possible, from what Terry Eagleton characterizes as the Mayakovskyan model of political poet suggested by the skinhead, and into the modes of elegiac and romantic compensation.[16] Harrison retreats not only to home but also to "my woman," and, finally, "to bed / where opposites are sometimes unified" (15). Only at the end of *v.* does Harrison set this poetics against the skinhead (and against his own opening assumptions) and offer any kind of judgment on it.

Harrison's second defense of poetry, to which he dedicates the last part of the poem, offers the medium as a transformative force. He digs beneath the cemetery to the "cavernous" "great worked-out black hollow" of the mine that yawns "further underneath" and grounds his reimagination of poetry in the substance of coal. Given the poem's context (perhaps "paratext" is more precise) in the Miners' Strike, its coal imagery might suggest, as Harrison does elsewhere, the sense of mines as "the classic battlefield between capital and labour...where the expense of extracting coal was entirely in the sweated labour of men, women, and children."[17] Sandie Byrne argues that mining is "still important," but that its significance has shifted so that it is now "the classic battlefield between the capital-owning class which is closing [mines] down and the diminishing labour-force."[18] Harrison does refer to that battle in his catalogue of "all the versuses of life": "the unending violence of US and THEM, / personified in 1984 / by Coal Board MacGregor and the N.U.M." (5). Harrison's defense of poetry in *v.*, though, builds not on an intervention *in* this battle but on a suppression or evasion *of* it. Byrne is right that "the whole poem is literally grounded on the worked-out pit which once helped to support the economy of Leeds," but the poem fails to forge a causal link between the contemporary battle between capital and labor.[19] Instead, Harrison grounds his poetics on the domestic and the aesthetic *as opposed to* the public and the political that Byrne finds coal symbolizing.

In *v.*, coal figures a transformation wrought not through the heroic wand wielding with which the poem begins and not through the hard-won translation of historic suffering into beauty and meaning, but through a passive and almost gestational patience. "A 1000 ages made coal-bearing seams," Harrison writes, and later he adds that coal "was lush swamp club moss and tree fern / at least 300 million years ago" (16). As Spencer argues, "Harrison invokes geomorphology as a global and timeless process which, by affecting us all, can be regarded as a species of unifying destiny."[20] The urban blight the poet catalogues on his way out of Leeds happened within the lifetime of his father, and this pace of change suggests a political response. Instead, the poem becomes what Spencer describes as an "extended meditation on the insignificance of social ills under the aspect of eternity."[21] Harrison takes the long view: we'll all be coal in the end.

Geological time, however, is only part of coal's significance; coal also stands in for the domestic and aesthetic realms in which the poet finds some consolation for the violent disunity that characterizes the public sphere. Harrison first associates coal explicitly with the domestic and the feminine—coal is what he comes home to—and he directly opposes both home and woman to Leeds, memory, and the cemetery: "Home," he writes, "never to return" to Beeston Hill except as "bits of clinker scooped out of [his] urn" (16). Syntax and line-break consociate couple and coal—"in our hearth we burn." Moreover, home is where the bed is, that most intimate space in which, unlike the world full of recalcitrant "v."s out there, "opposites are sometimes unified." Harrison next juxtaposes coal and the aesthetic. The latter is represented here, as it is in the anecdote he recounts in the cemetery, by a soprano. The couple listens to opera (*Lulu*) while a coal fire warms the room: "Shillbottle cobbles, Alban Berg high D" (16). Removed from political space, though, art-as-soprano seems to offer not the "prick-tease of the soul" that so incensed young Tony but a satisfying resignation to "decay." This is, perhaps, because decay is precisely the ground of coal-as-figure. Waste and dead matter— "perished vegetation"—can, under the proper conditions, become a source of illumination and comfort, and this is the substance of the poem's final defense of poetry.

It turns out, then, that poetry *can* transform the skinhead's "UNITED;" the transformation, though, is not an alchemical miracle in which dross becomes gold but is instead a chthonic processing in which dead matter becomes fuel. In the coal-warmed environment of the bedroom, the poet turns off the televised images of political struggle and turns "to love," to "the bride / I feel united to" (17). As Haberkamm writes, for Harrison "love appears to be the only escape and resort."[22] While the world outside is riven by social, political, cultural, and racial conflict ("versuses"), Harrison cuddles in the warmth provided by coal-as-transformed-death and finds an anchor in "the ones we choose to love." Haberkamm argues that Harrison shows this "love" to be "dependent on socio-political events reaching far into private lives."[23] While the result of sociopolitical events (mined coal) construct the space in which intimacy transpires, though, the events themselves are suppressed; Harrison turns *off* the TV—which broadcasts news of the outside world's conflicts, including a typical episode from the miners' strike that the poem ostensibly addresses—before turning *to* his beloved.

The poem, finally, performs what it prescribes, a turn to the intimacy of romantic love in opposition to engagement in worldly strife. As Byrne writes, this section's subtext is the "defeat (of a social conscience)."[24] Harrison's resolution is rescued for Byrne by its lack of confidence in this solution: "The joys of this fleeting life are not offered as sufficient consolation for a system the poet cannot change, and the sense of unity in personal relationships is rapidly undermined."[25] Aside from the *Lulu* reference, though, it is difficult to see what he bases this reading on; the poem does turn to Harrison's contemplation of his own death, which threatens the consolations of the bedroom, but this is to turn from one poetic universal (love) to another (mortality). Harrison thereby escapes the present's pressing claims. As Eagleton writes, the poem seeks "solace and unity" solely through "sexual relationship," as if either the ends or the means are "abstractable from the destiny of nations."[26] Harrison imagines the skinhead's response in terms that suggest he's anticipating Eagleton's critique—"his aerosol vocab would balk at LOVE"—but he proleptically accepts this condemnation because he is at least partially reassured in his assumptions about poetry's power and value: it can turn death into warmth that in turn enables love. He at once resigns from the skinhead's pissing contest and, by locating "the skin's UNITED" as the substrate for his own "LOVE," wins it.

This kind of victory through resignation characterizes Harrison's attitude throughout the poem's last few pages and is central to the idea of poetry he implicitly offers as an alternative to his earlier, anxious, and aggressive defense against the skinhead. Looking ahead to the "next millennium," he admits his grave will be hard to find and accepts that it will be "graffitied." The anger that leads him to call those who spray-painted his parents' gravestone "cunts" has dissolved in an atmosphere of acceptance. Some art-lover, he imagines, might want to clean the obscenities from the stone, but Harrison urges such a person to "leave, with the worn UNITED, one small *v*." (18). Why? Because he acknowledges the "victory" of time and decay, the "vast

coal-creating forces / that hew the body's seams to get the soul."
But leaving the "v" also means leaving the various other meanings
that the poem has posited for that letter. On one hand, we might
read this as a continuation of the poet's acceptance of the feminine
(the soprano, the beloved, the domestic); after all, "v" has been made
(crudely) to stand for "vagina."[27] On the other hand, though, the
poet is also resigned to the perpetuation of conflict ("all the versuses
of life").

Harrison's resolution of the crisis provoked by the skinhead is
unsatisfying. The poem's language and form are less compelling in the
final pages than in the cemetery scene. The domestic refrain ("Home,
home to my woman") is embarrassingly cliché, and Harrison's diction
and syntax here settle down all too harmoniously in the quatrains
where both seethed and pressed against the stanza in the poem's
first half (as Eagleton writes, that struggle between diction and form
is part of the poem's meaning).[28] More importantly, the content of
the resolution itself fails to address the skinhead's accusations and
anxieties. Like Elpenor in the eleventh book of the *Odyssey* (and
in Pound's version in Canto I), the skinhead worries that his grave
will go unmarked and he will be forgotten. Harrison confesses that
he shares this concern. As darkness falls on Beeston Hill, Harrison
disavows fears of ghosts or even of death, but confesses to a deeper
dread: "what I fear's / that great worked-out black hollow under
mine." That hollow will eventually "swallow / this place of rest and
all the resters down" (14). What Harrison fears, then, is a void vaster
than that represented by his own grave; it is the loss (the "undermin-
ing") of the ground that would support his grave (and, we might
infer, the engraved monument that would mark it). As Harrison
informs us with his homonym, the "hollow" is a coal mine; its threatening characterization suggests that Harrison does not entirely trust
the resolution with which he has consoled himself and on which he
has grounded his vocation. While we are all united in mortality, and
while, from the perspective of geological time, we will become light
and heat, that into which we will be transformed will disappear in
turn when it's dug up, will escape "insubstantial up the flue," and its
mining will threaten with subsidence all the marks we've left. Since
coal is a vocational metaphor for Harrison, since it represents the
poetic transformation Harrison enacts by remaking the dead matter
of Gray's elegy, its disappearance threatens the verbal cemetery of *v.*
as much as the Beeston Hill Cemetery in Leeds.

Finally, Harrison simply retreats from public spaces fraught with
violent opposition into domestic spaces characterized by acceptance

and unity, and by so doing retreats onto the familiar terrain of W.H. Auden's elegy for Yeats, where "poetry makes nothing happen." When Harrison shifts his gaze from the coal fire's embers to the television and finds the "old violence and old disunity" of "police v. pickets at a coke plant gate" and "the map that's color-coded Ulster / Eire," he turns the set off so that both Miners' Strike and mad Ireland fade to a "blank screen." In the end, he models and implicitly advocates a poetry that works to accept what cannot be changed, to transform the world's waste—the "tiny coffin" carried at an Irish funeral—into ephemerally glowing evidence of our need for love. Spencer calls this "formal closure" "ingenious" since it unites skinhead and skald "in being equally subject to geological forces."[29] Surely, though, Eagleton is closer to the mark when he takes Harrison to task for his "dispirited political imagination"; given the choice between "being pained primarily by oppression and being pained primarily by division and disunity," he writes, the poet chooses the latter and resigns himself to being a "bruised metaphysician."[30] It is tempting to read the retreat into domestic space, the insistent passivity, and the acceptance of both high cultural pleasures and the continuity of historic conflict as the adoption of the "feminine" poetics briefly sketched in chapter 1. Indeed, Harrison provides a sanction for this reading when he suggests to the skinhead "a sort of working marriage . . . / a blend of masculine and feminine" (12). Even if we set to one side the problematic character of a gendered cultural binary system in which the aesthetic and domestic are feminized against the stringently masculine spheres of politics and history, though, what Harrison stages in the poem is not a "blend." Rather, it is an acceptance of the binary and of poetry's location on the feminine side.

Harrison wraps his poem up with a tightly epigrammatic quatrain. Like Gray's "Elegy," *v.* concludes with an epitaph, one Harrison has planned for his own grave and which he invites readers to come and see. Harrison's epitaph is a self-deprecating recapitulation of the poem's major themes that wittily sums up the poet's sense of his project:

> *Beneath your feet's a poet, then a pit.*
> *Poetry supporter, if you're here to find*
> *how poems can grow from (beat you to it!) SHIT*
> *find the beef, the beer, the bread, then look behind.*

Beef, beer, and bread return us to the poem's opening quatrain and its assumptions about poetry's value, "SHIT" recalls the skinhead's attacks, which provoke Harrison's reconsideration of those assumptions, and the pit beneath the poet repeats Harrison's certainty that poetry, like coal, is waste transformed, a certainty that reinstates his judgment of poetry's value.

As the epitaph suggests, a seam of coal runs beneath the entire poem, from its epigraph's quotation of Arthur Scargill to the pit named in its closing quatrain. When he addresses coal and the labor of mining explicitly, though, Harrison tries either to cancel them (by literally turning off images of the strike and by metaphorically turning coal into a figure for his own work so that miners' work is occluded) or to contain them in a series of metonymic connections (with other conflicts he hopes will be resolved—v's cum UNITED's—or with death). Harrison's suppression of the Miners' Strike enables his turn toward his bride, toward love (or "LOVE"). Some critics read the epitaph as uniting art and its "social foundations," as the poem's acknowledgment of the "material reality" out of which it grows.[31] To read the epitaph (to understand the poem), however, we must accept mortality ("face this grave") and reject the public sphere ("your back to Leeds"). Since Leeds throughout the poem has represented history, the depredations of capital, and the lived experience of political divisions (between races, religions, parties, and classes), the poem's conclusion suppresses (rather than acknowledging) its own conditions of possibility.

7

SEAMUS HEANEY'S "STATION ISLAND"

When Seamus Heaney sets out to perform his own rigorous self-examination, he heads not to his dining room, nor to the cemetery or the Caribbean, but, instead, for Station Island, in County Donegal's Lough Derg. According to legend (and to some medieval maps), a cave on the island is the opening to Hell. Also known as St. Patrick's Purgatory, the island has long been the site of a Catholic penitential pilgrimage whose ritual comprises vigils, fasting, and prayer while kneeling at and walking barefoot around a series of stone beds. When they have completed the "spiritual exercises," "pilgrims are granted a Plenary Indulgence applicable to the souls in Purgatory."[1] In Heaney's poem, both of these significances are in play, as the poet undertakes the pilgrimage (driven, apparently, by a need to repent)[2] and, like Dante in Hell and on the slopes of Purgatory, encounters a series of "familiar ghosts," the shades of relatives, friends, and other writers.

Heaney's twelve-part poem announces its descent from the Eliot of "Little Gidding" (and, of course, from Dante, who provides Eliot's own model) in both its form and its preoccupations. With terza rima of varying strictness and with the sonnet as the stanza in the poem's pivotal ninth section, Heaney formally echoes both Dante and Eliot, and, like his precursors, Heaney stages encounters between his poet/ speaker and a series of revenant spirits. These encounters dwell at length on the nature of the poetic vocation and, especially, the responsibilities such a vocation might entail in the political climate of Northern Ireland after 1968. This set of issues surfaces in the work of numerous Irish writers; indeed, it is so common that Declan Kiberd begins his chapter on "Irish Literature and Irish History" (in the Oxford *History of Ireland*) by summarizing the positions:

> The points in history at which literature and politics meet have been described as a "bloody crossroads." Romantic impulses, derived from literature, allegedly lead to carnage and terror in a city's streets. Conor Cruise O'Brien has gone so far as to deride the ancient Irish

collaboration between nationalism and art as "an unhealthy intersection." There is, however, a counter-argument to the effect that art
is too potent a force to be left entirely in the hands of its creators,
and politics too pervasive in its effects to be left in the sole control of
politicians.[3]

In his essay introducing *New Irish Writing*, the poet Eamon Grennan
provides the poet's perspective on the situation. After quoting South
African poet David Yali-Manisi and Joseph Brodsky on the question
of the poet's political responsibility (Yali-Manisi: "he must agitate";
Brodsky: the poet is responsible "to the language"), Grennan offers
his synthesis of these two apparently antithetical positions:

> Part of the writer's business must always be, through his or her own
> independent use of the language, to agitate us, shake up conventional
> assumptions, unsettle readers and listeners in those areas of the self
> where we reflect on being private humans, and in those areas of our
> selves where private and public borders cross, and cross-hatch.[4]

In "Station Island," Seamus Heaney works through the question
Grennan poses, arriving at his own provisional resolution of the
vexing and vexed question of poetic responsibility. He does so not
only by engaging the immediate circumstances he faces, but also by
casting his questioning in a synthetic form imbued with vocational
and penitential significance. In an essay on Dante, Heaney gestures
toward the two traditions he brings together in "Station Island."
On one hand, he writes of the way Dante "could place himself in
an historical world yet submit that world to scrutiny from a perspective beyond history," indicating the generation of the sequence
in the example of the *Divine Comedy*, while on the other hand
he enumerates the Irish writers who had preceded him to Lough
Derg: "William Carleton, Sean O'Faolain, Patrick Kavanagh, Denis
Devlin."[5] Heaney's sequence, then, participates in the necromantic
tradition he receives from Dante and Eliot, of course, but, through
its setting at Station Island, its structure's relationship with the rituals of St. Patrick's Purgatory, and its allusions to previous Irish
writers' texts on Lough Derg, the poem also locates itself within a
specifically Irish version of the *nekuia*, so that Heaney at once takes
on the "Great Tradition" and the local literary history by which
he is intimately formed. Like Boland's in "The Journey," Heaney's
descent plays out through a synthesis of traditions that foregrounds
the specific literary, political, and ethical issues he needs to work
through.

The poet's responsibility to and in his historical moment is not a new question for Heaney when he composes "Station Island" in the mid-1980s; his 1975 volume *North* is a sustained meditation on precisely this problem. I will say more below about the provisional resolution Heaney manages in that volume, but it is clear both in the poems' ambivalent tones and in the book's reception (Ciaran Carson's review in *The Honest Ulsterman*, for example, attacked Heaney for setting himself up in the book as "the laureate of violence" and "an anthropologist of ritual killing"[6]) that it is a resolution Heaney felt a need to revisit and revise. More than this, circumstances, both for Heaney and for Northern Ireland, changed between the mid-1970s and the mid-1980s in ways that led to a reconsideration of *North* (and *Field Work*, the 1979 volume that followed it). As Peggy O'Brien has written, just as "some troubled believers feel they must do the Station to make sense of a difficult time," Heaney in 1984 undertakes the "Station" to do "urgent cultural, personal, and poetic work that needed to be done when it was done."[7] In the years after publishing *North* and *Field Work*, Heaney (who had already left Northern Ireland for the Republic in 1972), had distanced himself from his home and its Troubles, taking an appointment at Harvard in 1981 and from then on spending one semester a year in Cambridge, Massachusetts. This shift in Heaney's personal situation coincided with an intensification of the Troubles in the North. In 1980 and 1981, Republican prisoners in Northern Ireland's Long Kesh prison staged a series of protests, attempting to regain "special status" as political prisoners. After protests involving refusals to bathe and the smearing of excrement in their cells, a number of the prisoners began a hunger strike; ten eventually died.[8] Riots in the cities of Northern Ireland ensued. Finally, Heaney's Harvard position brought him into regular close contact with two other émigré poets: Brodsky, who was at Mount Holyoke College in western Massachusetts, and Walcott, who was teaching just across the Charles River at Boston University. As O'Brien writes, these poets "would offer strategies for coping with varieties of Irish cultural problems."[9] In "Station Island," then, Heaney returns to the dangerous intersection of poetry and the political under (largely but not exclusively self-imposed) pressure to revise his earlier resolutions of the problem.

*   *   *

As Neil Corcoran has pointed out, Heaney's pilgrimage is framed by encounters with the shades of Irish writers. The poet meets William

Carleton and Patrick Kavanagh on his way to Station Island and finds Joyce waiting for him when he disembarks from the ferry that returns him to the mainland. Corcoran argues that Heaney discovers an "enabling and releasing alternative" to "the orthodoxies of the island" in his colloquies with these "exemplary artist figures."[10] This focus on what Helen Vendler has called the poem's "vocational colloqu[ies]" enables Corcoran and others to argue that "Station Island" ultimately affirms a Joycean attitude with respect to history's claims on poetry.[11] As Vendler puts it, Heaney concludes that he "must retain an intellectual and moral independence—symbolized by the work of Joyce—which resists the deflection of art by either politics or pity."[12] These readings miss the penitential and purgatorial point of "Station Island," for in the poem Heaney chastises himself precisely for his past resolutions that most resemble those Corcoran and Vendler describe. While these critics focus on the framing "vocational" encounters, the poem's most compelling vignettes are not those in which Heaney meets with the shades of writers; rather, they are the moments when nonwriters force Heaney to justify his vocation. Each of these encounters refers to and cancels an earlier attempt to harmonize the demands of poetry and politics. Confronting these failures in sections VII and VIII of "Station Island," Heaney must reimagine poetry's relationship with the political in sections IX, X, and XI. It is the resulting sense of poetry as a transformative engagement with its historical moment that Heaney ultimately articulates and defends in "Station Island."

While "Station Island" is framed by terza rima encounters with writers who urge Heaney to declare poetic independence from his historical situation, the poet's response to them is at best ambivalent. In section III, while listening to birdsong on the road to Lough Derg, Heaney is overtaken and challenged by the shade of William Carleton. A nineteenth-century novelist (1794–1869), Carleton began as a Catholic and a member of the Ribbon Society, made his own pilgrimage to Lough Derg when he was eighteen, but left the countryside for Dublin, converted to Protestantism, and made his literary career attacking the rural, Catholic, and Republican culture of his youth. He represents the determined rejection of a background Heaney explicitly recognizes as very much his own. In his advice to abandon the pilgrimage, Carleton invites Heaney to join him in this rejection. "I made the traitor in me sink the knife," he says. "And maybe there's a lesson there for you."[13]

Nothing in section III suggests, though, that Carleton's is a lesson Heaney will learn. Heaney recognizes that he has much in common with Carleton: both grew up amidst sectarian prejudice, both left the northern countryside for the environs of Dublin. But attitude, language, and career trajectory separate the two. Carleton's speech insistently returns to violence, his sensory memories are of "gun butts...cracking on the door," "hanged bodies rotting," death, decay, and the threats of "hard-mouthed Ribbonmen and Orange bigots" (65). Heaney acknowledges the continuing presence of these political divisions—"Orange drums" and "neighbors on the road at night with guns"—but emphasizes other aspects of landscape and culture, especially abundance and community. Where Carleton is driven to anger and the production of scathing literary representations (*Lough Derg Pilgrim*), Heaney disavows "the angry role," and posits his hometown "band of Ribbonmen [who] played hymns to Mary" as a source of poetry: "obedient strains like theirs," as opposed to the Fenian "harp of unforgiving iron" that provided both soundtrack and provocation for Carleton's cultural betrayal, were the poet's formative tunes (65). In this stance toward the Ribbonmen of his youth, Heaney implies his position regarding the pilgrimage; he accepts its meaning and associations, its whole cultural matrix, as a source of inspiration.

Heaney's obstinate unwillingness to follow Carleton's anti-Vergilian lead away from the island "Purgatory" manifests in tone as well as explicit statement. Carleton is characterized by anger and hardness; these qualities shape his actions and language. Heaney describes the shade as fast and determined, "aggravated," "raving," "hammering." Carleton is brusque and dismissive when Heaney mentions his destination, unresponsive when the poet points out their common ground. He interrupts with vivid descriptions of violence and its aftermath, and offers tart rejoinders when Heaney articulates his own sensibility. The poet's actions and language, on the other hand, characterize him in opposite terms. Heaney is passive and pacific in Carleton's company, opposing the generative corruption of nature ("earthworms") to the destructive corruption of violence, answering Carleton's hard speech with his own soft consonants, long phrases, and inactive verbs. Moreover, Heaney aligns himself with the frail and the feminine; he notes that the spot where Carleton overtakes him is the place where he "overtook the women," and he describes himself as "tuned" to the "obedient strains" of the Ribbonmen who undertake their own "frail procession" in fringed sashes and "collarettes."

An allusion suggests that while Heaney identifies himself with everything against which Carleton sets himself, he does not devalue himself or his sensibility by so doing. In Carleton's mouth he puts the imperative to "Remember everything." The command echoes a crucial line from *Translations*, the 1980 play by Heaney's friend, colleague, and fellow Northern Catholic, Brian Friel. In the play, Hugh, the master of an Irish hedge school soon to be wiped out—along with its village—by the British army of the 1830s, advises his son that "To remember everything is madness."[14] Carleton, whose career consisted largely of remembering (and caustically reporting) everything about rural, nationalist, Catholic Ireland, is therefore subtly marked as mad (in both senses), and the pilgrim poet registers no great sense of loss when the shade turns away and heads "up the road at the same hard pace" (66).

In section XII, a final shade—that of James Joyce—appears as Heaney steps off the ferry and returns to the mainland. A number of critics have concluded that Joyce embodies Heaney's newfound sense of aesthetic freedom. In his dismissal of the pilgrimage (a "common rite" that fails to discharge the poet's "obligation"), in his recommendation that Heaney "write for the joy of it," in his offer of wisdom ("Let go, let fly, forget") that echoes Stephen Dedalus's triadic aesthetic epiphany of "silence, exile, and cunning," Joyce effectively closes the frame Carleton opened and sums up a compelling resolution of the question of poetry's responsibility.[15] The final revenant Heaney confronts in "Station Island," Joyce appears to get the last word, and that word is emphatic: "it's time to swim // out on your own and fill the element / with signatures on your own frequency" (94). As Henry Hart writes, though, it is unclear whether Heaney "wants to take the rather cold, skeletal hand of Joyce in the first place."[16] Hart points out a number of differences between pilgrim and shade: Joyce is "cool to the artist's social, religious and political commitments" while "Heaney is warm"; Joyce's artistic trajectory is away from the vernacular and toward greater "verbal intricacy" while Heaney "has simplified"; Joyce celebrates "willful detachment" while Heaney values "the artist's ambivalent attachment."[17] Finally, Hart argues that the Joycean artist's "silence, exile and cunning" are, for Heaney, "temptations to be confessed rather than ecstatically embraced."[18]

We need not take Hart's word, though; the poem itself registers Heaney's ambivalence. Heaney characterizes the space opened up by Joyce's advice as one in which he is "alone with nothing that I had not known." Joyce's is an old solution to the problems Heaney has explored. Moreover, it only *appears* that Joyce gets the last word, for the poem goes on after Joyce falls silent: "The shower broke in a cloudburst, the tarmac / fumed and sizzled" (94). The rain, as opposed to Joyce's sea imagery, is related to reality. Earlier in the section, rain

awakens Heaney and accompanies his resistance to Joyce's "Let go,
let fly, forget." Its reappearance here implies that that resistance continues. While the sea is an element Heaney might fill, the rain is water
in contact with earth. While he will get no less wet standing in it, the
poet encounters the water differently from if he dove in and swam;
the rain is agent rather than empty element. It creates an infernal
atmosphere—the fuming and sizzling of the tarmac—and, in its final
act, in the poem's concluding single line, it walls Joyce off, creating
screens around the shade's straight walk which at once resembles the
tangent he recommends to the poet and is antithetical to the circular
walking Heaney has engaged in over the course of "Station Island."
In the last analysis, Joyce's is a resolution Heaney works hard to contain. What lasts beyond the end of "Station Island" is the defense
of poetry elaborated in the climactic sections VII–XI, the defense
demanded at once by Heaney's specific historical circumstances and
by his deployment of the necromantic topos.

* * *

Some critics privilege the obviously "vocational" colloquies
between Heaney and other writers, but as I have shown, Heaney is
ambivalent about those writers' models of poetic responsibility (or lack
of it). In what follows, I argue that the real heavy lifting of Heaney's
defense of poetry against the claims of history takes place not in the
encounters with Carleton and Joyce but in a series of encounters with
shades who press those claims. These occur in the poem's seventh
and eighth sections where, as Hart writes, the poet meets "ghosts of
a specifically Irish inferno."[19] These sections announce their concern
with the question of poetic responsibility by referring—sometimes
quite explicitly—to earlier poems in which Heaney has taken up that
problem, especially his 1975 volume, *North*, his most sustained and
thorough engagement with the question of engagement.

Section VII opens with an echo of that volume's title poem. In
both cases Heaney comes to water; in each he fails to find what he
at first expects: no reflection in the mirror on Station Island, no
spiritual presence but only the Atlantic's "secular powers" on the
strand in "North." In addition, and most importantly, the similar
settings introduce poems in which Heaney confronts "man's inhu-
manity to man." "North" is concerned with the unbroken chain of
violence and betrayal in Irish history back to (and perhaps beyond)
its brutal colonization by Vikings. This episode of "Station Island"
deals with one specific instance, narrated at length by the victim

(William Strathearn's speech runs unbroken for two pages, longer than any other shade's) and includes details that enhance its pathos (the last words exchanged between the victim and his wife). Where "North" offers a resolution to the poet, however, the seventh section of "Station Island" concludes with self-accusation and suffering. The earlier poem has the tongue of the Viking longboat speak this now famous wisdom into the face of humankind's bloody history: "Lie down / in the word-hoard."[20] It was ever thus, the longboat says. People have always betrayed and murdered each other. The violence of conquest and the vigor of commerce (and even the visions of cartography) are perpetrated by the same hands. In the face of this truth, a poet can only turn inward, lie down in language, where all literary ladders start, and cultivate the fertile ground of his own memory and experience. By looking keenly and carefully, by attending to the tactile presence of "what nubbed treasure [his] hands have known," the poet might capture moments of illumination, and while these will not change the human tendency toward destruction, they might somehow compensate for it.

The longboat's case is easy to make in the abstract (which is how Heaney makes it in "North") and in the absence of any concrete manifestation of human nature's consequences. In section VII of "Station Island," Heaney finds himself face to face with just such an embodiment, the shade of William Strathearn, a childhood friend of the poet who, as an adult, was beaten to death by off-duty police in County Antrim.[21] Where the longboat speaks metaphorically of "Thor's hammer," Strathearn is all too literal: "His brow / was blown open above the eye and blood / had dried on his neck and cheek" (77). In spite of Strathearn's "Easy now," the poet's "shock" at the sight persists not only throughout the narrated moment but all the way through the moment of narration; Heaney writes that it "is in me still." When confronted with Strathearn unchanged "except for the ravaged // forehead," when encountering a specific (formerly) flesh and blood "perfect, clean, unthinkable victim," Heaney seems to reject the counsel of the longboat's tongue, repenting his "timid circumspect involvement" (80). The shade replies not with absolution but with his own request for forgiveness, his apology for the ruined face with which he confronts Heaney, and then fades in "a stun of pain," a brutal suggestion that his suffering endures.

Heaney's self-accusation in VII, which questions the resolution of "North," is the beginning rather than the end of this poem's exploration of the poet's responsibilities, a rigorous questioning of whether, as O'Brien writes, "there is something simply in being an artist that puts the soul in jeopardy."²² Section VIII goes further. Heaney first meets the shade of Tom Delaney, a friend who worked as an archaeologist.²³ The shade's work recalls Heaney's early *ars poetica*, "Digging" ("The squat pen sits in my hand, snug as a gun. I'll dig with it") as well as the archaeological poems of *North*.²⁴ A metaphor buried in Heaney's description, though, suggests the danger to himself posed by this friendly shade. The archaeologist looks at the poet "with the same old pretence of amazement," and his expression includes his hair falling over his brow in a way Heaney likens to that of a "woodkerne." This is an easy reference to miss (O'Brien misreads it, writing that "the archaeologist is remembered in terms of a bird"²⁵). A "woodkerne" (or "wood-kerne"), though, is not a bird but is instead, according to the OED, "an Irish outlaw or robber haunting woods or wild country." Delaney speaks to the poet of how he was driven by "love" to "dig in for years...in a muck of bigotry," just as Heaney found himself compelled to dig first into familial and national history (in his earliest work), and then, in *North*, into the human species' apparently innate proclivity for violence and betrayal—figured in the bodies of Neolithic victims preserved in Scandinavian bogs.²⁶ But Delaney's digging implicitly rebukes Heaney's. Instead of burrowing in the word-hoard of linguistic history or even in the "good turf" of familial history, Delaney dug in the middens of sectarian violence. Poet and archaeologist arrived at different conclusions: where the bog poems of *North* discover evidence for atavistic and eternally recurring violence as something like a universal human condition, Delaney comes upon the concrete specificity of Irish defeat at English hands in the seventeenth century, the cannon balls hurled by William III's army into Catholic towns like Derry; the "muck of bigotry" is found "under the walls," where Delaney picks through "shards and Williamite cannon balls" (82). And this difference finally leads to diametrically opposed results. Heaney transforms the long view of *North* into powerful poetry, but Delaney says that no such transformation occurs on the materials of more recent history; "[A]ll that," he concludes, "we just turned to banter" (82).

    This inefficacious speech leads me to what is most important in Heaney's encounter with Delaney: his emphasis on his own failures to speak. Recalling his last meeting with Delaney, as the archaeologist lay dying, Heaney writes "I said nothing," and remembers feeling he had "somehow broken / covenants, and failed an obligation." The poet unable to speak in the face of mortality is the poet who cannot do his job, it seems, and Delaney's spirit offers no comfort; Heaney's silent "long gaze and last handshake" did nothing to help him meet his death.

The poet's failure or unwillingness to engage the concrete evidence of specific historical violence and suffering renders him again silent—"I could not speak"—and leads to the poem's most direct and astringent address of an earlier poem in which Heaney responded to the violence of his time and place; when he looks again for Delaney's shade he finds the archaeologist has disappeared and in his place stands "a bleeding, pale-faced boy, plastered in mud" (82). This is the spirit of Heaney's cousin Colum McCartney, murdered by Protestants and memorialized by Heaney in the 1979 poem, "The Strand at Lough Beg."[27] That earlier poem includes its own confrontation with McCartney, one worth glancing back at before going on to Heaney's reexamination of it. Turning to find his dead cousin, still covered with the blood and "roadside muck" of his murder, Heaney washes the body with dew and wipes it clean with moss. "I lift you under the arms and lay you flat," he concludes, and "With rushes that shoot green again, I plait / Green scapulars to wear over your shroud."[28] The poet's duty here is to clean and prepare the corpse, to clothe it in the eternal renewal and preservative of nature (those rushes are not only green but green "again"). More than this, the poet's response is to transform flesh into word, blood and muck into emblems of eternity. Heaney's baptism of his cousin's corpse acknowledges the end of its worldly life and announces its rebirth into an otherworldly life. The washing is accomplished with the materials of the landscape, so that the earth effects this change. With rushes that figure the renewal of spring, Heaney weaves a garment (scapulars) that, at the simplest interpretive level, professes faith, a badge of affiliation with a religious order. That this is to be worn "over your shroud" suggests that it is meant to transform McCartney's death into something of eternal and consolatory significance. More specifically, though, the green scapulars are, in Catholic tradition, God's means for reconciling those who have lost their faith, and a guarantee that they will receive a "happy death."[29] When Heaney weaves green scapulars for McCartney, then, he is trying in retrospect to make his cousin's death "happy" by reconciling him to God. At the same time, though, this Catholic significance, which might be seen as an escape from the political conflict that has brought about McCartney's death, is itself politically colored; the green scapulars woven of the rushes and worn (forever) bring to mind Yeats's "Easter 1916" ("wherever green is worn / A terrible beauty is born") so that McCartney becomes, through the poet's ministrations, a paradoxically nationalist and Catholic figure for the spiritual/aesthetic *transcendence* of sectarian violence.

On Station Island (and in "Station Island"), McCartney gets a chance to resist this fate and by so doing he provides Heaney (or, rather, Heaney, through McCartney, provides himself) an opportunity to reconsider this confused resolution of poetic responsibility. At the climax of Heaney's sojourn on this "Purgatory" (St. Patrick's), McCartney castigates him for his misuse of another *Purgatory* (Dante's) in his elegiac handling of the cousin's death. In reply, Heaney must defend poetry, and especially his own specific poetics, against claims that they evade and cover up the truth and are therefore politically useless if not politically reprehensible. Still bearing the blood and mud the poet imagined he had cleared away, McCartney's shade first chides Heaney for having stayed "with poets" when he got news of his cousin's death, already implying that Heaney's loyalty is to the wrong clan, the aesthetic artificers rather than the political victims. Heaney replies "I was dumb," admitting once again his verbal failure in the face of death and historical reality, then attempts to justify himself with his poetic vision: "I kept seeing a grey stretch of Lough Beg / and the strand empty at daybreak." This provokes McCartney's most lacerating accusation, Heaney's most acute self-accusation: "You saw that, and you wrote that—not the fact. / You confused evasion and artistic tact" (83). Instead of reporting on reality, "you whitewashed ugliness," the shade says, and, with allusions to Dante and poetic polish, "saccharined" a murder victim's "death with morning dew" (83). The poet's vision, refracted through the images, the verbal repertoire, and the cultural project of the pastoral elegy, is here opposed to "the fact," the brute reality of political violence. More than this, that elegiac vision is characterized through images of veiling (whitewashing and blind-drawing) rather than revelation.[30] What the poet sees, McCartney argues, is not the truth but a fabrication that avoids the truth and artificially sweetens history's bitter pill. Most important of all, the argument here has to do not simply with truth versus falseness or reality versus illusion, but also, as McCartney's accusation makes clear, with culpability. While the gun-wielding Protestant is directly responsible for McCartney's death, the blurred vision of Heaney and the tradition he inherits and promulgates is indirectly responsible because it has for too long made such bloody and mucky deaths palatable by viewing them "through the lovely blinds of the *Purgatorio*" (whose opening lines Heaney used as the epigraph for "The Strand at Lough Beg").

Heaney makes no answer to McCartney's parting shot; he does not even explicitly name the speechlessness that has plagued him throughout section VIII. Instead, he spends the last four sections of "Station Island" at once performing his penance and re-resolving the questions of poetry's proper relationship with the political. The poet's progress begins during the long night of section IX, when Heaney first hears the shade of Francis Hughes, a IRA hunger striker who died in the Maze prison in 1981.[31] Heaney does more than listen to this shade, though; he imaginatively *identifies* with him, seeing and smelling what Hughes must have seen and smelled during the flight through the Derry countryside that preceded his capture in 1978. Heaney imagines himself into Hughes's senses, seeing "woodworm" and smelling "mildew / From the byre loft where he watched and hid"(84). This leads to the poem's nadir, when Heaney dreams a flood of muck and faces upon it a "Strange polyp...like a huge corrupt / Magnolia bloom," an embodiment of the poet's "blanching self-disgust." This vision provokes his most abjectly penitent moment:

> I repent
> My unweaned life that kept me competent
> To sleepwalk with connivance and mistrust. (85)

What are these sins? A life "unweaned" because still dependent upon some source of nourishment meant for the immature, because still unable (or unwilling) to digest harder fare? A lyrical competence that maintains a half-willed ignorance of back-stabbings and betrayals? A pattern Hart describes as "unintentionally condoning rather than actively deterring atrocities"?[32] The section concludes by first qualifying this renunciation; as Hart writes, Heaney "renounces old ways" even as he "affirms their inevitable continuity."[33] Heaney recognizes that the poet cannot change that which constitutes him as what he is, just as "the cairnstone could [not] defy the cairn," but then resolves, in an almost Beckettian manner, to go on (86).

In "Little Gidding," the compound ghost warns Eliot that he has acted in ways he will regret, that he has, in effect, done wrong; that necromantic moment is imbued with the purgatorial energies that animate the poem as a whole. Sections VII, VIII, and IX perform a similar function in "Station Island." In spite of advice from the shades of William Carleton and Patrick Kavanagh, Heaney undertakes his pilgrimage to St. Patrick's Purgatory and confronts what he sees as his own wrongdoing. The seriousness of his self-examination, the viciousness of his self-accusation, militate against Hart's claim that "Station Island" "employs a pilgrimage more like a 'frame narrative' than a central dramatic event," that the journey to Lough Derg "provides the occasion for the characters to speak out, so that the poem in the end is more a collage than a flowing synchronized story."[34] Sections VII, VIII, and IX are saturated with real guilt; as Seamus Deane summarized in his review of *Station Island*, the poem shows that "Heaney gets better and better as time goes on and guiltier and guiltier about being so."[35] Heaney is not, therefore, simply using the pilgrimage as a metaphor (as Corcoran claims), nor is he using it simply to castigate Irish Catholicism for its "constrictions" and to suggest how "through art, a newly enabling freedom might be gained."[36] "I hate how quick I was to know my place," Heaney cries out in IX; he means not only, as Corcoran suggests, that he hates the ease with which he founded a career on his identification with "a particular territory" or with which he "meekly accept[ed] a servitude to the mores of a community," but also that he regrets having too quickly subscribed to exactly the model of aesthetic autonomy from the demands of that territory's historic and contemporary conflicts that both Corcoran and Vendler argue he spends the poem arriving at.[37]

Sections X and XI, two parts of the poem to which neither Corcoran nor Vendler pay much attention, sketch a new solution to the problems the poem has explored. This solution synthesizes in the key term "translation" the vision and fact McCartney's shade poses as irreducible opposites. Heaney's understanding of translation is rooted in precisely the Irish Catholicism Corcoran finds him trying to critique and escape. Stefan Hawlin is surely right when he argues that "a Catholic sacramental sense seems to be working in the background" of section X.[38] Here, Heaney recalls (sees, actually) a simple earthenware mug from his childhood home, a mundane vessel "patterned with cornflowers" and patiently standing on a shelf out of the boy's reach day after day after day. Hart reads the mug as an "emblem of wholeness" that Heaney reaches after his Jungian plunge into the Underworld of the collective unconscious on a quest for individuation.[39] He misses the point of the episode, though, for the mug on the shelf is not an archetype but is instead just a mug, "unchallenging" and "unremembered."[40] Once, though, the mug had been taken down and used as a prop by actors: "a couple vowed and called it their loving cup" (87). After the performance, the mug returns to its customary place, but it has been altered by that moment of aesthetic estrangement.[41] While it is still what it is (as Heaney recognizes himself to be irrevocably what he is and history to be inalterably what it is at the end of IX), the mug has at the same time become something else, something more: "Dipped and glamoured with this translation" (87). The baptismal symbolism is up and running here, as Hart suggests, but the baptized is not Heaney as he awakens from the dark night of IX. Rather, it is the everyday cup transformed (or "translated," to use Heaney's term) by aesthetic attention.

The poem's penultimate section (XI) exemplifies Heaney's "translation." In a moment of illumination, he recalls a monk who "spoke again about the need and chance // to salvage everything, to re-envisage..." (89). Heaney's language directs us to the intertwined acts of digging and recovering and of seeing, and the monk's quoted speech explicitly connects those acts, in their synthesis as translation, to poetry, prayer, and penance; "Read poems as prayers," he says as he orders the poet to translate "something by Juan de la Cruz" (89). The remainder of the section is Heaney's translation of St. John of the Cross's "*Cantar del alma que se huelga de conoseer a Dios por fe*" (Song of the soul that is glad to know God by faith). In it, Heaney carries the object (the Spanish poem's meaning) into another space and condition (the English language) through a speech act (poetic translation) that at once preserves and transforms it.

The translation of XI, though, is less important for an understanding of Heaney's defense of poetry than are some specific aspects of translation as he illustrates it in section X. First, Heaney's language in X suggests that McCartney's accusation still stings, that the translation he names here is formulated, at least in part, in response to it. The mug is "Dipped" and then likened to the psalter of St. Ronan, miraculously unharmed after a day in "lough water." Both images echo the bathing of McCartney's corpse in "The Strand at Lough Beg" so that what Heaney claims for the mug (its simultaneous [and miraculous] sameness and difference) might be true of the dead cousin as well. Another significant element of diction here is "translation" itself, for Heaney seems to have in mind both of the term's primary meanings. The OED defines "translation" first as "removal or conveyance from one person, place, or condition to another" (including the removal of a person to Heaven without death), and only second as "the action or process of turning from one language into another." The mug has been carried from one space (the everyday space of the shelf) to another (the aesthetic space of the stage), and from one condition (utilitarian) to another (aesthetic), and it has been changed (changed utterly) in the process. A key component to that change is language; the spatial estrangement that finds the mug on the stage instead of its shelf apparently would not transform the mug without the actors' lifting it and transforming it with their speech (calling it their "loving cup"). And the speech act that has this efficacy is a specifically *literary* one, the composed speech of actors in a play. The agent of translation, then, is *poetry*, a kind of speech act that preserves what McCartney calls "fact"—here the material signifier of the mug—even as it transforms that fact into a vision that confers upon or draws out of it some deeper and compensatory significance.

But it isn't just any aesthetic attention that performs this work, and I want to conclude by pointing out how both the nature of Heaney's "translation" and the illustrative object here echo the Catholic Mass's transubstantion of the wine in a chalice (through a specific set of speech acts) into the salvific blood of Christ. Moreover, the baptismal symbolism is a peculiarly Irish model, an allusion to the legend of King Sweeney, in which Sweeney throws the monk Ronan's psalter into the lough, from which it is recovered undamaged, and for this offense is cursed to wander Ireland under the delusion that he is a bird. Heaney's defense of poetry, then, is not one based, as Corcoran and Vendler would have it, on an escape from his cultural roots but is instead constructed (as "Station Island" itself is constructed) out of that culture's specific linguistic, narrative, and symbolic resources. Just as in "The Strand at Lough Beg," Heaney finds here a culturally specific means for effecting his poetic purposes. But where that poem's purposes are largely decorative, here he offers a more thorough poetic transformation of the materials of everyday life, a transformation calculated to answer the charges he has leveled at himself in Colum McCartney's voice. While they cannot be escaped or changed, the truths of human history, of that history as it manifests even in contemporary politics (in the broken and bloody bodies of sectarian victims), can be translated into something rich and strange, preserved and transformed in the paradoxical work of poetic vision. The poet's responsibility in circumstances like those of Northern Ireland in the 1970s and 1980s is therefore to see and to translate, at once registering the costs and making available the compensations.

EPILOGUE

I have focused in part 2 on some of the most searching, self-critical, and powerful late twentieth-century poems deploying the topoi of Underworld descent and invocation of the shades in order to trace the ways these intertwined narratives have helped poets to work through their varying senses of the medium's responsibility in and to the poet's specific historical moment. There are, it must be said, other necromantic and katabatic poems in the archives of postwar poetry in English, and many others, from Robert Frost's "Acquainted with the Night" to Robert Duncan's "Often I Am Permitted to Return to a Meadow" to Walcott's *Arkansas Testament* that can be profitably read with the Underworld descent as an interpretive horizon. What will probably strike readers more profoundly than the absence of any of these poems, however, is the absence from this book of those twentieth-century poems modeled on Underworld descents other than those of Odysseus, Aeneas, and Dante. What, one might ask, of Orpheus? Or Persephone? Or Inanna? I realized early in my work on this project that the book simply could not address the whole range of descent narratives, and I was driven by my own interests— both in individual poets like Heaney and Walcott and in the problematics of poetic responsibility—to focus on the descent of the epic hero or questing poet. I am mindful of the blindnesses entailed by and enabling whatever critical insights I have managed to develop through my attention to these poems, to this particular strand of the descent tradition, and I would like, in this Epilogue, to offer some glimpses of those Underworld rivers into which I have not yet deeply waded.

The myth of Orpheus's descent in pursuit of his beloved Eurydice has, of course, captivated poets and other artists for millennia. The Orphic legends were enshrined in cults and rituals about as far back as scholars have been able to travel in ancient Greece. The canonical version of the Orpheus story is Ovid's in the *Metamorphoses* and is quite familiar: Orpheus, gifted with such musical talent that he can control animals and the elements with his songs, loses his beloved Eurydice when she is bitten by a snake. He descends into the Underworld,

calming the guard-dog Cerberus with his song, and musically moves
Hades to allow him to bring Eurydice back to the world. The only
condition the god imposes is that Orpheus must not look back at
Eurydice until they have left the Underworld. Orpheus fails to meet
this condition, looking back at the last moment, and Eurydice disappears again into the land of the dead. The figure of Orpheus appears
in the attempts of early Christians to make Christ comprehensible to
pagan audiences, in the songs and lays of medieval minstrels, and,
repeatedly, in the Surreal fever dreams of Jean Cocteau, who explored
the myth in several plays and films.

Among twentieth-century poetic treatments of the myth, perhaps
the most famous are those of the German poet, Rainer Maria Rilke,
whose career is almost book-ended by Orpheus poems—"Orpheus.
Eurydice. Hermes" in 1904, when the poet was twenty-nine, and the
spectacular "Sonnets to Orpheus" in 1922, just four years before his
death. The earlier poem was written in Rome, where Rilke wrote a
number of poems on classical themes ("The Tombs of the Heterae,"
"Alcestis," "The Archaic Torso of Apollo"). "Orpheus. Eurydice.
Hermes" opens with an evocative description of the Underworld,
one that focuses not on the evaluative geography familiar from Vergil
and Dante but instead on the uncanny character of the landscape
(indeed, in the first line Rilke calls the place "*der Seelen wunderliches
Bergwerk*," which Stephen Mitchell translates as "the deep uncanny
mine of souls").[1] Like H.D.'s "Eurydice," Rilke's poem on the Orphic
descent focuses largely on the experience of the one who is being
taken from the Underworld and on her bewilderment when she is
brought out of the "new virginity" she had found among the dead,
but Rilke's description of Orpheus emphasizes both the difficulty of
his task (he strains to hear Eurydice behind him and is convinced that
he hears only the echoes of his own footsteps), and, most importantly,
his strong identification with poetry itself (the lyre he carries is represented as actually growing out of his arm "like a slip / of roses grafted
onto an olive tree").

It is that identification that Rilke elaborates on at great length in
the sequence of fifty-five sonnets he wrote during February, 1922. In
letters, Rilke wrote that these poems came to him as "dictation," that
he was powerless to resist and could only "submit" to them, though
he was preparing at the time to continue with the *Duino Elegies* on
which he had been working for some time.[2] The sequence is complex, with references not only to Orpheus but also to a range of other
myths, but a recurrent motif is poetry, especially its difficulty and its
relationship to death (both of which, of course, find expression in

the myth of Orpheus). The third sonnet of the first part (Rilke broke the sequence into two parts, of twenty-six and twenty-nine poems), for example, intertwines poetry's difficulty with its demand for the nonbeing of death: "Song, as you have taught it, is not desire," he writes. Instead, "song is reality."[3] As we have seen other poets do, we see Rilke here justifying a specific poetics through the performance of the Underworld descent. While the songs that arose from himself enabled Orpheus to seek Eurydice, it is the song that arises from his loss that continues to inspire poets ages and ages hence. In just that way, Rilke offers "True singing" as the song born not of desire but of desire's end, not of passion but of passion's aftermath.

The passion of Rilke's engagement with the Orpheus myth is matched (or complemented) by the irony of John Ashbery's in his 1977 "Syringa." The contrast is discernible from the very first lines of Ashbery's poem: "Orpheus liked the glad personal quality / Of the things beneath the sky. Of course. Eurydice was a part / Of this. Then one day, everything changed."[4] While he establishes a wry distance from the myth's pathos, though, Ashbery, like Rilke, uses the myth to work through and to enact a specific set of poetic priorities and practices. On one hand, Ashbery writes, there is an imperative to sing "accurately" so that the notes of the song (the words of the poem) rival the elements of the natural world. Such singing enables a fuller understanding of the world because it "encapsulates / The different weights of the things." On the other hand, however, "it isn't enough / To just go on singing." Even an accurate song can only be judged, can only really be known, when it is over; to isolate a note and judge it in isolation is impossible, just as it is impossible to capture, evaluate, and keep a single moment of passing time. Yet the accurate song attempts just this impossible feat, dooming itself thereby to irrelevance. Ashbery wonderfully parodies the Orphic poet's ambition (as acidly as but much more humorously than H.D. does in "Eurydice"): "Stellification / Is for the few, and comes about much later."[5] Ashbery skewers the poetic "star system" here almost as effectively as Walcott does in Souffriere's pit of poets. In his poem's own musical meandering, though, he demonstrates a humbler but perhaps superior kind of singing, one that follows the tortuous paths of thought, association, allusion, and narrative logic, but that does so with a gentle irony that allows humor to invite the reader in. Where Orpheus, and Rilke after him, sing desire and death, Ashbery proffers poetry as play.

Like Orpheus, Persephone is a very old figure, her story a very old story. The story's earliest versions narrate the abduction and (partial) rescue of Kore, the maiden. This figure takes on the identity of the daughter of the harvest goddess Demeter, and transforms the innocent maiden into Persephone (which means something like "Destroyer"), and her story becomes the foundation for the Eleusinian mysteries, around which a huge cult grew up in pre-Hellenic Greece. Also like the Orpheus myth, though, the story of Persephone has its canonical form in Ovid's *Metamorphoses*. Persephone, the daughter of Demeter, is picking flowers when the earth opens and Hades arises to drag her down with him to the Underworld. Grief-stricken, Demeter refuses to let the earth flower so that winter falls, threatening people with starvation. Zeus intervenes and Hades relents, but when Persephone is preparing to leave the Underworld, the gardener shows up with a pomegranate missing six seeds. It turns out that Persephone ate the seeds and as a consequence of eating the food of the Underworld, she is forced to return for half of every year (during which Demeter brings winter to the world, with spring accompanying Persephone's annual return to her mother). If remarkable poems on Orpheus and Eurydice are to be found here and there in the work of twentieth-century poets, remarkable poems on Persephone (or Proserpine) and Demeter (Ceres) are to be found all over the place. Fortunately, a handful of the most powerful—by such poets as Eavan Boland, Rita Dove, and Louise Glück—have been collected and published together in a beautifully printed limited edition by Elm Press, and it is to this anthology, *To Persephone*, that I want to call attention here. While it will not be immediately accessible to readers, the poems included in it are (and I provide their publication information for those I discuss in the notes). It will be worth the trouble for those readers who find a rare book library with a copy in its possession, though, because the book itself is a breathtaking artifact, a demonstration that there are real pleasures to be found in Hell.

To Persephone is oversize, printed on vellum paper, and bound in cloth-covered boards; six glass pomegranate seeds are recessed into the front cover. The poems are accompanied throughout by Enid Mark's lithographs; one lithograph, at the center of the book, stands alone, depicting a desolately rocky landscape that melts imperceptibly into clouds (perhaps the Sinai Desert, since Mark's acknowledgments thank Peter Mark for use of negatives "shot during expeditions" there), with red pomegranate seeds tumbling down the gutter of the book. The poems included demonstrate the range of interpretations to which the Persephone myth is susceptible. Eavan Boland's "The Pomegranate" and Rachel Blau DuPlessis' "Pomegranate" both suggest bonds between mother and daughter that the myth informs and sanctions.[6] "Love and blackmail," Boland writes, "are the gist" of the Proserpine story, the "only story I have ever loved." She goes on to catalogue the ways the story has seemed relevant to her, from her childhood "in exile" to a moment when she thought her daughter had been lost, when she could not find her.[7] Mothers and daughters, the poem suggests, are bound by what they withhold from each other as much as by what they share; Boland's speaker resolves at the poem's end to not tell her daughter the myth, but silently to bequeath it to her instead. For DuPlessis, the pomegranate seeds Persephone eats, the bit of infernal food that binds her to an annual return to Dis, are "a taste of the mother," the only means available for the girl to maintain a sense of her mother's presence. They are also the necessary price she pays for speech, so that DuPlessis grounds both maternal relationship and poetry itself in the absence and loss entailed by the eaten pomegranate seeds.

At the other end of the continuum, Laurie Scheck and Louise Glück find distance, separation, and irony in the familiar story.[8] In "Persephone," Scheck takes the title figure from her arrival in the Underworld, still bearing aspects of her earthly origin—the dead "can smell the earth / on her skin, the white narcissus, the wheat, the rain-wet soil"—and from her longing for the world above and for her mother to the condition of the Queen of the Underworld. By the end of the poem, Persephone "no longer thinks of her mother." She remembers instead "a woman so ugly no one would want to touch her." Scheck does not reveal this woman's identity, and while we are led by her description to imagine Demeter (the woman "smearing dirt on her naked face / and singing to the flowers"), we might be led by the same images (Persephone was gathering flowers when she was abducted, after all) to see here the Underworld queen's bitter memory of her own earthly self. "Persephone" is accompanied by a lithograph, tipped in on a translucent sheet so that it is visible on both sides of the page, depicting a split pomegranate, a few seeds spilled between its halves, as if to represent the permanence of Persephone's reign as Queen of the Dead. Glück's poem, "Pomegranate," aims its irony at precisely the mother-daughter bond at the heart of Boland's and DuPlessis' poems. Her (unnamed) Hades meets Persephone's refusal of his heart (figured as a pomegranate) with a gesture toward Demeter (also unnamed) and her grief: "Now *there* / is a woman who loves / with a vengeance." Persephone sees that her mother's grief has robbed the world of color and smell, while the Underworld is bursting with fruit: pomegranates flame on the branches of their trees. Hades concludes his case by urging Persphone to "examine / this grief" and to remember that her grieving mother "is one to whom / these depths were not offered." The poem does not indicate Persephone's response. Mark's lithograph maintains the poem's ambivalence: a hill-top temple, columns standing and fallen, seen from below with trees in the foreground and clouds towering over, seems to acknowledge Hades' power and the forceful temptation of his kingdom, even as a huge tree on the left answers the poem's description of trees "turning to" Demeter in her grief.

The descent stories of Orpheus and Eurydice and Persephone and Demeter are known widely and well, familiar to school children for-tunate enough to encounter the D'Aulaires' spectacularly illustrated compendium of Greek myths and to students fortunate enough still to be assigned Ovid's *Metamorphoses*. The story of Inanna and her descent into the Underworld to visit her sister Ereshkigal, the god-dess of the dead, is, though older than any other descent narrative dis-cussed in this book, far less familiar to most readers. One of the small handful of Mesopotamian stories to find its way from the deep past to the present (the epic of *Gilgamesh* is another), the story of Inanna's descent appears in slightly different versions (Sumerian, Akkadian, Assyrian). In its broad outlines, though, the story is the same across these variations: Inanna, the Queen of Heaven and Earth, goes to visit Ereshkigal, the Queen of the Great Below. At each of seven lapis gates, Inanna must remove an article of her royal clothing or another sign of her royal status, so that she is naked when she finally confronts Ereshkigal, who promptly hangs her from a stake (or imprisons her in some other way). The goddess remains imprisoned for three days before her minister, Nincubura, is able to persuade one of the gods to force her release. As a condition of her release from the Underworld, Inanna must find a substitute; she settles on her consort, the shepherd Dumuzi, whom she finds enjoying himself in her absence. Dumuzi is sent to take Inanna's place for half of every year (his sister takes his place for the other half).[9] What might most immediately strike us here is the resemblance to the myth of Persephone (or the Greek myth's resemblance to the Mesopotamian, to put them in proper temporal order), but what I want to emphasize here is the progressive stripping away of earthly or celestial authority that Inanna must endure on her way to the Underworld. This aspect, too, finds its way into late Underworld descent narratives; Aeneas must sheathe his sword, for example, and refrain from the martial conduct that is his forte. It is unclear why Ereshkigal's minions demand that Inanna strip herself in this way (perhaps it is simply resentment of the goddess of erotic love, perhaps Inanna intends to conquer the Underworld).

No twentieth-century poem that I know of follows the narrative of Inanna's descent as closely as some poems follow the narratives of Odysseus, Aeneas, or Dante, but Alice Notley's book-length poem, *The Descent of Alette*, comes close. In a poem that is perhaps superficially off-putting to some readers (phrases are separated by quotation marks throughout the poem so that, as Rachel Falconer has put it, "the lines fairly bristle with punctuation."[10] Whatever difficulty this poses for the reader (and Notley suggests in her "Author's Note" that she intends a somewhat difficult reading experience) is worthwhile, for the poem's four sections, each comprising about forty "cantos" ranging in length from four to nine unrhymed stanzas (most four or five lines), detail a fascinating, dreamlike (or, more often, nightmarish) descent into an Underworld that is at once contemporary patriarchal and capitalist culture and the speaker's often fragmented self. The poem begins in conventional epic style (in *medias res*), and, more specifically, with an apparent allusion to Dante:

> "One day, I awoke" "& found myself on" "a subway, endlessly"
> "I didn't know" "how I'd arrived there or" "who I was"
>   "exactly"[11]

By the end of the first canto, the speaker understands that the subway is a kind of Underworld, a " 'world of souls' " run by a "tyrant," and that the tyrant would demand " 'all of you & more' " to allow her to leave:

> " 'Money will not" "be enough,' " "a woman said to her," "Not
>   just money,"
> "he wants your things," "your small things," "your emblems,"
>   "all your
> trappings" "You must give up" "to the tyrant" "all your
>   flowers"
> "all your carnations" "Or your cut hair" "Give him your hair"
> "You must give him your jokes" "your best jokes" "he takes
>   whatever"[12]

She surveys this Underworld in the first part, describing its population and their sufferings, the latter all attributable to the tyrant, whom she learns she must kill. Like Inanna, Alette must lose all of her accoutrements not only if she wants to " 'go upstairs,' " but also in order to descend deeper and confront the tyrant. This imperative to strip away the objects that guarantee identity is repeated over and over; indeed, Alette must lose her form itself, for as she is told by a desperate and exhausted woman painter in the subway, the tyrant invented form itself, he "'owns form.'"[13] Alette becomes a shadow (41), temporarily loses her sex (57), and finally gives up her body itself in order undertake the necessary further descent (41–42). Moreover, she is surrounded by others who are also stripping, being stripped, giving up their possessions, their sex, and their bodies. Such losses seem to be, as the guard tells Inanna at the first lapis gate, the way of the Underworld.

Loss is also, for Notley as for Eliot in "Burnt Norton," the solution to this Underworld, for in loss known and accepted Alette regains her identity and Notley suggests the nature of the truth to be found in her version of the Underworld descent. In a climactic confrontation with the tyrant, who has been shown to own not only shape and form but also transcendence and inspiration, Alette (in the form of an owl) is able to rescue from the river of his blood a black fabric fragment that turns out to be her memory, discarded some time before because it had been too painful to keep. Swallowing the cloth to keep it from the tyrant, she regains her knowledge of herself and of what she has lost (ultimately the same): "'My name is Alette'" / "'My brother'" "'died in battle.'" The form and transcendence and inspiration owned by the tyrant reduce, finally, to war, to his insistence on its intensity, the "'proximity to life & death'" that so stimulates the creative imagination. Alette refuses this, refuses the tyrant's science and art and politics, even the way he is moved by her grief for her brother. Instead, she hunts down the tyrant's roots and pulls them up, destroying the reality growing from his convictions and locating the possibility of change in dreams, in negation, in all that is not of the tyrant's reality.

All of these poems—and many others—draw on the array of gestures associated with the Underworld descent. In them we see the poets' references to their own art, their reckoning with poets who have come before. We see the poets criticizing aspects of their societies by representing them as part of the Underworld and therefore dead, outmoded, or infernal. We see the poets wondering about the value of their chosen form, about its power or lack thereof, about what responsibilities poetic power might entail. In the poems that allude to descent narratives other than the classical medieval *nekuia* or *katabasis*, the epic hero or questing poet's invocation of the dead and travels through the Underworld, we also see new avenues for exploration. The Orphic descent seems to invite a different kind of attention to poetry and its purposes, while the Persephone descent foregrounds specific kinds of relationships and the conditioning power of gender.

The Inanna descent emphasizes askesis and abnegation, finding positive value in the negative in ways that also intersect powerfully with discourses of gender. These are fit subjects for studies of their own, fit oracles to be consulted in further critical descents. Perhaps you will go down now into one of these textual Underworlds. As Vergil writes (*Facilis descensus Averno...*), it's easy.

NOTES

INTRODUCTION

1. Douglas Oliver, *In the Cave of Suicession* (Cambridge, UK: Street Editions, 1974), 2.
2. Oliver, 2.
3. Oliver, 2, 4.
4. Oliver, 18.
5. Of course, Hell is popular among the authors of nonpoetic texts throughout the twentieth century as well. To take just one strand of the infernal tradition, the scene of the sinner's judgment in the Underworld informs Fritz Lang's 1931 film *M*, in which Peter Lorre's serial killer is tried by the criminal gangs whose harmonious relations with the police he has disturbed, and in the more comical circumstances of a Walt Disney cartoon that grants a dream vision straight out of the medieval *Vision of Tondal* to the aptly named dog Pluto and a Simpsons episode that has Homer tried by a jury of infamous evildoers after selling his soul to the Devil (not surprisingly, Ned Flanders). For a treatment of serious narrative deployments of the Underworld descent in the twentieth century, including the only substantial discussion of Notley's *Descent of Alette* of which I am aware, see Rachel Falconer's *Hell in Contemporary Literature: Western Descent Narratives since 1945* (Edinburgh: Edinburgh University Press, 2005). Serious critical treatment of the numerous popular cultural deployments of the Underworld Descent has yet to be undertaken but would be the subject of a fascinating book.
6. In his influential 1914 *Studies in the Odyssey*, the classicist J.A.K. Thomson devotes a chapter to "the Boeotian Odyssey," arguing that character names and lineages, elements of ritual, and the centrality of Tiresias all locate the roots of the Homeric *nekuia* in Boeotian culture. (J.A.K. Thomson, *Studies in the Odyssey* [Oxford: Clarendon, 1914], 21–24, 93.) I discuss Thomson in more detail below.
7. Vergil, *The Aeneid*, trans. Robert Fitzgerald (New York: Random House/Vintage, 1990), 164 (ll. 189–90).
8. Ronald Macdonald, *The Burial-Places of Memory: Epic Underworlds in Vergil, Dante and Milton* (Amherst: University of Massachusetts Press, 1987), 42. For Macdonald's full discussion of the encounter with Palinurus, see 34–37.
9. David L. Pike, *Passage through Hell: Modernist Descents, Medieval Underworlds* (Ithaca: Cornell University Press, 1997, 8).

10. Macdonald, 49.
11. Dennis D. Buchholz, *Your Eyes Will Be Opened: A Study of the Greek (Ethiopic) Apocalypse of Peter* (Atlanta: Scholars Press, 1988), 197–201. The passage is taken from Buchholz's literal translation of the text, 6:7–7:10. A more readable translation, along with translations of other late antique and medieval visions of Hell, is to be found in Eileen Gardiner's valuable *Visions of Heaven and Hell before Dante* (New York: Italica, 1989). For a critical analysis of these late antique apocalypses, see Martha Himmelfarb, *Tours of Hell: An Apocalyptic Form in Jewish and Christian Literature* (Philadelphia: University of Pennsylvania Press, 1983), especially 16–19 and 62–66).
12. Roger S.Wieck, "The Visions of Tondal and the Visionary Tradition in the Middle Ages," in *The Visions of Tondal from the Library of Margaret of York* (Malibu, CA: Getty Museum, 1990), 3.
13. Wieck, 6.
14. Gardiner, 163–64. For a study of *Tondal* that compares the text to other visions of Hell, see Howard Rollin Patch, *The Otherworld: According to Descriptions in Medieval Literature* (Cambridge, MA: Harvard University Press, 1950), 112–19.
15. Alice K. Turner, *A Brief History of Hell* (New York: Harcourt, Brace, 1993), 159.
16. All included, along with others, in Gardiner.
17. Dante, *Inferno,* trans. Allen Mandelbaum (New York: Bantam, 1982), 3.
18. Pike, 2.
19. George DeForest Lord, *Trials of the Self: Heroic Ordeals in the Epic Tradition* (New York: Archon, 1983), 219.
20. Lord, 220.
21. Falconer, 5.
22. Pike, 2.
23. Macdonald, 31–32.
24. Macdonald, 8.
25. Macdonald, 8.
26. David L. Pike, *Subterranean Cities: The World beneath Paris and London, 1800–1945* (Ithaca: Cornell University Press, 2005), 1.
27. Pike also provides thorough and fascinating treatment of the sewers and cemeteries in both cities, in both of which more people spent time than is typically remembered now, from ragpickers and criminals to political revolutionaries.
28. Rosalind Williams, *Notes on the Underground: An Essay on Technology, Society and the Imagination* (Cambridge, MA: MIT Press, 1990), 55.
29. Williams, 72, 54.
30. Pike, *Subterranean Cities,* 30.
31. Pike, *Subterranean Cities,* 48.
32. Pike, *Subterranean Cities,* 53, 55.

33. Though Williams does briefly argue that the Underworld descent narrative is "rooted in the structure of the human brain," this argument is neither fully developed nor central to her thesis, which involves the underground's capacity to illustrate the displacement of the natural environment by the technological one. See Williams, 4, 7–8.

34. Thomson, vii. I must here acknowledge that I was led to the Oxbridge classicists and their treatments of the *nekuia* by Ronald Bush, who argues for their probable influence on Ezra Pound as he worked on the early versions of the opening *Cantos*. See Bush, *The Genesis of Ezra Pound's* Cantos (Princeton: Princeton University Press, 1976), 126–29).

35. Jane Harrison, *Prolegomena to the Study of Greek Religion*, second edition (Cambridge: Cambridge University Press, 1908), 74–76.

36. For a survey of nineteenth-century poets' engagements with Dante, see Steve Ellis, *Dante and English Poetry: Shelley to T. S. Eliot* (Cambridge: Cambridge University Press, 1983).

37. Ellis, 142.

38. Ellis, 158.

39. Robert Graves, *Fairies and Fusiliers* (London: Heinemann, 1917), 63.

40. Graves, 64.

41. Wilfred Owen, *The Collected Poems of Wilfred Owen*, ed. C. Day Lewis (New York: New Directions, 1965), 35.

42. Jon Stallworthy, *Wilfred Owen* (Oxford: Oxford University Press, 1974), 243–54. Along with the mining disaster and the war, Stallworthy locates the sources of "Strange Meeting" in Shelley's *Revolt of Islam*, Siegfried Sassoon's "The Rear Guard" (which Owen had published as editor of *The Hydra*), and Henri Barbusse's *Under Fire* (256).

43. Stallworthy, 257.

44. Paul Fussell, *The Great War and Modern Memory* (Oxford: Oxford University Press, 1975), 3–35. Irony is the key bequest of the Great War in Fussell's argument, made throughout the book. An exemplary statement of his claim is the conclusion of his introductory chapter: the "one dominating form of modern understanding" is "essentially ironic" and it "originates largely in the application of mind and memory to the events of the Great War" (35).

45. Owen, 35.

46. Doug Anderson, *The Moon Reflected Fire* (Farmington, ME: Alice James, 1994), 44. Anderson also has a poem on Achilles's arrival in the Underworld ("Descent," 42), though since it narrates the journey of one of the dead it falls outside the purview of the Underworld descent tradition proper.

47. Anderson, 45.

48. Jon Stallworthy, "War Poet," *Times Literary Supplement*, 7 November 2008.

49. Stallworthy, unpublished MSS.

1 DECLARATIONS OF INTERDEPENDENCE: THE NECROMANTIC CONFRONTATION WITH TRADITION

1. Myles Slatin, "A History of Pound's Cantos I–XVI, 1915–1925," *American Literature* 35 (May 1963), 183–95: 183. Frank Lentricchia suggests that Pound was planning a "long poem of epic size" "perhaps as early as 1904, while a student at Hamilton College." See *Modernist Quartet* (New York: Cambridge University Press, 1994), 215.

2. Pound published his *Three Cantos* in the June, July, and August, 1917, issues of *Poetry* (one canto per issue). They then appeared, with some revisions, in the American edition of his *Lustra* (October 1917). For a thorough publication history of *Three Cantos*, see Bush, xiii. For fairly brief accounts of Pound's revision of *Three Cantos* into the first three of *The Cantos*, see Slatin, "A History of Pound's Cantos I–XVI, 1915–1925," John L. Foster, "Pound's Revision of Cantos I–III," *Modern Philology* 63 (1966), 236–45. Bush provides a longer and more sophisticated treatment (183–263), as does Christine Froula in *To Write Paradise: Style and Error in Pound's Cantos* (New Haven: Yale University Press, 1984), 11–52. The most readily available text of *Three Cantos* is the one included in *Personae: The Shorter Poems*, ed. Lea Baechler and A. Walton Litz (New York: New Directions, 1990).

3. Quoted in Slatin, 183.

4. Pound, *Literary Essays*, ed. T.S. Eliot (New York: New Directions, 1968), 86.

5. Bush, 83.

6. As Michaela Giesenkirchen argues, Pound found in Browning's poem at once a way of dramatizing "the author's own making and meta-poetic meditations," a model for realizing a "poetic objectivity that would synthesize the poet's subjectivity with transpersonal truth," and a set of specific strategies—the accumulation and paratactic relation of textual and historical details, the imposition upon those details of a narrative obedient not to chronology but to the poet's thematic needs, the presence of a stage-directing narrator—for embodying these aims. Michaela Giesenkirchen, " 'But Sordello, and My Sordello?': Pound and Browning's Epic," *Modernism/Modernity* 8.4 (November 2001), 623–42: 624–5.

7. For more extended and eloquent descriptions of this form and Pound's way to it, see Bush, Chapter 2. Bush later offers this shorter summary:

> As Pound conceived his "long poem" in 1915, it would have to be both epic and modern. That is, although it might partake of "a unity in the outline" of a "beautiful tradition," it would have to meet post-symbolist standards of acceptability. Part of that problem…could be solved by making the poem… "Vorticist"—constructing it out of a pattern of "radicals in design." In 1915, however, Pound had been too long a dramatic poet to be fully content with achieving merely a Vorticist surface. He was then more interested in dramatic technique than in structure, and he attempted to model *Three Cantos* after the most sophisticated example of dramatic narration he could discover. (75)

See also Lentricchia, 209.

8. See, for example, Giesenkirchen, 624. See also Leon Surette, " 'A Light from Eleusis': Some Thoughts on Pound's *Nekuia*," *Paideuma* 3 (1974), 191–216 [198].

9. Bush, 132.

10. Pound, "Three Cantos" 3, *Poetry* 10.5 (August 1917), 250–51.

11. Pound, "Three Cantos" 3, *Poetry* 10.5 (August 1917), 251.

12. Pound, *Personae*, 60. For example, Hugh Kenner, *The Pound Era* (Berkeley: University of California Press, 1971), 148–49; Bush, 131; Lentricchia, 221.

13. *The Letters of Ezra Pound, 1907–1941*, ed. D.D. Paige (New York: Harcourt, Brace and World, 1950), 274.

14. Kenner, 148.

15. Kenner, 149.

16. Surette, 197–98.

17. Hugh Witemeyer, *The Poetry of Ezra Pound: Forms of Renewal, 1908–1920* (Berkeley: University of California Press, 1969), 160.

18. Quoted in Bush, 128.

19. Quoted in Bush, 129.

20. Bush, 127.

21. Bush, 133.

22. Kenner, 149.

23. Kenner, 150.

24. The narrator of "The Seafarer" worries precisely that his final deeds will be unknown and he will therefore be unremembered. Without a witness, his "Daring ado" will not lead to the expected conclusion ("So that all men shall honour him after / And his laud beyond them remain 'mid the English, / Aye, for ever, a lasting life's blast, / Delight 'mid the doughty" (*Personae*, 62).

25. Lentricchia, 200.

26. *The Odyssey*, trans. Robert Fitzgerald (London: Heinemann, 1961).

27. Pike, *Passage through Hell*, 5.

28. Pike, *Passage through Hell*, 5.

29. Lentricchia, 220.

30. See, for example, Jerome McGann's discussion of *A Draft of XVI Cantos* in *The Textual Condition* (Princeton: Princeton University Press, 1991), 122–25, 130–37.

31. Pound, "Three Cantos" 3, *Poetry* 10.5 (August 1917), 253–54.

32. Pound, *The Cantos* (New York: New Directions, 1973), 3.

33. McGann, *Textual Condition*, 129. The phrase is from the title of Chapter 6, in which McGann also describes the material bibliographic texts of various early editions of the poem (e.g., *A draft of XVI cantos*). McGann's discussion of transmission is also germane at this point:

> the transmission of such works is as much a part of their meaning as anything else we can distinguish about them. Transmission is an

elementary kind of translation, a reenactment (and often one kind of completion) of the poetic act which the artist sets in motion. (149)

34. Foster, 243. It also highlights the Eleusinian reference Surette finds in the *Cantos*, since Aphrodite can be seen at once as figuring Persephone in the Underworld and representing the fertility forces the rites were to engage (Surette 205; 207).

35. Witemeyer, 160.

36. Surette, 207.

37. Froula, 22. See also her detailed discussion of Pound's refinements of the technique as he revised Canto IV (24–33).

38. Grieve, 149.

39. Lawrence Rainey, *Ezra Pound and the Monument of Culture: Text, History, and the Malatesta Cantos* (Chicago: University of Chicago Press, 1991), 4. Rainey continues, writing that the Malatesta work "enabled Pound to discover poetic techniques essential to the formal repertory of *The Cantos*, such as the direct quotation of prose documents, a device that effectively dissolved the distinction between verse and prose—a crucial development in the history of modern poetry" (4).

40. Froula, 15.

41. Jewel Spears Brooker and Joseph Bentley, *Reading* The Waste Land: *Modernism and the Limits of Interpretation* (Amherst, MA: University of Massachusetts Press, 1990), 138. I read the frames and framed slightly differently from Brooker and Bentley; where they find the fish-men in St. Magnus Martyr lines to be the central episode in "The Fire Sermon," an episode they argue is framed by Tiresias' vision of the typist and the clerk on one side and Elizabeth and Leicester on the other, I find Tiresias' vision itself at the heart of the section (and the poem). For their fuller discussion, see 146–47.

42. T.S. Eliot, *The Waste Land*, ed. Michael North (New York: W.W. Norton, 2001), 23.

43. Dante, *Inferno*, xxvii, 61–66. Translation quoted from B.C. Southam, *A Guide to the Selected Poems of T.S. Eliot* (sixth edition) (New York: Harcourt Brace, 1994), 47.

44. Eliot, *Collected Poems*, 6.

45. Eliot, "Tradition and the Individual Talent," in *The Sacred Wood: Essays on Poetry and Criticism* (London: Methuen, 1920), 47–59: 53–54.

46. Eliot, "Tradition," 53–54.

47. Eliot, "Tradition," 48, 49.

48. Eliot, "Tradition," 49.

49. Eliot, "Tradition," 52–53.

50. Bernard F. Dick offers a useful set of terms for reading the poem as a descent into the Underworld; he writes that the "descent model" includes an initiator, a quester, a specific location for the Underworld, a realistic chronology, and "a result measured by the quester's ability to apply the lesson learned in the other world to the quester's own

life" (109). Unfortunately, Dick's reading is marred by an insistence that Tiresias is the poem's quester/speaker throughout. See Dick, "*The Waste Land* as a Descent into the Underworld," in Jewel Spears Brooker, ed., *Approaches to Teaching Eliot's Poetry and Plays* (New York: Modern Language Association, 1988): 109–114.

51. For example, Michael Levenson in *A Geneaology of Modernism*.
52. Southam, 133–34.
53. T.S. Eliot, *The Waste Land* (New York: Boni and Liveright), 9. Subsequent quotations refer to this edition and are cited in text.
54. See also Southam, 151.
55. Macdonald, 31–32.
56. Maud Ellmann, *The Poetics of Impersonality: T.S. Eliot and Ezra Pound* (Cambridge, MA: Harvard University Press, 1987), 95.
57. Nancy Gish makes a similar comment on the frame, though her reading of the episode focuses on the typist's and the clerk's absence of feeling as exemplary of the loveless desire that blights the land and on Tiresias' "contemptuous and judgmental" tone as indicative of Eliot's "revulsion." See The Waste Land: *A Poem of Memory and Desire* (Boston: Twayne, 1988), 78–79.
58. Southam, 174–75.
59. The association of Moorgate, Margate, and exhaustion makes sense in the context of Eliot's biography: Moorgate, in the City's financial district, is associated with Eliot's banking work, while Margate is the resort on the Thames estuary to which Eliot retreated to rest and recover from nervous exhaustion.
60. Southam, 178–79. In addition, Michael North's gloss on the second line in the Norton Critical edition points to the tradition of the epitaph, offering as an example Suetonius's epitaph to Vergil (*The Waste Land*, 15, n. 9).
61. In "A Game of Chess," Eliot introduces the Ovidian narrative into his poem. He recurs to it in "The Fire Sermon," after the Mrs. Porter passage: "Twit twit twit / Jug jug jug jug jug / So rudely forc'd / Tereu." The narrative is most complexly and productively deployed at the end of "What the Thunder Said." There Eliot quotes the anonymous Latin poem "*Pervigilium Veneris*," which refers to Tereus and Philomela. This appearance of the narrative bears with it a context of speechlessness; the Latin poem's speaker wonders when she / he will be like the swallow and no longer voiceless. The fragment also appears here amidst a welter of allusions that either trouble communication by appearing in other languages (Dante's Italian, Nerval's French, the Sanskrit of the Upanishads) or refer to such linguistic pastiche (Kyd's *Spanish Tragedy*). One bit of English ("O swallow swallow") clarifies the Philomela story's function here. According to Southam, the words are Tennyson's; they open the fourth section of his *The Princess* and begin the Prince's plea for the bird to be his messenger. The swallow is also Procne, who can speak for Philomela, while the latter cannot but makes her story known by other means. The

self-reference is impossible to miss. Eliot is threatened with speechlessness by the tradition but is able, by weaving the tradition's own unraveled threads and by giving his story to other voices, to communicate.

62. H.D., *Selected Poems*, ed. Louis Martz (New York: New Directions, 1988), 36. Subsequent citations in text.

63. Helen Sword suggests Richard Aldington as the referent behind Orpheus in the poem, which makes sense given their recent history at the time of the poem's composition (Aldington had been unfaithful and the couple had disintegrated). Whether Pound or his disciple Aldington, the important point is that H.D.'s Eurydice cries out against an Orpheus who clearly stands for a male poet contemporary with the poet. (See Sword, *Engendering Inspirations: Visionary Strategies in Rilke, Lawrence, and H.D.* [Ann Arbor: University of Michigan Press, 1995]), 185.

64. Sword, 185.

65. Cheryl Walker offers a similar reading of this moment, writing that the mirror is like the male gaze, "which promises subjectivity to the woman only to betray that promise in the end…The young woman cannot know herself by looking in this mirror." (See Walker, *Masks Outrageous and Austere: Culture, Psyche and Persona in Modern Women Poets* [Bloomington, IN: Indiana University Press, 1991], 154.)

66. Edna St. Vincent Millay, *Collected Sonnets* (New York: Washington Square Press, 1959), 54.

67. Millay, 52. Walker analyzes the scene in terms not only of ideology but also of masochism, deploying Mary Ryan's sense of the term ("where gratification comes from an activity which is stressful and self-defeating") (153).

68. Sandra Gilbert, "Female Female Impersonator: Millay and the Theatre of Personality," in William B. Thesing, ed., *Critical Essays on Edna St. Vincent Millay* (New York: G.K. Hall, 1993), 303.

69. David Kalston, *Five Temperaments: Elizabeth Bishop, Robert Lowell, James Merrill, Adrienne Rich, John Ashbery* (New York: Oxford University Press, 1977), 146.

70. Wendy Martin, "From Patriarchy to the Female Principle: A Chronological Reading of Adrienne Rich's Poems," in Barbara Charlesworth Gelpi and Albert Gelpi, eds., *Adrienne Rich's Poetry* (New York: W.W. Norton, 1975), 175–88. 185.

71. Nancy Milford, "This Woman's Movement," in Gelpi and Gelpi, 189–202, 201.

72. Milford, 201. Ellipses in Milford.

73. For example, Alicia Ostriker, for whom what Rich calls "the wreck and not the story of the wreck / the thing itself and not the myth" is the new myth inaugurated by the unity of mermaid and merman (Ostriker, "The Thieves of Language: Women Poets and Revisionist Mythmaking," in Elaine Showalter, ed., *The New Feminist Criticism* [New York: Pantheon, 1985], 314–38]). It is precisely this "revisionist mythmaking" that dissatisfies some critics. Charles Altieri, for example, criticizes the poem

for evading real philosophical or political thought and opting instead
for "mythic answers to psychological and political problems," while
Cary Nelson concludes that the poem "demonstrates that one can sup-
press difficult feelings by mythologizing them." (See Altieri, *Self and
Sensibility in Contemporary American Poetry* [New York: Cambridge
University Press, 1984], 189, and Nelson, *Our Last First Poets: Vision
and History in Contemporary American Poetry* [Urbana, IL: University
of Illinois Press, 1981], 156.)
74. Elizabeth Hirsh, "Another Look at Genre: *Diving into the Wreck* of
Ethics with Rich and Irigaray," in Lynn Keller and Cristannne Miller,
eds., *Feminist Measures: Soundings in Poetry and Theory* (Ann Arbor:
University of Michigan Press, 1994), 117–38, 118, 134.
75. Barbara Eckstein, "Iconicity, Immersion and Otherness: The Hegelian
'Dive' of J.M. Coetzee and Adrienne Rich," *Mosaic* 29.1 (March 1996),
57–71. 58.
76. Quoted in Cheri Colby Langdell, *Adrienne Rich: The Moment of Change*
(Westport, CT: Praeger, 2004), 117.
77. Colby, 117.
78. Langdell, 120.
79. Adrienne Rich, *The Fact of a Doorframe: Poems Selected and New, 1950–
1984* (New York: W.W. Norton, 1984), 163.
80. Sword, 187.

2 *KATABASIS* AS CULTURAL CRITIQUE

1. Bush, 251.
2. Wendy Stallard Flory, *Ezra Pound and the Cantos: A Record of Struggle*
(New Haven: Yale University Press, 1980), 34
3. James Bronterre O'Brien, *A Vision of Hell, or, Peep into the Realms
Below, Alias Lord Overgrown's Dream* (London: GG Holyoake, undated
[early 1850s]), np. (British Library shelf mark 11651a.69.)
4. O'Brien.
5. O'Brien.
6. O'Brien, 14. O'Brien also earlier writes that Overgrown wishes himself
"again with Guelph" (5).
7. Caroll F. Terrell, *A Companion to the Cantos of Ezra Pound* (Orono:
National Poetry Foundation, University of Maine), 65.
8. Terrell, 9.
9. *The Selected Letters of Ezra Pound*, ed. D.D. Paige (London: Faber and
Faber, 1971), 191.
10. Pound, *Selected Letters*, 239.
11. Terrell, 65.
12. Matthew Hofer suggests possible identities for some of the individuals whose names are "censored" in these cantos, among them T.S.
Eliot. See Hofer, "Modernist Polemic: Ezra Pound v. 'the Perverters of
Language,'" *Modernism/Modernity* 9.3 (2002), 463–89, 474–79.

13. Kevin Corrigan, *Reading Plotinus: A Practical Introduction to Neoplatonism* (West Lafayette, IN: Purdue University Press, 2005).
14. Ovid, *Metamorphoses,* trans. Mary M. Innes (Middlesex, UK: Penguin, 1971).
15. Countee Cullen, *My Soul's High Song: The Collected Writings of Countee Cullen, Voice of the Harlem Renaissance* (New York: Doubleday, 1991), 79.
16. Hart Crane, *The Bridge* (1929) in *Poems of Hart Crane,* ed. Marc Simon (New York: Liveright, 1987), 98. Subsequent references in text.
17. Susan Schultz, "The Success of Failure: Hart Crane's Revisions of Whitman and Eliot in *The Bridge,*" *South Atlantic Review* 54.1 (January, 1989), 55–70, 55, 61.
18. Schultz, 64.
19. Hart Crane, "The Tunnel," *The Criterion* 6 (November 1927), 398–402. For a discussion of Crane in the context of *The Criterion,* see Edward Brunner, *Splendid Failure: Hart Crane and the Making of* The Bridge (Urbana, IL: University of Illinois Press, 1985), 100–102.
20. Millay, 5.
21. T.S. Eliot, *Four Quartets* (1943) (New York: Harcourt, 1971), 17. Subsequent references in text.
22. Charles Olson, *Selected Poems,* ed. Robert Creeley (Berkeley: University of California Press, 1997), 15. Subsequent citations in text.
23. Thomas F. Merrill, *The Poetry of Charles Olson: A Primer* (Newark: University of Delaware Press/Associated University Press, 1982), 103.
24. Walter Kalaidjian, *Languages of Liberation: The Social Text in Contemporary American Poetry* (New York: Columbia University Press, 1989), 67, 70.
25. Robert von Hallberg, *Charles Olson: The Scholar's Art* (Cambridge, MA: Harvard University Press, 1978), 143–50; Andrew Ross, *The Failure of Modernism: Symptoms of American Poetry* (New York: Columbia University Press, 1986), 95–157. In an exemplary passage in his reading of Olson, Ross writes

> Despite Olson's commitment to an experimental methodology, he courts an idealist conviction about the ends of a radical realism, a *proper* humanist discourse will rectify the social and cultural injustice whereby "man is estranged..." In effect, he holds out for the messianic return of subjectivity to its *authentic* epistemological space, a naturally ordained position with easy access to the discourses of freedom. (99–100).

von Hallberg's argument is almost diametrically opposed, emphasizing Olson's resistance to the subjectivity Ross describes and his insistence on the self as indeterminable process.
26. Charles Olson, "Projective Verse," in Robert Creeley, ed., *Charles Olson: Selected Writings* (New York: New Directions, 1967), 15–30 [26].
27. Merrill, 106; see also von Hallberg, 149–50.
28. Merrill, 106.

29. von Hallberg, 143.
30. Merrill, 107; von Hallberg, 148–49.
31. Sterling A. Brown, *The Collected Poems of Sterling A. Brown* (New York: Harper, 1980), 89. Subsequent references in text.
32. John Edgar Tidwell, "Sterling Brown," in William L. Andrews, Frances Smith Foster, Trudier Harris, eds., *Oxford Companion to African American Literature* (New York: Oxford University Press, 1997), 104–6. 105.
33. Joanne V. Gabbin, *Sterling A. Brown: Building the Black Aesthetic Tradition* (Westport, CT: Greenwood, 1985).
34. Patricia Bernstein, *The First Waco Horror: The Lynching of Jesse Washington and the Rise of the NAACP* (College Station, TX: Texas A & M University Press, 2005), 4–6.
35. Tidwell, 105.
36. Mark A. Sanders, *Afro-American Aesthetics and the Poetry of Sterling A. Brown* (Athens: University of Georgia Press), 146.
37. B.A. Botkin, ed., *Folk Say IV: The Land Is Ours* (Norman, OK: University of Oklahoma Press, 1932), 252, 254, 256.
38. James E. Smethurst, *The New Red Negro: The Literary Left and African American Poetry, 1930–1946* (New York: Oxford, 1999), 64, 62.
39. Smethurst, 79.
40. Smethurst, 60.
41. Sanders, 146.
42. Here I am in complete disagreement with Mark Scroggins, who concludes his fine reading of "Mantis" by arguing that "the knowledge Zukofsky hopes to convey through his poetry is not a primarily political knowledge" (*Louis Zukofsky and the Poetry of Knowledge* [Tuscaloosa, AL: University of Alabama Press, 1998], 328). As my reading makes clear, Zukofsky's attempt to reveal the ideological work behind "natural" or taken-for-granted economic logics cannot be characterized as anything but primarily political; for all that is right about his reading of the "Mantis" poems, Scroggins' conclusion here exemplifies Michael Davidson's "critics [who] have tried to protect Zukofsky from his own political commitments during the 1930s" (*Ghostlier Demarcations: Modern Poetry and the Material Word* [Berkeley: University of California Press, 1997], 134). For Scroggins' reading of the poems, see 311–20.
43. Louis Zukofsky, *All: The Collected Short Poems, 1923–1964* (New York: W.W. Norton, 1971), 77. Subsequent citations in text.
44. Davidson, 122.
45. For comparisons of the cultural work of Zukofsky's sestina with Pound's, see Davidson, 119–20, and Scroggins, 313.
46. Davidson puts this well: "it is the 'invoked collective' of disarranged and recombined facts that reestablishes contact, not to stop history with a verbal icon but to keep it alive and tangible in the present" (123). See also Scroggins, 319.
47. A copy of Rukeyser's FBI file is in her papers at the Library of Congress.
48. Muriel Rukeyser, *U.S. 1* (New York: Covici and Friede, 1938), 146.

49. Roy Campbell, *The Collected Poems of Roy Campbell,* vol. 2 (London: Bodley Head, 1957), 87. Campbell refers several times to this composite figure: as "joint MacSpaunday" (87, 89), "Brave MacSpaunday" (90), and "poor MacSpaunday" (92). Marilyn Rosenthal calls "Talking Bronco" "no more than an epigraph to *Flowering Rifle,*" Campbell's 1939 "fanatical view of the Spanish Civil War." See Rosenthal, *Poetry of the Spanish Civil War* (New York: New York University Press, 1975), 108.

50. Louis MacNeice, *Autumn Journal* (London: Faber and Faber, 1939), v. Subsequent citations in text.

51. This impressionism is part of what has bothered many critics of the poem. John Lehmann, for example, criticized the poem for "rather too conspicuously elaborating the picture of an easy-going but attractive personality" instead of representing depth of thought and political commitment (Lehmann, *New Writing in Europe* [Harmondsworth, UK: Allen Lane, 1940], 116). For an overview of the poem's reception focused on critics' disagreement over whether MacNeice was "unable to commit himself to idealistic belief and political action" or "a sophisticated skeptic," see Beret Strong, *The Poetic Avant-Garde: The Groups of Borges, Auden, and Breton* (Evanston, IL: Northwestern University Press, 1997), 188–192.

52. For a comprehensive treatment of the events that inspired Rukeyser's sequence, see Martin Cherniack, *The Hawk's Nest Incident: America's Worst Industrial Disaster* (New Haven: Yale University Press, 1986). See also the hearings of the subcommittee of the House of Representatives' Labor Committee, from which Rukeyser drew some of the poems' language as well as much of the factual information to which the poems refer: *An Investigation Relating to Health Conditions of Workers Employed in the Construction and Maintenance of Public Utilities* (Washington, DC: Government Printing Office, 1936).

53. Robert Shulman, *The Power of Political Art: The 1930s Literary Left Reconsidered* (Chapel Hill, NC: University of North Carolina Press, 2000).

54. For other important readings of the sequence, see Walter Kalaidjian, *American Culture between the Wars: Revisionary Modernism and Postmodern Critique* (New York: Columbia University Press, 1993), Cary Nelson, *Repression and Recovery,* and Thurston, *Making Something Happen: American Political Poetry between the World Wars* (Chapel Hill, NC: University of North Carolina Press, 2001), 169–210.

55. John Wheelwright, "Review of *U.S. 1,*" *Partisan Review* 4 (March 1938), 54–56.

56. Quoted in Jon Stallworthy, *Louis MacNeice* (London: Faber, 1995), 233.

57. Robyn Marsack, *The Cave of Making* (Oxford: Oxford University Press, 1982), 48.

58. Stallworthy, *Louis MacNeice,* 230–31.

59. In a letter dated 7 February 1939, T.S. Eliot wrote to MacNeice that he admired *Autumn Journal* ("I think it is very good indeed. At times I was much moved..."), but criticized the poet's handling of the Oxford

by-election. While he agrees that the election "has a definite symbolic value…as one of the historic points during the last autumn," Eliot deplores MacNeice's suggestion that "the supporters of Quintin Hogg were mostly a pack of scoundrels." "As a matter of fact," Eliot goes on, "the alternative [Lindsay] offered was obsolete" (quoted in Stallworthy, *Louis MacNeice*, 237).

60. Edna Longley, *Louis MacNeice: A Critical Study* (London: Faber, 1988), 67.
61. Stallworthy, *Louis MacNeice*, 234.
62. Louis MacNeice, *The Strings Are False* (New York: Oxford University Press, 1966), 176–96. Especially interesting is MacNeice's account of the Metro air-raid shelter, cast in katabatic terms and evocative of the Tube station shelters in which Londoners would take refuge in a couple of years: "The great dim station was the real underworld of dreams, in dreams I had seen it all before—the long lines of sleepers with their heads against the wall, five children under one blanket, the resigned faces that were lost to the sun…a limbo of weakening tissue" (192). See also MacNeice's journalistic report of his experience of bombardment (194–95).
63. Margot Heinemann, "Three Left-Wing Poets," in Jon Clark, Margot Heinemann, David Margolies, and Carole Snee, eds., *Culture and Crisis in Britain in the 30s* (London: Lawrence and Wishart, 1979), 103–32: 114. Here I must note a disagreement with Samuel Hynes, who writes in his otherwise fine reading of the poem that *Autumn Journal* is "a passive poem, a record of private life carried on the flood of history. It has no personal momentum, no important decisions are made…Nor does it propose any positive values, any programme for confronting the future…beyond a vague solidarity of resistance against the common enemy" (Hynes, *The Auden Generation: Literature and Politics in England in the 1930s* [Princeton: Princeton University Press, 1976], 372. The resolution to support the values embodied by the Spanish Republic not only by writing his identification with Spain but by narrating his journey there seems a somewhat stronger statement of commitment (and advocacy of a political position) than Hynes suggests.
64. H.D., *Trilogy* (New York: New Directions, 1973), 108.

3   IN *NEKUIA* BEGINS RESPONSIBILITY: "LITTLE GIDDING" AND THE POSTWAR NECROMANTIC TRADITION

1. Eliot, *Four Quartets*, 52. Subsequent citations to "Little Gidding" or other of the *Four Quartets* will be in text in parentheses, with an abbreviated title followed by the line number(s) for the quoted passage (e.g., LG 75–78).
2. Strong readings of "Little Gidding," by which my discussion is informed even when it is not in direct dialogue with them, include

Harry Blamires, *Word Unheard: A Guide through Eliot's* Four Quartets (London: Methuen, 1969), Ronald Bush, *T.S. Eliot: A Study in Character and Style* (New York: Oxford University Press, 1983), 224–37, and Albert Gelpi, *A Coherent Splendor: The American Poetic Renaissance, 1910–1950* (New York: Cambridge University Press, 1987), 141–55.

3. For exemplary readings of "Little Gidding" in explicit social and political contexts, see Steve Ellis, *The English Eliot: Design, Language and Landscape in* Four Quartets (London: Routledge, 1991), John Xiros Cooper, *T. S. Eliot and the Ideology of* Four Quartets (Cambridge: Cambridge University Press, 1995), and Jed Esty, *A Shrinking Island: Modernism and National Culture in England* (Princeton: Princeton University Press, 2004).

4. See *The Waste Land*, ll. 215–50; see also my discussion of the "violet hour" passage in chapter 1.

5. See especially Bush, *T.S. Eliot*, 199–200.

6. Peter Middleton, "The Masculinity behind the Ghosts of Modernism in *Four Quartets*," in Cassandra Laity and Nancy K. Gish, eds., *Gender, Desire, and Sexuality in T.S. Eliot* (Cambridge: Cambridge University Press, 2004), 83–106: 89.

7. Middleton, 100.

8. On metonymy as the master trope in *The Waste Land*, see Brooker and Bentley.

9. Critics typically point out the echoes of Dante, Yeats, and Mallarmé, about which I will have more to say below. Harry Blamires offers the most thorough catalogue of allusions and echoes; see 148, 154, 156–58.

10. *Inferno* XV, line 26 (*"per lo cotto aspetto"*) and line 30 ("'*Siete voi qui, ser Brunetto*'"), the latter appearing in more complete form in Eliot's early drafts of the poem (see Helen Gardner, *The Composition of* Four Quartets [New York: Oxford University Press, 1978], 174–76.

11. Stéphane Mallarmé, *Poems,* trans. Roger Fry (New York: New Directions, 1951), 108.

12. William Butler Yeats, *The Collected Poems*, ed. Richard J. Finneran (New York: Macmillan, 1989), 245.

13. Yeats, 246.

14. T.S. Eliot, "What Dante Means to Me," in *To Criticize the Critic and Other Writings* (New York: Farrar Straus and Giroux, 1965), 125–135 [128].

15. Quoted in Gardner, 176. For Gardner's discussion of Yeatsian echoes in the early drafts, see pp. 186–189.

16. Jonathan Nauman, "Eliot and Yeats's Anti-Self: 'Ego Dominus Tuus' and the Ghost of 'Little Gidding'" (*Yeats Eliot Review* 11.3 [Summer 1992]), 67–68.

17. Yeats, 332.

18. "Hotel Normandie Pool" appears in Walcott's 1981 collection *A Fortunate Traveller* (New York: Farrar Straus and Giroux, 1981). The first appearance of "The Journey" in a collection of Boland's is her 1987 *The Journey and Other Poems* (Manchester: Carcanet, 1987), but it was first published in a limited, illustrated small-press edition four years earlier (Deerfield, MA: Deerfield Press; Dublin, Ireland: Gallery Press, 1983).

19. For background on and readings of Boland, see Patricia L. Hagen and Thomas W. Zelman, *Eavan Boland and the History of the Ordinary* (Bethesda, MD: Maunsel, 2004), and the special issue of *Colby Quarterly* devoted to Boland (35.4 [December 1999]), especially the introduction by Jody Allen Randolph (205–9) and Albert Gelpi's "'Hazard and Death': The Poetry of Eavan Boland" (210–28).

20. Eavan Boland, *An Origin Like Water: Collected Poems 1967–1987* (New York: W.W. Norton, 1996), 182. Subsequent citations to this poem will be in text.

21. See, for example, the title poem's catalogue of violence and treachery, or the artistic and mythic acknowledgments of violence throughout human history in the "Summer 1969" section of "Singing School" (Heaney, *North* [London: Faber, 1975], 11, 63).

22. Patricia Haberstroh, *Women Creating Women: Contemporary Irish Women Poets* (Syracuse, NY: Syracuse University Press, 1996), 82.

23. For example, Carolyn Forche's anthology *Against Forgetting: Twentieth-Century Poetry of Witness* (New York: W.W. Norton, 1993). See Boland's essays in *Object Lessons: The Life of the Woman and the Poet in Our Time* (New York: W.W. Norton, 1995), especially "Outside History" (123–53).

24. Paul Breslin, *Nobody's Nation: Reading Derek Walcott* (Chicago: University of Chicago Press, 2001), 50. "Hotel Normandie Pool," *New Yorker* 5 January 1981, 30–31.

25. Rei Terada reads the nine-line stanza as an embodiment of the poem's key image of the pool, the stanza's forty-five metrical feet analogizing the pool's cubic feet of water. See *Derek Walcott's Poetry: American Mimicry* (Boston: Northeastern University Press, 1993), 138.

26. John Thieme, *Derek Walcott* (Manchester: Manchester University Press, 1999), 166; Walcott, 65.

27. Ovid has become a popular figure for the poet in exile in recent decades, showing up not only in Walcott's poem but also, for example, in Derek Mahon's "Ovid in Tomis," which also dwells on linguistic estrangement, loneliness, and geographical displacement. Mahon also shows the poet resolving to create in spite of, and out of, these conditions (Mahon makes an analogy between the exiled Roman poet and his own suburban "exile"). (Mahon, *Selected Poems* [London: Penguin, 1993], 181). While it is up to something different, Geoffrey Hill's "Ovid in the Third Reich" is another remarkable poem that borrows the exiled Roman poet and uses him to comment on the

place of the poet vis-à-vis history (Hill, *New and Selected Poems, 1952–1992* [Boston: Houghton Mifflin, 1994], 49).

28. There is no clear or obvious single referent here, but Walcott's language recalls his reaction to the 1970 Black Power revolution in Trinidad as well as his aversion to Afro-centric and postcolonial politicization of literature, often expressed throughout the 1970s. See Breslin, 49–50, as well as Walcott's essays from the mid- to late-1970s and his play, *Dream on Monkey Mountain* (New York: Farrar Straus and Giroux, 1970). Corruption as a product of even well-intentioned social change is much on Walcott's mind at the turn of the decade; his play, *Beef, No Chicken*, which premiered with the Trinidad Theatre Workshop in April, 1980, comically registers the political and economic corruption that spring up in a small town in the wake of social change. (Walcott, *Three Plays: The Last Carnival, Beef No Chicken, A Branch of the Blue Nile* [New York: Farrar Straus, 1986]). See also Bruce King, *Derek Walcott: A Caribbean Life* (New York: Oxford University Press, 2000), 400.

29. Walcott's explicit acknowledgment of his own mixed racial and cultural position is a recurrent theme over the course of his career and in every form in which he has written. While it is in play here, I take it up more fully in my discussion of *Omeros* in chapter 8.

30. Cf. Terada, 139.

31. Terada, 137.

32. Paula Burnett, *Derek Walcott: Politics and Poetics* (Gainesville, FL: University of Florida Press, 2000), 3.

33. Heaney, 51.

4   JAMES MERRILL'S "BOOK OF EPHRAIM"

1. The trilogy's parts appeared separately before they were published together in 1982: "The Book of Ephraim" concludes Merrill's 1976 *Divine Comedies*; *Mirabell: Books of Number* was published in 1978; *Scripts for the Pageant* came out in 1980, with the entire trilogy, together with a coda, first published in a single volume in 1982.

2. Richard Saez, "'At the Salon Level': Merrill's Apocalyptic Epic," in David Lehman and Charles Berger, eds., *James Merrill: Essays in Criticism* (Ithaca: Cornell University Press, 1983), 211–45, 218–19.

3. See Timothy Materer, *James Merrill's Apocalypse* (Ithaca: Cornell University Press, 2000), 110.

4. Helen Sword, *Ghostwriting Modernism* (Ithaca: Cornell University Press, 2002), 134, 141.

5. Ann Kenison, *Overheard Voices: Address and Subjectivity in Postmodern American Poetry* (New York: Routledge, 2006), 58.

6. Mutlu Konuk Blasing, *Politics and Form in Postmodern Poetry: O'Hara, Bishop, Ashbery, and Merrill* (Cambridge: Cambridge University Press, 1995), 176–178. Materer, 6.

7. Blasing, 176.
8. Rachel Jacoff, "Merrill and Dante," in Lehman and Berger, 145–58, 155. Peter Sacks, "The Divine Translation: Elegiac Aspects of *The Changing Light at Sandover*," in Lehman and Berger, 159–85, 162.
9. Brian McHale, *The Obligation toward the Difficult Whole: Postmodernist Long Poems* (Tuscaloosa: University of Alabama Press, 2004), 43.
10. Walter Kalaidjian, *Languages of Liberation: The Social Text in Contemporary American Poetry* (New York: Columbia University Press, 1989), 111, 99.
11. McHale, 48.
12. As Materer writes, the initial contact with the spirit world is registered in poems before "Ephraim." Most importantly, "The Will" "recounts the breakthrough of the spirit world into Merrill's consciousness," and in that poem Ephraim enjoins the poet to "SET MY TEACHINGS DOWN" (74–76).
13. James Merrill, *The Changing Light at Sandover* (New York: Knopf, 1993), 55. Subsequent citations in text.
14. Materer, 103–4. See also the poem's own occasional comments on its historical backdrop, for example, this passage from section "L": "Impeachment ripens round the furrowed stone / Face of a story-teller who has given / Fiction a bad name" (41).
15. Charles Berger, "Merrill and Pynchon: Our Apocalyptic Scribes," in Lehman and Berger, 282–97. 282.
16. McHale, 52.
17. James Merrill, "An Interview with Donald Sheehan," in J.D. McClatchy, ed., *Recitative: Prose by James Merrill* (San Francisco: Northpoint, 1986), 24–36. 28.
18. Nick Halpern, *Everyday and Prophetic: The Poetry of Lowell, Ammons, Merrill, and Rich* (Madison: University of Wisconsin Press, 2003), 162.
19. Merrill, "An Interview with Helen Vendler," in McClatchy, 49–52 [50].
20. Merrill, "An Interview with Helen Vendler," 51. He goes on to talk about the "doubleness of [poetry's] source, the concept of the "bicameral mind," and the way *Sandover* was produced "in two adjacent rooms" (52). See also "An Interview with Fred Bornhauser," in McClatchy, 53–61 and "An Interview with J.D. McClatchy" in McClatchy, 62–83: "There was truth on both sides…and the ability to see both ways at once isn't merely an idiosyncrasy but corresponds to how the world needs to be seen" (80).
21. Halpern, 162, 182–83. See also Jacoff, 155.
22. Lee Zimmerman, "Against Apocalypse: Politics and James Merrill's *Changing Light at Sandover*," in Guy Rotella, ed., *Critical Essays on James Merrill* (New York: G.K. Hall, 1996), 175–89, 185.
23. Zimmerman, 187.
24. See Sacks, 172.

25. See Merrill, *The Changing Light at Sandover*, 131. See also Robert Polito, *A Reader's Guide to James Merrill's* The Changing Light at Sandover (Ann Arbor: University of Michigan Press, 1994), 94, 58.
26. Merrill, "On Literary Tradition," in McClatchy, *Recitative*, 8–12, 8.
27. See Willard Spiegelmann's comment on this line break ("Breaking the Mirror: Interruption in Merrill's Trilogy," in Lehman and Berger, 186–210), 194.

5 DEREK WALCOTT'S *OMEROS*

1. Jahan Ramazani, *The Hybrid Muse: Postcolonial Poetry in English* (Chicago: University of Chicago Press, 2001), 58.
2. Ramazani, 58.
3. Ramazani, 68.
4. To be precise, I should say "amelioration" rather than "healing." Ramazani writes that "even after the climactic scene of healing, the wounds of history and language are shown to persist" (70). Ramazani's reading as a whole expands upon Rei Terada's brief discussion of metaphor and the provisional unifying of difference in the poem; see Terada, 181.
5. See, for example, Stefania Ciocia, "To Hell and Back: The Katabasis and the Impossibility of Epic in Derek Walcott's *Omeros*," *Journal of Commonwealth Literature* 35 (2000), 87–103; Gregson Davis, " 'With No Homeric Shadow': The Disavowal of Epic in Derek Walcott's *Omeros*," *South Atlantic Quarterly* 96.2 (1997), 321–34; Joseph Farrell, "Walcott's *Omeros*: The Classical Epic in a Postmodern World," *South Atlantic Quarterly* 96.2 (1997), 247–74; and Robert D. Hamner, *Epic of the Dispossessed: Derek Walcott's* Omeros (Columbia, MO: University of Missouri Press, 1997).
6. In this, I follow Charles Pollard, who argues that critics have focused so intently on the poem's relationship to Homer that they "have neglected the influence of Dante." (Charles W. Pollard, *New World Modernisms: T.S. Eliot, Derek Walcott, and Kamau Brathwaite* [Charlottesville, VA: University of Virginia Press, 2004], 150).
7. Pollard writes that Eliot and Walcott recast such scenes in order to "defend poetry's social utility" (151), which accurately captures part, though not all, of the matter. The climactic moment in which the Narrator is chastised in the Underworld of Soufriere is animated by the need to define rather than defend poetry's "social utility," and that definition entails a sense of the poet's responsibility to and in his specific social / historical moment.
8. John B. Van Sickle, "The Design of Derek Walcott's *Omeros*" (*Classical World* 93 (1999), 7–27 [7–8]).
9. Van Sickle, 10.
10. These similarities lead some critics simply to call the Narrator "Walcott." We are reminded by the poem, though, that "every 'I' is a fiction" (28),

that this Walcott-like character is indeed a character, a figure for the poet distinct from the poet. I will, therefore, follow the lead of those critics who discuss the (capitalized) Narrator.

11. Van Sickle, 19.
12. Derek Walcott, *Omeros* (New York: Farrar, Straus and Giroux, 1990), 70. Subsequent references will be cited by page number in the text.
13. Ramazani, 49.
14. The key term has broader implications for Walcott's Homeric project as well. As Terada writes, "To 'reverse' means to 'verse again' and therefore connotes continuity, but also means 'to undo' and so connotes rebellion and discontinuity" (205).
15. Van Sickle adds quotation marks after "my father said," clearly ascribing the language that follows to the barber, noting that Walcott penciled this addition into Van Sickle's copy of *Omeros* when asked who spoke the words. See Van Sickle, 19 (n. 47).
16. Walcott, "The Muse of History," in *What the Twilight Says: Essays* (New York: Farrar Straus and Giroux, 1998), 36–64 [44].
17. Walcott, *Collected Poems, 1948–1984* (New York: Farrar Straus and Giroux, 1986), 269.
18. Pollard, 162.
19. While Jonathan Martin criticizes Walcott's "morally distasteful comparison," both Pollard and Paul Breslin defend the analogy by arguing that Walcott envisions a reciprocal relationship between the women and the poet. I would argue that Martin simply misses the point; Walcott posits the women not as laborers whose work is comparable to the poet's but as the source, inspiration, and, crucially, obligation of poetry. (Jonathan Martin, "Nightmare History: Derek Walcott's *Omeros,*" *Kenyon Review* 14.3 [1992], 197–204, 203–4; Pollard, 163; Breslin, 260).
20. Hamner titles his chapters on the middle books of the poem "The Middle Passage to Europe," "The Middle Passage to Africa," and "The Middle Passage to North America."
21. Of course, Seven Seas has already been a protean character by this point in the poem, having appeared as an African griot and a Sioux shaman, among other guises.
22. Note, though, that this synthesis of man and island itself enacts a cultural synthesis: the St. Lucian Narrator sees his island not only through its own eyes but, allusively at least, through the blind but miraculously visionary eyes of its namesake (St. Lucy, iconographically depicted holding her eyes); the view of the land from the land's own point of view is also the view of the land through the blind eyes indicated by the land's name, through its construction in the colonizing Christian European imaginary.
23. Daniel Maximin weaves a similar echo through his novel *Soufrieres* (Paris: Seuil, 1987).

24. Terada, 208.
25. Pollard, 170.
26. *Inferno*, Canto XXXIII.
27. T.S. Eliot, *Four Quartets*, 53.
28. In Allen Mandelbaum's verse translation of *Inferno*.
29. I am also inclined to read the shade as the embodiment of some condemned aspects of the Narrator because this fits best with the dialectical character of *Omeros* and much of Walcott's other poetry of the 1990s and after (e.g., *The Prodigal* [2004]).
30. Pollard, 171.
31. Breslin, 241.
32. Breslin, 249.
33. Breslin, 261. Pollard, too, writes that the renunciation of history's importance depends upon a prior "mastery" of the past (171).
34. See, for example, Hamner, 75.
35. *Aeneid* VI.919 (184).
36. Breslin, 259.
37. Walcott, "The Muse of History," 54, 44.
38. Amos Tutuola, *My Life in the Bush of Ghosts* (London: Faber and Faber, 1954); *The Wild Hunter in the Bush of Ghosts* (1948), ed. and intro. Bernth Lindfors (Washington, DC: Three Continents Press, 1982). For background on Tutuola, see Lindfors' introduction (xi–xx).
39. Tutuola, *My Life in the Bush of Ghosts*, 74–75.
40. Walcott, "The Muse of History," 39.
41. See Dabydeen, *Turner: New and Selected Poems* (London: Cape, 1994), 33.
42. Quoting Edmund Wilson to the effect that Philoctetes is "a literary man" productively alienated from his society and abhorrent to it, Terada writes that "the Achaian Philoctetes has often been seen as an archetype of the artist" (199). Wilson's comment might be too weak a hook on which to hang the claim, but Terada's reading of Philoctete as at once wounded and healed by language itself and her argument that "through the process of more specific allegorizations of Philoctete's infirmity Walcott confronts the infirmity of his own medium" are persuasive. Where Terada locates the infirmity of the medium in the inevitable disfigurement of language itself, though, I would argue that Walcott locates it instead in poetry's evasion of social responsibility.
43. My discussion here, as I imagine Terada's and Ramazani's must be, is informed by Jacques Derrida's analysis of the *pharmakon* as at once toxin and remedy and by his location of this undecidable simultaneity in language itself. See "Plato's Pharmacy," in *Dissemination*, trans. and ed. Barbara Johnson (Chicago: University of Chicago Press, 1981), 63–171.
44. Breslin, 258.
45. Ramazani, 58–59.

6 TONY HARRISON'S *V*

1. See, for example, Helmut Haberkamm, " 'These Vs Are All the Versuses of Life': A Reading of Tony Harrison's Social Elegy *V*," in C.C. Barfoot, ed., *In Black and Gold: Contiguous Traditions in Post-War British and Irish Poetry* (Amsterdam: Rodopi, 1994, 79–94 [90]); Luke Spencer, *The Poetry of Tony Harrison* (New York: Harvester/Wheatsheaf, 1994), 92–93. The most substantial comparison of Harrison's poem to Gray's is elaborated by Sandie Byrne in his "On Not Being Milton, Marvell, or Gray," in Byrne, ed., *Tony Harrison: Loiner* (Oxford: Clarendon, 1997), 57–83 [67–75].

2. Tony Harrison, *v. and Other Poems* (New York: Farrar, Straus and Giroux [Noonday], 1991), 3. Subsequent quotations from the poem will refer to this edition and will be cited parenthetically in the text.

3. Byrne, "On Not Being Milton, Marvell, or Gray," 67.

4. Jonathan and Ruth Winterton, *Coal, Crisis and Conflict: The 1984–85 Miners' Strike in Yorkshire* (Manchester, UK: Manchester University Press, 1989), 1. For a more journalistic but still thorough account of the strike, see Martin Adeney and John Lloyd, *The Miners' Strike 1984–85: Loss without Limit* (London: Routledge and Kegan Paul, 1986), which takes its subtitle, as Harrison does his epigraph, from Arthur Scargill, leader of the NUM during the strike.

5. Winterton, 1.

6. Tony Harrison, *v.*, second edition (Newcastle upon Tyne: Bloodaxe, 1989).

7. Spencer, 91.

8. Eagleton, "Antagonisms: Tony Harrison's *v.*," *Poetry Review* 76 (June 1986), Rpt. in Neil Astley, ed., *Tony Harrison* (Newcastle: Bloodaxe, 1991), 348–50: 350.

9. Haberkamm, 82, 79–80.

10. Byrne, 71.

11. Byrne, 71.

12. Critics have struggled a bit with how best to characterize the skinhead, who certainly speaks and acts as if real but is also clearly a ghostly version of Harrison's own younger (or alternative potential) self; Sandie Byrne's solution is the most cautious ("one [half] of its protagonist[s]" [69]), but I will settle for the simpler notion (also most consistent with the terms of this study) that the skinhead is a revenant spirit in the necromantic tradition.

13. Harrison, *Selected Poems*, second edition (London: Penguin, 1984), 123.

14. Haberkamm, 89; Jonathon Green, *Cassel Dictionary of Slang* (New York: Cassel, 1998), 301; Spencer, 94. It is worth recalling that "CUNTS" appears earlier in the poem in a graffito aimed at the racist National Front; the term is not only one in common use in northern England working-class culture, but is reserved for those one most reviles.

15. Haberkamm, 90. Partridge's *Dictionary of Slang and Unconventional English* defines "Greek" in terms of cheating ("card sharp") or ethnicity

("Irishman") (Ed. Paul Beale, London: Routledge, 2002, 499). Jonathon Green, though, in *The Cassel Dictionary of Slang*, offers as his fourth nominal definition "a person who engages in anal intercourse, not necessarily but usu. a homosexual," and as his second adjectival definition "a generic term for homosexual," dating both usages to the 1930s and after (533).

16. Eagleton, 350.
17. Harrison, "All Out" (review of Alan Bold, Ed., *The Penguin Book of Socialist Verse*), *London Magazine* 10.12 (1971), 87.
18. Byrne, 70.
19. Byrne, 70.
20. Spencer, 98.
21. Spencer, 97.
22. Haberkamm, 87.
23. Haberkamm, 87.
24. Byrne, 80.
25. Byrne, 81.
26. Eagleton, 350.
27. In his penultimate act of spray-painting, the skinhead "added a middle slit to one daubed V" to make a rudimentary image of a vagina.
28. Eagleton, 349.
29. Spencer, 98.
30. Eagleton, 350.
31. Haberkamm, 88; Spencer, 98.

7 SEAMUS HEANEY'S "STATION ISLAND"

1. Joseph Duffy, *Lough Derg Guide* (Dublin: Irish Messenger, 1980), 4. For a history of Lough Derg as a pilgrimage site and also as a locus often visited by Irish poets working through their relationship to the nation and aspects of its culture, see Peggy O'Brien, *Writing Lough Derg: From William Carleton to Seamus Heaney* (Syracuse, NY: Syracuse University Press, 2006), xiv–xix.
2. O'Brien writes that Heaney undertakes the "penitential exercise to expiate certain self-perceived poetic and moral lapses" (xv).
3. Declan Kiberd, "Irish Literature and Irish History," in Roy Foster, ed., *The Oxford History of Ireland* (New York: Oxford University Press, 1989), 230.
4. Eamon Grennan, "Introduction," in *New Irish Writing: Essays in Memory of Raymond J. Porter* (Boston: Twayne, 1989), xii.
5. Heaney, "Envies and Identifications: Dante and the Modern Poet," in Peter S. Hawkins and Rachel Jacoff, eds., *The Poet's Dante* (New York: Farrar Straus and Giroux, 2001), 239–258: 256. Earlier in the essay, Heaney marks his difference from Pound and Eliot and his affinity with Mandelstam as earlier readers, translators, and transformers of the Dantean donnée.

6. Carson, "Escaped from the Massacre?" *Honest Ulsterman* 50 (Winter 1975), 184.

7. O'Brien, 154.

8. See David Beresford, *Ten Men Dead: The Story of the 1981 Irish Hunger Strike* (New York: Atlantic Monthly Press, 1987), 15–20.

9. O'Brien, 156.

10. Neil Corcoran, *A Student's Guide to Seamus Heaney* (London: Faber and Faber, 1986), 166.

11. Helen Vendler, *Seamus Heaney* (Cambridge, MA: Harvard University Press, 1998), 97.

12. Vendler, 98.

13. Seamus Heaney, *Station Island* (London: Faber and Faber, 1984), 65 (subsequent citations in text). As Stefan Hawlin puts it, "Carleton's shade urges Heaney not to go on the pilgrimage because he wants him to become an outsider like himself, to transcend sectarianism by undergoing some similar distancing from his roots." (Hawlin, "Seamus Heaney's 'Station Island': The Shaping of a Modern Purgatory," *English Studies* 73.1 [1992], 35–50 [39]).

14. Brian Friel, *Selected Plays* (London: Faber and Faber, 1984). First performed by the Field Day Company, 1980.

15. Corcoran, 166.

16. Henry Hart, "Ghostly Colloquies: Seamus Heaney's 'Station Island,'" *Irish University Review* 18.2 (Autumn 1988), 233–50: 238

17. Hart, 238.

18. Hart, 238. See also O'Brien, 164.

19. Hart, 247.

20. Heaney, *North*, 11.

21. Corcoran, 162.

22. O'Brien, 195.

23. Delaney was a friend Heaney had met when both were at Queen's University in the 1960s. He worked in the Antiquities department of the Ulster Museum until his death, at age 32, in 1979. (Christine Finn, *Past Poetic: Archaeology in the Poetry of W.B. Yeats and Seamus Heaney* [London: Duckworth, 2004], 80–81).

24. Seamus Heaney, *Death of a Naturalist* (New York: Oxford University Press, 1966), 13.

25. O'Brien, 198.

26. A number of poems in *North* were inspired by P.V. Glob's 1969 book, *The Bog People*, a study of bodies discovered in bogs and determined to have been placed in the bogs after execution or sacrifice.

27. Corcoran, 130. Heaney was attending a literary festival when he received word of McCartney's death. Rather than attend the funeral, he remained at the festival (where he was obliged to introduce poets at their readings) and, as Peggy O'Brien writes, also spent the day "in an outing with other poets to Jerpoint Abbey, an aesthetic ruin" (161). Heaney often prefaces readings of "The Strand at Lough Beg" with an account of his

reaction to his cousin's death, including his failure to attend the funeral (he did so at a reading at Smith College in October, 2004).

28. Seamus Heaney, *Field Work* (New York: Farrar Straus and Giroux, 1979), 18.

29. This tradition derives from a series of appearances the Virgin Mary made to Sister Justine Bisqueyburu, a nun of the Daughters of Charity, in 1840. At her fifth and final appearance, the Virgin is supposed to have revealed a green scapular on which were her image and a prayer for her intercession at the moment of death.

30. O'Brien argues that McCartney here accuses Heaney of a sin of omission, of failing to accuse anyone directly when writing of McCartney's death. The passage's emphasis on seeing, though, suggests that the sin at the heart of McCartney's accusation is the more active sin of seeing and saying as a poet sees and says; the indictment, then, includes not only Heaney but also the traditions that have formed his vision. See O'Brien, 161. She is closer to the truth, I think, when she writes a few pages later that "Station Island" "is the moment when Seamus Heaney takes himself to task for poeticizing violence and pain" (166).

31. As Hawlin writes, Hughes "was captured in 1978 after a shoot-out with the SAS [British special forces]…After being badly injured in the hip, he managed to crawl into the undergrowth and hide, packing his wound with mud to stem the bleeding" (45). See also Beresford, 112–31.

32. Hart, 248.

33. Hart, 248.

34. Hart, 235.

35. Deane, "A Noble, Startling Achievement," *Irish Literary Supplement* (Spring 1985), 1. Also quoted in Hart, 242.

36. Corcoran, 164.

37. Corcoran, 164.

38. Hawlin, 47.

39. Hart, 248.

40. If the mug *does* bear any significance beyond the quotidian, it would derive not from any symbolism of "wholeness," but from the sequence's series of images and objects that represent the feminine: the "seaside trinket," a "toy grotto with seedling mussel shells / and cockles glued in patterns over it" in section III, the "basilica door," "space," and "dish" of VI, and the brass trumpet that rises from lough water in IX. Vendler writes that these were added late in the sequence's composition (94); the association forged in these sections between the feminine, sexual awakening, passivity, and death complicates the significance of Heaney's confrontations with masculine forebears and interlocutors.

41. O'Brien writes that the returned cup is "newly perceived as damaged," though this seems a relatively unimportant change in the cup's appearance to the poet. More bizarrely, she goes on to perform a sexual reading of the cup, with the couple who call it their loving cup referring to

Heaney's parents, a reading for which I simply cannot find warrant in the text (173).

EPILOGUE

1. *The Selected Poetry of Rainer Maria Rilke*, trans. and ed. Stephen Mitchell (New York: Random House [Vintage], 1984), 49.
2. Rilke, "Notes," 335–36.
3. Rilke, 231.
4. John Ashbery, *Selected Poems* (New York: Penguin, 1985), 245.
5. Ashbery, 247.
6. "The Pomegranate" was originally published in Boland's *In a Time of Violence* (New York: W.W. Norton, 1994). "Pomegranate" was originally published in DuPlessis' *Wells* (New York: Montemara, 1980).
7. Also the subject of Boland's "The Making of an Irish Goddess." See Boland, *Outside History*, 38–39.
8. Scheck's "Persephone" originally published in *10 at Night* (New York: Knopf, 1990). For Glück's "Pomegranate," see *The First Four Books of Poems* (Hopewell, NJ: Ecco, 1995).
9. See *The Electronic Text Corpus of Sumerian Literature* (http://www.etcsl.orient.ox.ac.uk/section1/tr141.htm)
10. Falconer, 161.
11. Alice Notley, *The Descent of Alette* (New York: Penguin, 1992), 3.
12. Notley, 5.
13. Notley, 28.

INDEX